Intel Wars

The Secret Sentry: The Untold History of the National Security Agency

INTEL WARS

The Secret History of the
Fight Against Terror

MATTHEW M. AID

BLOOMSBURY PRESS
New York • Berlin • London • Sydney

Published by Bloomsbury Press, New York

All papers used by Bloomsbury Press are natural, recyclable products made from wood grown in well-managed forests. The manufacturing processes conform to the environmental regulations of the country of origin.

LIBRARY OF CONGRESS CATALOGING-IN-PUBLICATION DATA

Aid, Matthew M., 1958–
Intel wars : the secret history of the
fight against terror / Matthew M. Aid.—1st U.S. ed.
p.   cm.
Includes bibliographical references and index.
ISBN 978-1-60819-481-0 (alk. paper)
1. Terrorism—Prevention—Government policy—United States—History.
2. Intelligence service—United States—History.   I. Title.
HV6432.4.A36 2012
363.325'1630973—dc23
2011023840

First U.S. Edition 2012

1 3 5 7 9 10 8 6 4 2

Typeset by Westchester Book Group
Printed in the U.S.A. by Quad/Graphics, Fairfield, Pennsylvania

To my family:
Harry, Rita, and Jonathan.
This book would not have been possible without them.

I'm so cocky I could swagger,
Things I know would make you stagger,
I'm ten percent cloak and ninety percent
    dagger.
Boo Boo Baby I'm a spy.
                    —Anonymous Office of Strategic
                        Services (OSS) officer

Contents

Introduction

*The one permanent emotion of the inferior man
is fear—fear of the unknown, the complex,
the inexplicable.*

—H. L. MENCKEN

After more than eight years spent looking for Osama bin Laden, the CIA finally got their first break in the hunt for the al Qaeda leader in August 2010, when Pakistani agents working for the CIA followed an al Qaeda courier from an Internet café in the city of Peshawar to an isolated compound just north of the city of Abbottabad, thirty-one miles northeast of the Pakistani capital of Islamabad.

Abbottabad has been a military garrison town since it was established by the British Army in 1853. After Pakistan obtained its independence from Great Britain in 1947, the Pakistani military took over the bases that had formerly been occupied by the British forces. Abbottabad is now the home of the regimental depots and training centers for two Pakistani Army regiments—the Baloch Regiment and the Frontier Force Regiment—with between two thousand and three thousand troops in residence at these bases at any one time. Just north of the city in the town of Kakul is the Pakistani Military Academy. The mysterious walled-in compound was located on a dirt road less than a mile from the front gate of the Pakistani Military Academy.

The CIA agents had no inkling at the time that Osama bin Laden and his family were hiding in the compound, but the extreme security measures in and around the complex suggested that someone important was hiding there.

As described in greater detail in chapter 4, the CIA had been searching for bin Laden ever since the Saudi terrorist leader and up to a thousand of his followers had fled across the border to Pakistan in December 2001 after the Battle of Tora Bora. When bin Laden's trail quickly went cold, the CIA changed its approach and tried to identify the couriers that bin Laden was using to carry his messages to his followers and sympathizers, reportedly including tapping the phones of the Islamabad bureau of the Arab news agency Al Jazeera to try to identify who was providing them with videotapes of bin Laden's speeches. In addition, a number of Pakistani journalists who were known to have had or suspected of having occasional contact with al Qaeda were placed under surveillance by the CIA in the hope that bin Laden or one of his lieutenants would contact them and lead the agency to their hideouts. None of these surveillance operations yielded any leads.

In 2003, a number of al Qaeda detainees, including al Qaeda's operations chief, Khalid Sheikh Mohammed, identified the person they thought was most likely Osama bin Laden's principal courier: a veteran al Qaeda operative who went by the nom de guerre of Abu Ahmed al-Kuwaiti. In 2004, another al Qaeda leader who had been captured in Iraq, Hassan Ghul, confirmed the identification. Years later, the CIA finally learned that al-Kuwaiti's real name was Sheikh Abu Ahmed, and he was a Pakistani national who had been born in Kuwait.

Over the next six years, agents of the CIA's Islamabad station mounted a dragnet looking for al-Kuwaiti inside Pakistan, even circulating a composite photograph of the man to Pakistani intelligence and security forces. But the search produced no results.

It was not until early 2010 that an intercepted cell phone call led a team of Pakistani agents working for the CIA to al-Kuwaiti. The agents found him in the northern Pakistani city of Peshawar delivering, according to an intelligence source, a packet of materials to a Pakistani journalist known to be sympathetic to al Qaeda. The CIA's Islamabad station hastily put together a surveillance team of Pakistani operatives to follow al-Kuwaiti, with orders that he was not to be captured, and that the Pakistani intelligence service, the ISI, was not to be told of the discovery. The surveillance team was ordered to closely monitor his movements in the hope that he would lead them to bin Laden. He did. Right to the isolated compound outside the city of Abbottabad.

One of the secrets coming out of the entire bin Laden affair is that over the past several years, the CIA has secretly recruited and trained a small but very capable cadre of Pakistani operatives, many of whom were formerly police officers. These agents do much of the fieldwork inside Pakistan that the CIA officers in the agency's Islamabad station cannot do because they are under surveillance around the clock by operatives of the ISI. These Pakistani agents run agent networks, conduct physical and electronic surveillance, install wiretaps, operate cell phone intercept equipment, and much more. According to an intelligence source, they were to end up doing much of the work that led to the killing of Osama bin Laden.

A team of these agents rented a house just down the road from the compound, which they converted into a sophisticated clandestine observation post, complete with infrared cameras capable of taking pictures at night, sophisticated video equipment, powerful telescopes connected to the latest generation of digital cameras, and cell phone intercept receivers. And they did all of this without alerting any of the neighbors as to what they were doing inside the house.

The CIA was unable to determine who was hiding inside the compound other than al-Kuwaiti and his brother, another longtime al Qaeda operative, and their families, but all the signs indicated that there was someone else living on the top floor of the residence inside the compound. The question was, who was he? By mid-February 2011, intelligence from a variety of sources convinced Obama administration officials that some senior al Qaeda leader was holed up inside the mansion at Abbottabad, but no one was sure who it was. The betting was that it was bin Laden.

So on Friday morning, April 29, 2011, Barack Obama gave the go order that launched a commando operation with personnel from SEAL Team Six to attack the Abbottabad compound; then the president left for a long-planned trip to Florida. The level of distrust of the Pakistani government was such that the decision was made in Washington not to tell the Pakistani government or the ISI anything about the operation in order to ensure that it would not be compromised by Pakistani officials sympathetic to al Qaeda.

Halfway around the world at Forward Operating Base Fenty, located on the eastern outskirts of the city of Jalalabad in southeastern Afghanistan, five helicopters set off on the beginning leg of the dangerous 150-mile flight across Pakistan to Abbottabad. Three of the helicopters were huge CH-47 Chinooks; each large enough to carry a Humvee jeep; they now carried a team of twenty-five SEAL commandos who would act as a reserve force during the operation. Two smaller UH-60M Black Hawk helicopters, fitted with the latest stealth and noise suppression technology, carried the attack team of twenty-three SEALs who would conduct the actual assault on the compound.

Even before Obama gave the go order, the U.S. intelligence community had secretly begun deploying an array of collection platforms to monitor the compound and the surrounding area. A top secret stealth unmanned drone based in Afghanistan flew over Pakistan and took up station high over Abbottabad, relaying an uninterrupted stream of video imagery via satellite to the CIA operations center at Langley, Virginia, about everything going on in and around the compound. NSA SIGINT (signals intelligence) operators based at Fort Gordon, Georgia, were able to confirm that the flight of the drone had not been detected by Pakistani radar operators.

The CIA surveillance team based just a few hundred yards from the compound in their clandestine observation point watched the building with infrared cameras and sophisticated cell phone intercept gear, while other teams watched the front gates of the various Pakistani military bases and police stations in Abbottabad and Kakul to ensure that the Pakistanis would not interfere with the operation. SIGINT platforms based across the border in Afghanistan monitored Pakistani military, air defense, and police radio traffic to determine whether Pakistani forces posed any threat to the helicopter-borne commando force.

At 11:00 P.M., Pakistani radars detected the five helicopters taking off from Jalalabad airfield and heading in the direction of the Pakistani border. Then, according to Pakistani military sources, the helicopters disappeared off the Pakistani radar screens. How the U.S. military was able to hide the flight of five helicopters across Pakistani territory to Abbottabad, then back to Afghanistan, remains one of the great mysteries of the mission. In fact, the version of the events of that spring weekend released by the government and corroborated by various media accounts has been criticized for possible inaccuracies and elisions. In all likelihood, we will never know with full certainty what happened from April 29 to May 1, other than the basic reality of Osama bin Laden's death.

Just before 1:00 A.M. on Sunday morning, May 1, 2011, the two Black Hawks landed the twenty-three-man SEAL team just outside the eighteen-foot-high walls of the compound. One of the Black Hawks suffered a catastrophic mechanical malfunction and had to be blown up after the operation was completed. It took fifteen minutes to storm the house inside the compound. Bin Laden was killed on the top floor. The commandos then spent the next twenty minutes going through the house seizing computers, documents, and anything else that might be of intelligence value before loading bin Laden's body and the captured material into the helicopters and starting the flight back to Afghanistan. The commandos spent thirty-eight minutes on the ground in Abbottabad; not one of them got so much as a scratch to show for the ordeal.

The operation was immediately hailed as a resounding success for the U.S. military and intelligence community. The Navy SEALs seized a huge cache of documents, such as bin Laden's handwritten daily dairy, which was found to be filled with details of planned or ongoing operations. Also seized were five computers, ten computer hard drives, and more than a hundred flash drives. All told, intelligence sources estimated the take at more than 2.7 terabytes of data, with 1 terabyte being the equivalent of 2,000 hours of audio or 220 million pages of text. At the time that this manuscript goes to press, the analysts are picking their way through this material looking for leads to current al Qaeda operations or those still in the planning stage.

The victory may be a short-lived one. Some intelligence analysts in Washington believe that bin Laden's death signals the end of what is left of al Qaeda in Pakistan. Others are not so sure. On June 15, 2011, al Qaeda announced that its new leader was bin Laden's longtime deputy, Ayman al-Zawahiri. Born in Egypt, Zawahiri has been a member of al Qaeda for over twenty years, serving as the organization's ideologue and strategist. Analysts have noted that Zawahiri does not have bin Laden's name recognition or force of personality, and his prickly nature and propensity for making decisions on a whim have sometimes gotten him into trouble with his fellow al Qaeda commanders. But a veteran CIA counterterrorism analyst stated in a 2011 interview that, despite all his faults, Zawahiri commands enormous respect within the organization because of his managerial talent, his uncompromising attitude, and his determination to continue the fight against the West.

But it probably does not really matter who is the new leader of al Qaeda. If history is any guide, bin Laden's death probably will not change much. The war on terrorism will start all over again tomorrow, and will continue unabated for the foreseeable future.

Despite the present-day recognition of its vital importance in protecting the security of the United States, historically spying has been viewed in America as one of the most odious and disreputable of professions. In 1984, Michael J. Barrett, then the assistant general counsel of the CIA, wrote that "espionage is the world's second oldest profession and just as honorable as the first."

Spying has been around since the beginning of time, and will almost certainly continue to be practiced well past most other human endeavors because as long as nations want to know "what the other guy is doing," there will be a need for spies. Spying is not just limited to nation-states. Corporations do it under the guise of "competitive intelligence." Fishermen in New England secretly monitor their competitors to see which fishing grounds are producing the best catches. Narcotics traffickers in Mexico and Colombia have for decades infiltrated government agencies, the military, and police in order to counter narcotics interdiction efforts. Arguably the most accomplished spies in the world are journalists, who, just like their clandestine counterparts, collect information obtained from open and secret sources and publish their findings in their newspapers or broadcast them on the nightly news. During the American Civil War, General William Tecumseh Sherman famously said, "I hate newspapermen. They come into camp and pick up their camp rumors and print them as facts. I regard them as spies, which, in truth, they are. If I killed them all there would be news from Hell before breakfast."

Some historians and commentators have compared spying to combat, suggesting that the endeavors of the average spy are somehow comparable to the struggles of a soldier on the battlefield. The analogy may be apt. But unlike in a typical war, which usually has a clearly defined beginning and end, and a recognized victor, in the intelligence business you can never declare victory and go home, because even after the soldiers have all gone home, the spies remain at their posts. Years ago, a now retired senior American intelligence official told me, "War is hell. Spying is much, much worse. Wars you can win. But in espionage, there are no winners because it never ends."

Which is where we find ourselves today. A decade after 9/11, the U.S. military is still engaged in two full-time wars—Afghanistan and the war on terrorism—and a host of smaller conflicts, such as our continuing involvement in the Libyan civil war. Parallel to the American military's efforts, the U.S. intelligence community has been engaged in a twilight struggle across the globe finding America's enemies, determining their plans and capabilities, and, in some cases, killing them by whatever means are available.

The principal purpose of this book is to provide the reader with a snapshot of what the U.S. intelligence community has been doing at home and abroad since Barack Obama entered the White House on January 20, 2009. What the chapters that follow show is that over the past three years America's 210,000-plus spies have been busier than ever. Take for example the following intelligence items from leaked State Department cables sent to Washington since Obama was inaugurated:

- In November 2009, the U.S. embassy in Bogotá, Colombia, reported to Washington that information developed by the CIA station (the phrase used in diplomatic cables to denote information from the CIA is "sensitive reporting") revealed that the Colombian government had secretly opened "a dialogue" with the Marxist FARC and ELN insurgent groups who had been trying to overthrow the government for decades. But the cable stated that "these efforts appear to be far from fruitful."

- In December 2009, a CIA source inside the Yemeni government in Sana'a reported, "We have learned . . . that Yemen may be pursuing sizable arms deals with several other Eastern European countries for $30 million to $55 million each."
- In January 2010, U.S. reconnaissance satellites operated by the National Reconnaissance Office revealed that the Chinese military had just conducted a successful test of an antiballistic missile weapon system in western China.
- In February 2010, the CIA station in Saudi Arabia told the State Department that al Qaeda's "ability to raise funds [in Saudi Arabia] has deteriorated substantially."
- In March 2011, the U.S. government admitted that the intelligence community had for months been secretly flying high-altitude reconnaissance missions using U.S. Air Force Global Hawk unmanned drones over northern Mexico in order to monitor the activities of the Mexican drug cartels.

These reports, while suggestive of the breadth of the intelligence community's global efforts, are just the tip of the iceberg. There have been two notable intelligence success stories over the past three years. The war in Iraq was officially declared a victory when the last American combat brigade departed in August 2010, which allowed the intelligence community to draw down its commitments in that country and shift those resources to Afghanistan; followed by the killing of Osama bin Laden in May 2011.

As will be described in greater detail in this book, however, the U.S. intelligence community has been struggling on other fronts.

- In a nationally televised address on the evening of June 22, 2011, President Obama announced that, in effect, the war in Afghanistan had been won, and that he had ordered the withdrawal of 10,000 U.S. troops from Afghanistan by the end of the year. Another 23,000 troops would return home by the summer of 2012. In justifying his decision to withdraw the troops, Obama stated that "the tide of war is receding" in Afghanistan. In reality, the opposite appears to be the case as the tempo of combat with the Taliban continues to increase rather than decrease, and there are sharply conflicting differences between the White House and the intelligence community over whether the war is going well.

- Intelligence cooperation with Pakistan came to a near-complete standstill in early 2011, calling into question whether Pakistan can ever again be trusted as a full and valued partner in the global fight against terrorism.
- The intelligence community failed to provide any discernible warnings prior to the collapse of the pro-American regimes in Egypt and Tunisia in early 2011.
- The U.S. intelligence community did a creditable job of monitoring the activities of Muammar Qaddafi's military during the six-month-long Libyan civil war in 2011. But very little of this information was ever given to the frontline Libyan rebel fighters because of questions about their reliability. Despite this, the rebels still managed to beat Qaddafi's forces and capture Tripoli on their own.
- The CIA's counterterrorism operations against al Qaeda affiliates in Yemen and Somalia have been stalled for two years. In Yemen, for instance, since the spring of 2011 anti-government tribal forces have seized more territory from government forces. After Yemeni president Ali Abdullah Saleh was gravely wounded on June 3, 2011, and left the country for medical treatment, the security situation deteriorated even further. Street protests in the capital of Sana'a and in other major Yemeni cities intensified as various opposition groups united for the first time against the Saleh regime. And the al Qaeda affiliate in the country has taken advantage of the situation to expand its zone of control in the southern part of the country.
- Iran continues to work diligently on building a nuclear weapon despite the imposition of harsh economic sanctions and the interdiction efforts of the U.S. intelligence community.
- The threat of domestic homegrown terrorism has continued to evolve in more dangerous directions since Obama became president, but the intelligence community has not shown any sign that it is adapting to meet the new threat.

Rather than describe, as other books have already done, the role played by President Obama and his national security team in Washington, this book instead focuses on the role played by the intelligence community on the battlefields in Afghanistan, Pakistan, Yemen, Somalia, and Iran, just to name a few.

The book also seeks to answer some fundamental questions, such as: Is the U.S. intelligence community finally working as it should ten years after 9/11? Does the intelligence community currently have the kind of strong, authoritative leadership needed to perform its vital mission? Have the vast number of appendages that comprise the U.S. intelligence community ever been merged into a fully functioning and cohesive organization? Is the intelligence community producing the kind of information needed by the U.S. government and military? Have the White House and the rest of the U.S. government's national security establishment made full and effective use of the material that has been produced by the intelligence community?

CHAPTER 1

Lipstick on a Pig

Warning Signs in Afghanistan

*Guard against arrogance, avoid underestimating
the enemy, and be well prepared.*
—MAO TSE-TUNG, NOVEMBER 1949

British prime minister Winston Churchill is purported to have said that "Americans will always do the right thing . . . once they have exhausted all the alternatives," which is a nice way of saying that we Americans have a nasty habit of repeating different variations of the same mistake over and over again until, usually by sheer happenstance, we finally get it right.

Churchill's words are as meaningful today as they were seventy years ago. Newly declassified documents and leaked Pentagon and State Department cables show that at the time Barack Obama was inaugurated in January 2009, the U.S. and NATO militaries were still making exactly the same mistakes in Afghanistan that American commanders had made in Vietnam over forty years earlier, and that, with some slight variations, the Soviets had repeated during their disastrous war against the mujahideen in Afghanistan during the 1980s. A decade after the U.S. invasion of Afghanistan, the White House is still, to paraphrase Churchill, exhausting all the alternatives in the search for a formula for victory. This is the story of how we got there, as seen through the eyes of American and NATO intelligence officials.

The summer of 2008 was an uneasy time for America. The economy was in a state of free fall, ultimately leading to the near-total collapse of the U.S. banking sector four months later. Nearly every evening, the network news led with stories about falling home prices and the collapse of a number of major mortgage lending institutions. The stock market was beginning to fluctuate wildly; prices for basic foodstuffs, such as bread and milk, were rising rapidly; and companies across the country were beginning to lay off thousands of workers as orders for goods and services began to dry up.

In the midst of the financial meltdown, on June 3, 2008, a formerly obscure first-term senator from Illinois named Barack Obama became the Democratic Party's presumptive candidate for president of the United States. But the election that would pit Obama against the Republican Party's presidential candidate, Senator John McCain of Arizona, was still five months away. The vast majority of Americans headed off on their summer vacations, not intending to pay much attention to the race for the White House until after the summer was over.

Almost seven thousand miles from Washington, the war against the Taliban, which had been raging without respite for almost seven years, was not going well.

On June 3, 2008, the same day that Obama became the Democratic candidate for president, General David D. McKiernan assumed command of the International Security Assistance Force (ISAF) in Kabul, and with it command of all U.S. and NATO troops in Afghanistan.

A grizzled combat veteran with thirty-six years of service, McKiernan was widely viewed within the U.S. military as one of the army's top field commanders. He had participated in the liberation of Kuwait (Operation Desert Storm) in 1991, then commanded U.S. forces in Bosnia in the mid-1990s and led troops during the war in Kosovo in 1999. He had earned plaudits for commanding all U.S. and coalition ground forces during the 2003 invasion of Iraq, leading some inside the Pentagon to whisper that he was destined to become the army chief of staff. In February 2008, McKiernan was offered the command of the 52,000 U.S. and NATO forces in Afghanistan, which on the surface was a prestigious assignment. But the choice of McKiernan puzzled many in the Pentagon because, despite his numerous accomplishments, he was a tank man who had no experience whatsoever with Afghanistan or with counterinsurgency warfare.

At McKiernan's first staff meeting, on the morning of June 4, 2008, in the wood-paneled conference room at ISAF headquarters in Kabul, his acting intelligence chief, Lt. Colonel Patrick "Pat" McNiece, told him in no uncertain terms that the 52,000 heavily armed American and NATO forces that he now commanded, backed by artillery, tanks, and limitless air power, were slowly but inexorably being driven back by a much smaller force of Taliban guerrillas, most of whom were illiterate villagers and farmers with no formal military training armed with nothing heavier than AK-47 assault rifles and rocket-propelled grenade (RPG) launchers left over from the war with the Soviets in the 1980s.

As the PowerPoint slide briefing progressed, it became increasingly clear to those in the room just how serious the situation was. Taliban attacks in the American zone of operations in eastern Afghanistan during the first six months of 2008 were up 40 percent over the previous year. In the NATO zone in southern Afghanistan, attacks had jumped by 60 percent. In the previously quiescent Italian zone of operations in western Afghanistan, Taliban attacks had jumped a startling 50 percent. The casualty figures for U.S., NATO, and Afghan troops killed or wounded in action were well above what had been experienced in 2007.

The bleakness of the briefing took many in McKiernan's party by surprise because it differed so markedly from what they had been told in Washington. One of the general's aides turned to a colleague and muttered, "Oh my God, what have we gotten ourselves into!"

Back in Washington, the Bush White House and the Pentagon were in a "state of denial," doggedly proclaiming that the trajectory of the war in Afghanistan was headed in the right direction despite much evidence to the contrary. The Pentagon and NATO's respective public relations machines furiously countered the incessant bad news about the war by giving the public a steady drumbeat of "all good news, all the time," insisting that the security situation in Afghanistan was actually improving and that the war against the Taliban insurgency was being won. Take for example the illusory assessment contained in a June 2008 Pentagon report to Congress that assured the lawmakers that "the security situation in [Afghanistan] was improving."

There were others who, at least publicly, thought that the war in Afghanistan was going well. One such person was General Dan K. McNeill, the man whom Dave McKiernan had replaced as commander of U.S. and NATO forces in Afghanistan, who wrote that "Afghanistan is clearly on the road to recovery; a president and parliament elected by the people; a constitution that is among the best in central and south Asia; an Afghan National Army and National Police that are growing in capability by the day; and reconstruction and development that are steadily improving the quality of life of the Afghan people." McNeill caustically dismissed as alarmist much of what was then appearing in the press about the increasing number of armed attacks, telling a group of amused reporters that these incidents were not the work of the Taliban but rather a reflection of what he described as increased "criminal activity, narcotics trafficking and tribal disputes."

The classified diplomatic and intelligence reporting reaching Washington from Afghanistan told a much grimmer story, one almost completely at odds with what was coming out of the White House and the Pentagon press briefing rooms, or General McNeill's assessment of the situation. According to the late Richard C. Holbrooke, President Obama's special adviser for Afghanistan and Pakistan, "There has always been a disconnect between what was being reported internally [about Afghanistan] and the talking points that the White House and Pentagon officials worked off for the Sunday talk shows . . . You would never know we were talking about the same war."

It is certainly true that in every war since the dawn of time, governments have sought to put the best possible spin on events, especially when a war is unpopular. During the Vietnam War in the 1960s and 1970s, the administrations of Lyndon Johnson and Richard Nixon, plus the U.S. military in Vietnam, played fast and loose with the facts in order to justify an increasingly unpopular war. And just as with Vietnam, the Bush administration and the American commanders in Kabul refused to accept the bad news, and would not admit to the public that the war in Afghanistan was not going well, proving correct Senator Hiram Johnson's famous assertion that truth is the first casualty of war.

An excellent example of this disconnect was the portrayal of President Hamid Karzai's Afghan government. Publicly, the U.S. government was characterizing Karzai's government as being the epitome of a vibrant new democracy.

In fact, the Afghan government was a train wreck. Seven years of ineptitude, corruption, and misrule by the Karzai regime had opened the door to the Taliban's resurgence. Angry Pashtun tribesmen, many of whom had been preyed upon by venal Afghan government officials or policemen, were flocking to the Taliban's banner by the thousands.* Not because they believed in what the Taliban stood for. Rather, they just wanted a modicum of justice and security in their lives. According to an internal planning document prepared

---

* The Pashtuns are the single largest ethnic group in Afghanistan. According to the CIA, there were an estimated eight million Pashtun tribesmen in Afghanistan in 2008, 42 percent of the country's population. Most of the Pashtuns live in the southern and eastern parts of the country, which collectively are referred to as the "Pashtun Belt."

by the U.S. embassy in Kabul, "In many areas, the Afghan population neither trusts nor respects a government they perceive to be involved in abuse of power, rampant corruption, and predatory behavior with few opportunities for redress . . . Key groups have become nostalgic for the security and justice Taliban-rule provided."

Afghanistan was, according to the watchdog group Transparency International, the second most corrupt nation on earth. Only the failed state of Somalia was worse. Longtime observers of Afghanistan are quick to point out that corruption has always been a fixture in Afghanistan society. In order to get anything done in Afghanistan, whether fixing a speeding ticket or getting a permit to sell kebabs on a street corner, payment of a small bribe (baksheesh) is a necessity. But the level of corruption in Afghanistan, especially within the Afghan government and military, has grown unchecked since the U.S. invasion of the country in 2001. By 2008, not only was corruption pervasive, it was endemic at all levels of the Afghan government, with a Pentagon document admitting that it "went beyond even cultural norms."

Centuries ago, the Italian writer Niccolò Machiavelli wrote that "the first method of estimating the intelligence of a ruler is to look at the men he has around him." In the view of many officials in the U.S. intelligence community, the open corruption of the clique of officials who constituted Karzai's kitchen cabinet spoke volumes about the regime the U.S. government and military were fighting to protect and the man who led it. The venality of many of Karzai's closest advisers was so transparent that one of the staunchest supporters of the war General Barry R. McCaffrey, President Bill Clinton's drug czar, was forced to admit that Karzai "has a collection of ruffians in his inner circle."

One notable example was the hilariously inept effort by President Karzai's political allies to rig the August 2009 Afghan presidential elections. Election monitors noticed that 3 million Afghans voted for Karzai or his political allies, but no ballots could be found for these voters. So Karzai officials hurriedly manufactured 3 million ballots to account for these "ghost voters." The fraud was quickly exposed, but of course none of the officials involved were ever punished, and Karzai's election to another term in office was certified despite what had just occurred. According to Dr. Thomas H. Johnson, a longtime Afghanistan watcher at the Naval Postgraduate School in Monterey, California, "The Kabul government is so corrupt, dysfunctional, and incompetent that even its election rigging is buffoonish."

With a few significant exceptions, Afghanistan's provincial and district governors, all of whom were political appointees named by Karzai, were taking advantage of their positions to shamelessly line their pockets by stealing reconstruction aid provided by the U.S. government, as well as through organized crime activities, narco-trafficking, smuggling, and a host of other illegal schemes. Little effort was made to hide these activities. A classified 2009 State Department survey of corruption in Ghazni Province in southeastern Afghanistan found that graft was so pervasive that the report concluded that the local provincial government was a "criminal enterprise masquerading as public administration." And the governor of neighboring Paktia Province, Juma Khan Hamdard, was deemed to be so corrupt that a secret State Department cable described him as "detrimental to the future of Afghanistan."

The Afghan National Army (ANA), which the Pentagon was loudly claiming was "a significant success story," was in fact riddled with corruption at all levels of the chain of command. Captain Carl Thompson, a Maryland Army National Guard officer who served as an adviser with the ANA from May 2006 to May 2007, recalled that his Afghan brigade commander siphoned off half the fuel out of every shipment his unit received and diverted it to gas stations owned by his family; and one of the brigade's logistics officers stole thousands of prepackaged meals (MREs) meant for his soldiers and sold them on the black market.

Corruption in the poorly trained and ill-disciplined 98,000-man Afghan National Police (ANP) was much worse, with Afghan policemen in many instances openly preying on the Afghan villagers they were supposed to protect. The predations of the ANP were most apparent in Kabul. On the road into downtown Kabul from the airport, Afghan policemen routinely stopped taxi drivers at checkpoints to demand bribes for alleged minor driving infractions. You could rid yourself of this hassle by paying a 1,000-afghani ($20) bribe to the police commander at the first checkpoint leading to the airport, who then radioed all other checkpoints down the road to let you pass without incident. A prominent Kabul businessman only half-jokingly admitted that he could not leave home without a thick wad of 100-afghani bills in his pocket so that he could bribe all of the policemen who routinely stopped him on the way to work. The situation was so apparent that a 2008 National Intelligence Estimate (NIE) on Afghanistan described the ANP as "a predatory force plagued by systemic problems beyond lack of professionalism, equipment, and training."

The U.S.-government-run reconstruction effort in Afghanistan was both underfunded and horrendously mismanaged. Tens of millions of dollars of U.S. taxpayer money intended to help rebuild Afghanistan was being stolen from right under the noses of the U.S. government agencies that were supposed to oversee these programs. A British aid official interviewed in 2010 recalled one particularly egregious example in which the U.S. Agency for International Development (USAID) paid some politically connected Afghan construction contractors $600,000 to build a grammar school in downtown Kabul that should have cost only $30,000. The remaining $570,000 ended up in the Dubai bank accounts of the contractors and their patrons in the Afghan government. A March 2010 report estimated that every weekday, couriers carrying $10 million in stolen financial aid left on the daily Ariana Airlines flights from Kabul International Airport bound for offshore banking centers in Dubai, Turkey, Yemen, and even the United States.

But corruption was only a small part of the problem. Another factor driving the Taliban insurgency forward was that Afghanistan economically was a basket case. The United Nations still ranked Afghanistan as the fifth-poorest nation on the face of the earth, despite the billions of dollars of U.S. financial aid that had been poured into the country since the 2001 U.S. invasion. More than 41 percent of the Afghan populace still lived below the poverty line, and unemployment stood at a staggering 40 percent. Food shortages were widespread, and malnutrition was pervasive. Seventy-two percent of all Afghans could not read or write, the lowest literacy rate in the world. The average life expectancy of an Afghan was still only forty-two years, and twenty-six out of every hundred Afghan children died before they reached the age of five, the worst infant mortality rate in world.

The efforts of the U.S. government and the international community to reduce the illegal narcotics trade in Afghanistan had been an abysmal failure. Almost seven years' worth of eradication efforts had been for naught, and billions of dollars wasted with little to show the effort. As of the summer of 2008, 2 million Afghan farmers were still openly growing opium poppies, and nobody wanted to do anything about it because opium farming and cultivation accounted for a staggering 30 percent of the Afghan gross domestic product. Even the Pentagon's "emphasize the positive" 2008 annual report to Congress had to admit that "the overall counternarcotics efforts in Afghanistan have not been successful."

Socially, the already weak threads that bound Afghanistan together as a nation were fraying. Organized crime was pervasive everywhere, and armed robbery and prostitution, all but unheard of during the Taliban regime, were now widespread problems in Kabul and the other big Afghan cities. Drug addiction had reached epidemic proportions, with a 2009 United Nations study estimating that there were at least 900,000 drug addicts in Afghanistan. A report prepared by the ISAF Rule of Law adviser revealed that in Helmand Province alone, "provincial officials believe nearly 60% of Helmand's police force abuse drugs and that there are at least 70,000 addicts now living in Helmand."

Security conditions in "the Lumpy Suck," the less than affectionate nickname given to Afghanistan by American GIs, had become so bad that the country had replaced Iraq as the most dangerous on the face of the planet. Taliban attacks across the country had jumped by one third, clearly indicating that the Afghan insurgents had become far more aggressive than had been the case in previous years. Declassified Department of Defense statistics show that as of June 2008, there were more combat incidents taking place in Afghanistan than in Iraq. And in the fall of 2008, another grim milestone was reached. According to the authoritative casualty database compiled by icasualties.org, beginning in May 2008 and continuing for the rest of the year, more Americans were killed every month in Afghanistan than in Iraq.

In southern Afghanistan, the Taliban had managed to consolidate their stranglehold on significant parts of four key provinces that were garrisoned by troops from Great Britain, Canada, the Netherlands, and Romania. The Dutch general commanding the NATO forces in southern Afghanistan, Major General Mart de Kruif, reported that the 23,000 soldiers under his command controlled, at best, 60 percent of the territory he was responsible for, and this was an optimistic assessment. And in the American-controlled sector in southeastern Afghanistan, the Taliban had managed to advance almost to the gates of Kabul, capturing large parts of three provinces (Logar, Wardak, and Ghazni) to the south and west of the Afghan capital, and had made significant inroads into the two provinces northeast of the city (Kapisa and Laghman provinces).

Even in the Afghan capital of Kabul the situation was perilous. Customs officials at Kabul International Airport admitted to visitors that they saw flak jackets and Kevlar helmets in almost all of the checked baggage that they inspected coming off incoming flights. All of the Western-style luxury hotels in Kabul had their own private security force, bomb squad, and SWAT team equipped with heavy weaponry that would be the envy of any Third World army. Guests at hotels in Kabul were frisked and their baggage searched upon checking in. Once they got to their rooms, they found on the nightstand next to their beds detailed instructions on what to do in case the hotel was bombed or attacked by Taliban gunmen. But these extraordinary security measures are little more than window dressing, as was proved by the bloody Taliban attack on the InterContinental Hotel in Kabul on June 29, 2011, which killed at least ten guests and wounded dozens more.

Even the 2008 edition of the *Lonely Planet* tourist guidebook for Afghanistan urged visitors to memorize how to say "Help!" (*Komak!*), "Is it safe?" (*Khatar day?*), "Are there landmines?" (*Dalta nazhde kum mayn sha?*), "bomb" (*bam*), "rifle" (*topak*), "rocket" (*raket*), "soldier" (*askar*), and "fighting" (*jang*).

As of the summer of 2008, the U.S. intelligence community had been trying for six years to warn the White House and the Pentagon that the security situation in Afghanistan was headed in the wrong direction, but no one in Washington was listening or seemed to want to hear what the spies were saying.

In September 2002, as the U.S. military prepared for the invasion of Iraq, the CIA issued a National Intelligence Estimate which expressed the concern of the U.S. intelligence community that all was not well in Afghanistan. In the year since the downfall of the Taliban regime, armed clashes among and between warring Afghan ethnic and tribal groups had increased. Organized crime and narcotics trafficking, absent during the Taliban regime, had returned. And roving bands of Taliban guerrillas were once again operating in southern Afghanistan, attacking isolated American outposts and killing Afghan government officials and policemen.

Secretary of Defense Donald Rumsfeld asked U.S. Central Command commander in chief General Tommy Franks to write a rebuttal. Voicing the view of the White House and the Pentagon, in October 2002 Franks issued his own estimate, which asserted that "the CIA assessment overstates the immediate risks to stability and security, and understates the positive developments underway to bring stability to Afghanistan." For the next six years this was to be the position of the White House and the Pentagon whenever the intelligence community raised concerns about the deteriorating security situation in Afghanistan.

Six years later, no one in the White House was paying attention to what the intelligence analysts were saying. The U.S. intelligence community was still being blackballed because many senior Bush administration officials believed that CIA officials had tried to undermine the White House and pin the blame for the 2002–3 Iraqi weapons of mass destruction (WMD) intelligence fiasco on President George W. Bush and his senior advisers. In retaliation, CIA director George J. Tenet was stripped of his access to the Oval Office and eventually forced to resign in June 2004. In his memoirs published after he left office, Tenet openly criticized a number of Bush's advisers, among them Secretary of Defense Rumsfeld, for what he described as "cherry picking" intelligence to support their desire to invade Iraq. Four years after Tenet's resignation, the White House and the intelligence community had still not patched up their differences. Much of what the intelligence community was reporting to the White House about Afghanistan was, according to a former CIA official, still being "shit-canned."

This was not the first time that the CIA had been blackballed by the White House. In 1964, CIA director John A. McCone had incurred the wrath of President Lyndon B. Johnson by disagreeing with the White House's plans to expand the U.S. role in the war in Vietnam. President Johnson punished McCone by shunning him and denying him access to the White House, leading to McCone's resignation in April 1965. As a declassified CIA history put it, "McCone found resignation preferable to being ignored."

In the rarefied climes of the U.S. intelligence community, being ignored by the Oval Office is nothing short of a catastrophe. Without access to the president, and with senior policymakers either refusing to read its reports or openly questioning the veracity of their contents, by 2008 the U.S. intelligence community's ability to effectively perform its principal mission of informing and advising the executive branch of the U.S. government had been reduced to a very low order.

Virtually no one in official Washington, except perhaps for a few senior officials in the State Department, was paying much attention to what the intelligence community was reporting about Afghanistan in the summer of 2008. A former official who was then involved in the Afghan policymaking process admitted in a 2010 interview that Afghan president Hamid Karzai "could have run through the West Wing [of the White House] with his hair on fire and nobody would have paid much attention."

Once the Washington bureaucracy becomes fixed in a herd mentality, nothing short of a major catastrophe can shake it. According to Paul R. Pillar, the CIA's national intelligence officer for the Near East and South Asia from 2000 to 2005 and a thirty-year intelligence veteran, "Experience has shown that major policy changes tend to come only from actual disasters."

For example, the 1968 Tet Offensive in Vietnam laid bare for everyone to see all of the fallacies of the Johnson administration's Vietnam War strategy. The disastrous two-day battle in Mogadishu, Somalia, in October 1993 made famous by the book *Black Hawk Down* and the film of the same name, which resulted in eighteen American soldiers killed and seventy-three wounded, led the Clinton administration to accept that the war was not winnable and pull U.S. forces out of Somalia. But nothing comparable had yet happened to wake the somnolent Washington bureaucracy up to what was happening in Afghanistan.

What is now referred to as the "Taliban resurgence" began in February 2006, when thousands of newly recruited Taliban guerrillas swarmed across the border from Pakistan into southern Afghanistan and launched their first nationwide offensive. Their timing could not have been better. On February 22, 2006, just as the Taliban's offensive was kicking off, Iraqi insurgents bombed the al-Askari mosque in the city of Samarra, one of the holiest shrines for Iraqi Shiites. In the months that followed, Iraq was swallowed up in wave after wave of sectarian violence, which produced carnage on a scale never seen before in Iraq. As this was happening, the Taliban overran huge portions of four key provinces in southern Afghanistan, including Helmand Province, the heart of the Afghan illegal narcotics industry.

The 2006 Taliban nationwide offensive took the U.S. intelligence community, and virtually every senior U.S. military commander and diplomat in Kabul, by surprise. Nobody in the U.S. government or intelligence community then thought that the Taliban were capable of mounting a nationwide offensive, much less capturing huge chunks of the southern part of Afghanistan. During the summer of 2006, the CIA station chief in Kabul, John C. "Chris" Wood, sent a number of cables to Washington warning that the military situation in Afghanistan was now deteriorating. Wood's cables were ignored by the White House and the Pentagon, who were focused on the rapidly escalating cycle of violence in Iraq.

A small number of Pentagon officials were alarmed by what was taking place in Afghanistan. In August 2006, Defense Policy Board official Marin Strmecki wrote a memo to Secretary of Defense Donald Rumsfeld warning that "the deteriorating security situation in 2006 was principally the result of the combination of two factors: A decision by the Taliban and its external supporters to escalate the scope and character of enemy operations; and weak or bad governance, particularly in southern Afghanistan, that created a vacuum of power into which the enemy moved." But Strmecki's memo was ignored.

It did not help that the U.S. ambassador to Afghanistan, Ronald E. Neumann, was telling Washington the exact opposite of what Wood and Strmecki were reporting, telling Washington that the war was still being won and that the rise in Taliban attacks was only a temporary phenomenon. According to

Neumann, "The violence does not indicate a failing policy; on the contrary we need to persevere in what we are doing . . . We are on the right track."

In November 2006, the office of the director of national intelligence (DNI) had issued a classified National Intelligence Estimate on the security situation in Afghanistan, the first that had been published on this subject in over three years. Written under the supervision of Dr. Nancy Jo Powell, a career diplomat who was the national intelligence officer for South Asia in the office of the DNI, the report took serious issue with Ambassador Neumann's rosy prognosis, warning that the Taliban had made substantial progress on the Afghan battlefield over the preceding nine months, capturing the vast majority of the strategically important Helmand Province and large parts of neighboring Kandahar Province in southern Afghanistan. The report also noted that the Taliban guerrilla forces were not only larger and more capable but becoming far more aggressive, and that the escalating numbers of insurgent attacks were threatening to destabilize the entire southern part of the country and bring the already stalled reconstruction effort to a complete halt.

A secret NATO intelligence summary confirmed the gist of Powell's assessment, stating that "the Taliban, despite not winning any clear-cut battles, has nevertheless been able to increase its influence, particularly in southern Afghanistan. Helmand province continues to be the focus of the Taliban, where they are consolidating safe areas; they also hope to cut off or capture Kandahar city. The morale and confidence of fighters remains high. Funding to the Taliban has increased significantly over the last year, including from Arab countries, while revenues from the opium trade are likely to increase in 2007."

Other classified reporting from Afghanistan confirmed that the Taliban's battlefield successes were further damaging the reconstruction efforts in the south, with a leaked cable from the U.S. embassy in Kabul to Washington confirming that "the Taliban campaign in outlying areas has convinced significant portions of the local population the GOA [government of Afghanistan] cannot deliver governance and that ISAF [International Security Assistance Force, the combined U.S.–NATO command headquarters in Kabul] and international resolve are withering."

These stark warning signs, none of which were ever released to the public, were ignored by the White House and other Bush administration policymakers because, according to Paul D. Miller, a senior CIA intelligence analyst who headed the National Security Council's Afghan desk from 2007 to 2009, the White House and the Pentagon were so focused on the events then taking place in Iraq that no one was paying much attention at all to what was going on in Afghanistan. "Some policymakers were not aware of the deteriorating situation in Afghanistan," Miller later wrote in the CIA's internal journal. "Others were aware, but chose to give more attention and resources to Iraq because they judged it to be a higher strategic priority or in greater danger of outright failure."

Another problem was that a powerful coterie of officials in the White House and the Pentagon, centered around Vice President Dick Cheney, firmly believed that the U.S. intelligence community was being alarmist and overstating the seriousness of the situation in Afghanistan. These officials were more inclined to believe the reporting coming from the U.S. ambassador to Afghanistan and the senior U.S. military commander in Kabul, General Dan McNeill, whose views on the war were on the whole much rosier than what the intelligence community was reporting.

The years 2007 and 2008 were a time of repeated clashes between the White House and the Pentagon on one hand and the intelligence community on the other over what was the true state of affairs in Afghanistan. For instance, at a classified 2008 briefing for a congressional oversight committee, Pentagon officials argued that the Taliban could not win the war in Afghanistan because the insurgents were split into three major factions, each with different agendas and goals. The intelligence community agreed that the Taliban were not a unified, monolithic force but told the lawmakers that the classified reporting they were getting showed that despite their loose organization, the fighters belonging to the various Taliban factions were closely cooperating on the battlefield inside Afghanistan, especially in the American zone in southeastern Afghanistan, and were becoming increasingly effective.

At the same time, the Pentagon was telling Congress that large numbers of al Qaeda fighters were operating alongside Taliban guerrillas inside Afghanistan. Weary CIA officials had to go up to Capitol Hill again to refute these allegations because the classified reporting they were seeing showed that al Qaeda had become a virtually nonexistent player in Afghanistan, with no more than a hundred al Qaeda fighters operating inside Afghanistan at any one time in 2008. It was an all too typical case of the Pentagon hyping the threat in Afghanistan by fudging the facts.

In fact, the senior leadership of the Taliban and al Qaeda vehemently disagreed on the fundamental goals of their respective organizations. These divergent goals were spelled out in a January 2007 interview with Taliban leader Mullah Mohammed Omar, who stated unequivocally that his organization only wanted to drive U.S. and foreign troops out of Afghanistan, which conflicted with al Qaeda's goal of waging global jihad against the West. Resentment of al Qaeda by senior Taliban commanders ran deep. Mullah Sabir, a senior Taliban commander in southeastern Afghanistan, told *Newsweek* "If they [al Qaeda] want to hide and fight here with us, we won't stop them. But they have no bases here, and we will not let them use our territory as they did before their strikes on the United States . . . Today we are fighting because of Al Qaeda. We lost our Islamic state. Al Qaeda lost nothing."

The propensity of the White House and the Pentagon for "emphasizing the positive" about the war in Afghanistan was a constant source of frustration within the U.S. intelligence community. In a 2010 interview, a senior U.S. intelligence official who formerly served on the National Intelligence Council, the organization that wrote all of the National Intelligence Estimates that were sent to the president and his top national security advisers, said, "We gave the White House all the news that was fit to print, good and bad, about what was going on in Afghanistan. The problem was that somewhere between the time we sent over our assessments to the White House and the time our material ended up on the president's desk, the bad news somehow disappeared . . . It sure looked to me like someone was washing any material that might give the president heartburn out of our reporting."

Thirty years earlier, President Lyndon Johnson's national security adviser, Walt Rostow, had done exactly the same thing, cleansing all reporting coming out of the intelligence community of any information that ran contrary to the administration's position that the war in Vietnam was going well. In early 1967, Rostow asked the CIA to prepare a list of accomplishments that had been achieved in Vietnam that President Johnson could cite in a forthcoming speech. The CIA very reluctantly complied with the request, providing Rostow with a list of both achievements and what were described as "setbacks and losses." Rostow knew that the president did not want to hear any bad news, so he cut out the section of the CIA report on "setbacks and losses" and forwarded the rest of the document to President Johnson.

The U.S. intelligence community's reporting on Afghanistan was deficient in many important respects. While the high-level National Intelligence Estimates proved to be remarkably prescient in accurately predicting the downward trend in security conditions in Afghanistan, much of the underlying analysis and reporting often amounted to little more than educated speculation. According to Major General Mike Flynn, the chief of military intelligence in Afghanistan from 2009 to 2010, his intelligence analysts in Kabul were so starved for information that many admitted that "their jobs feel more like fortune telling than serious detective work . . . It is little wonder then that many decision-makers rely more upon newspapers than military intelligence to obtain ground truth."

The simple reason for this was that high-level intelligence about the Taliban was extremely hard to come by. There were no high-grade intercepts of Taliban leaders talking on their cell phones, nor had the CIA or any of its foreign partners ever managed to insert an agent into the Taliban's high command in Quetta, Pakistan. The CIA stations in Kabul and Islamabad had tried just about everything they could think of to penetrate the high command, but without much success to show for all the time and vast sums of money spent on these efforts.

A CIA case officer recalled that midway through the Bush administration's second term in office, the agency's Kandahar base in southern Afghanistan was running an agent network comprised of Afghan and Pakistani truck drivers who drove Russian-made 2.5-ton "Jingle" trucks loaded with cargo back and forth between Kandahar and Quetta, which is widely believed to be where Taliban leader Mullah Omar and the rest of his fellow insurgent leaders have been hiding since the fall of the Taliban regime in December 2001. Upon returning to Kandahar, the truckers would report to their CIA handlers any signs of Taliban activity they observed at the police checkpoints, petrol stations, and truck stops between the border crossing point at Spin Boldak and Quetta. The truckers produced reams of material about price gouging at local gas stations and corruption among local Pakistani police, but nothing about the Taliban. After a short period of time, the CIA station in Kabul judged the operation to be unproductive and shut it down.

Over time, among the most important and productive, if unlikely, sources of intelligence information for the U.S. intelligence community about the Afghan insurgents have proven to be the Taliban's Web sites, such as the English-language *Voice of Jihad*. These Web sites are monitored twenty-four hours a day, seven days a week by CIA and ISAF intelligence analysts for any new information that might reveal the Taliban's short- or long-term plans, or insight into the thinking of the Taliban's leadership in Quetta.

For instance, every year in April, the Taliban's leadership posts a communiqué on these sites announcing the launch of their annual nationwide offensive inside Afghanistan. American commanders in Kabul initially scoffed at these pronouncements, but the laughter quickly died when the communiqués proved to be accurate. The Taliban also post on the sites detailed battlefield updates, which have also been found to be generally accurate.

The most valuable information comes from the Taliban's glossy online magazine *al-Samoud*, which depending on which dictionary you consult translates as either "Resistance" or "Resilience." American and NATO intelligence analysts are nearly unanimous in their opinion that *al-Samoud* has proven to be a particularly rich source of information about the inner workings of the Afghan insurgents, with each issue including interviews with senior Taliban officials and commanders, giving the names, backgrounds, and even color photographs of the Taliban's "shadow governors" and senior field commanders in Afghanistan, as well as providing descriptions of Taliban combat operations and obituaries of commanders killed in action.

During the Bush administration, Pentagon officials pressed the U.S. intelligence community to jam or disrupt the Taliban's Web sites, all of which had been traced long ago by NSA to computer servers inside Pakistan. Intelligence officials absolutely refused, on the grounds that these sites were among the best sources of intelligence information on the Taliban that they had available to them. The sites have been allowed to continue to operate unmolested ever since.

In some key areas, the U.S. intelligence community knew virtually nothing about the enemy we were fighting in Afghanistan. The quality of the intelligence on the Taliban was so deficient that even Afghan president Hamid Karzai wondered aloud how good U.S. intelligence on the Taliban was, asking the then commander of U.S. Central Command, General David H. Petraeus, "if we really knew who we were fighting."

For instance, the U.S. intelligence community had no clear idea how many Taliban guerrillas our soldiers were up against. In 2008 there were literally dozens of estimates floating around the U.S. intelligence community on the number of Taliban guerrillas, but not one of them was based on any hard factual information. It was all pure guesswork. When asked about this problem, General Dan McNeill, a former commander of U.S. and NATO forces in Afghanistan, had to admit to Pentagon reporters, "I don't know the answer."

The further down the chain of command you went, the more apparent it became how little we knew about our enemy. According to Captain Daniel Helmer, a twenty-six-year-old Rhodes Scholar who served as a U.S. Army adviser to the Afghan National Police, then helped establish the Afghan

Counterinsurgency Academy in Kabul, "We have only the most trivial understanding at the local level of who the insurgents are and what their narratives,
networks, motivations, demands, and support structures are. We have an even
poorer understanding of the human terrain, such as tribes and other networks,
and their dynamics . . . While we possess some national-level understanding
of the insurgency, we know little about how various pieces of the puzzle fit
from one region into another. We have not been able to predict what the enemy will do, nor have we been able to disrupt his decision cycle."

We did not even know much about the men leading the Taliban insurgency
in spite of the puff profiles the analysts were reading on the Taliban's Web
sites. This was made abundantly clear in 2010, after an incident in which a
man claiming to be a senior Taliban official named Mullah Akhtar Mohammed Mansour was secretly flown to Kabul ostensibly to negotiate peace terms
with the Afghan government on behalf of Taliban leader Mohammed Omar.

Mansour should have been well known to U.S. intelligence. He had been the
commander of the Taliban's air force prior to the collapse of the Taliban regime
in December 2001, and since 2003 he had been a member of the Taliban Leadership Council in Quetta as well as the Taliban's "shadow governor" of Kandahar
Province.

But it turned out that the man claiming to be Mansour was an impostor.
The con was only uncovered weeks later when an Afghan government official
who knew Mansour alerted the Afghan intelligence service that the man on
the other side of the negotiating table was not Mullah Mansour. The impostor
immediately disappeared, but not before collecting suitcases of cash from
NATO and Afghan officials to compensate him for his services. According to
Robert Baer, a veteran CIA clandestine services officer, the incident was yet
"another worrying sign that we're fighting blind in Afghanistan."

More often than not, Western newspapers and reports put out by nongov-
ernmental organizations have done a better job of correctly assessing the security situation in Afghanistan than the classified reporting being produced
by the U.S. intelligence community in Washington or the Kabul-based intelligence analysts. The former chief of intelligence in Afghanistan, Major General Mike Flynn, has admitted that some of his battalion intelligence officers
had told him that they were getting "more information that is helpful by reading U.S. newspapers than through reviewing regional command intelligence
summaries."

In November 2007, a widely respected London-based nonprofit organization, the Senlis Council, issued a study based on the reporting they were receiv-

ing from their personnel on the ground in Afghanistan. Its central conclusion was that the Taliban guerrillas had extended their operations into 54 percent of the 398 districts in Afghanistan and were also "enjoying increasing control of several parts of southern, south-eastern and western Afghanistan, ever more complicating the NATO-ISAF stabilization mission in the country."

The report came under attack almost instantly, both publicly and privately, from a host of senior NATO defense officials and military commanders, including the commander of U.S. and NATO forces in Afghanistan, General Dan McNeill, all of whom disputed the report's conclusions and claimed that the Taliban held only a small sliver of largely desolate and sparsely populated rural districts in the southern part of the country, and as such posed no meaningful threat to security or the ongoing reconstruction efforts in Afghanistan. According to General McNeill's spokesman, Brigadier General Carlos Branco, the Taliban controlled only five of the fifty-nine districts in southern Afghanistan, and the territory they did control consisted only of "very small pockets without territorial continuity."

On the other hand, the U.S. intelligence community's Afghan specialists generally agreed with the conclusion of the Senlis report because it matched almost exactly what they had been saying for two years. In early 2008, the national intelligence officer for South Asia, Dr. Peter R. Lavoy, sent to policymakers a classified paper, which, in essence, came down on the side of the Senlis Council, concluding that security conditions in Afghanistan were indeed deteriorating. Instead of the five districts General McNeill's staff argued the insurgents held, Lavoy's paper concluded that the Taliban largely controlled about 10 percent of the country; and in the territory that they controlled they had established "shadow governments," including fully functional civil administration, police, and judicial systems, that were far more efficient and efficacious than the legitimate but corrupt and inefficient Afghan government.

A Dutch military intelligence officer with over a decade of experience gained in hellholes like Bosnia, Kosovo, and Eritrea, Jaap Maartens (pseudonym) was one of the more than 870 officers, enlisted men, civilians, and contractors from twenty-six NATO countries who worked on the staff of the International Security Assistance Force, the combined U.S.-NATO headquarters in downtown Kabul that commanded all 52,000 U.S. and NATO troops in Afghanistan.

The ISAF headquarters compound where Maartens worked was located in the heart of the heavily guarded section of downtown Kabul known as the

"Green Zone," a 300-acre island of relative serenity surrounded by twenty-foot-high whitewashed walls topped by barbed wire, security cameras, and imposing guard towers that were manned twenty-four hours a day. The American commander of ISAF, General David D. McKiernan, and his fifty-man command staff had their offices on the second floor of the "Yellow Building," a battered two-story mustard yellow structure that formerly housed the Afghan Military Sports Club until the Soviet invasion in 1979. In and around the Yellow Building were a number of first-class dining facilities, fast-food outlets, a modern fitness center complete with racks of free weights and Stair Masters, a baseball field, and a host of other modern amenities, including a pizza parlor, seven bars, and even a German beer garden in a Muslim country where the consumption of alcohol is strictly forbidden.

A member of the ISAF intelligence staff's "Red Cell," Maartens was tasked with keeping track of the Taliban's senior leadership, constantly trawling the intelligence databases that were available to him looking for new snippets of information about the men who were leading the insurgency in Afghanistan—who they were, their backgrounds, names of wives and children, education, prior military experience, and even trying to divine their motivations by what they told friends, family, and the occasional reporter. In short, his job was to put himself in the shoes of his enemy to try to figure out what made them tick.

Like the vast majority of his colleagues, Maartens personally loathed the Taliban. He thought that everything the Taliban stood for was abhorrent, and their extreme interpretation of Islam morally repugnant. He was convinced that if the Taliban should win the war, they would return Afghanistan to exactly the same kind of extremist form of government that had existed when Mullah Omar ran the country from 1996 to 2001. Regardless of his personal feelings, though, Maartens was a consummate professional and he had a job to do, which was to try to assess the military strength and capabilities of the Taliban insurgency without passion or prejudice.

By the summer of 2008, Maartens had become convinced from his reading of classified intelligence reporting that all the talk emanating from senior U.S., Canadian, and European politicians and generals that the coalition forces were winning the war in Afghanistan was, in the words of his supervisor, a British Army officer with long experience in Afghanistan, akin to "trying to put lipstick on a pig."

In the opinion of Maartens and his fellow intelligence analysts in Kabul, the Taliban were prevailing because they were fighting a smarter war than the U.S. and NATO forces, who were trying to fight a counterinsurgency campaign with a badly flawed military strategy, very limited resources, and little public support back at home.

The biggest problem was that U.S. and NATO troop levels in Afghanistan were far below what was needed to combat the growing number of Taliban guerrilla attacks in the south. Dr. Thomas Johnson of the Naval Postgraduate School, one of the leading scholars of the war in Afghanistan, has written that "the minimal U.S. troop presence in the south [of Afghanistan] means that the rugged, porous, and often ill-defined 2,450 km border between Pakistan and Afghanistan does not even constitute a speed bump to groups such as the Taliban and Al Qaeda seeking to increase their influence among the Pashtun tribesmen in the region."

Everyone agreed that poor leadership of the coalition war effort in Afghanistan was also a huge problem. Since 2002, a series of conventionally minded American generals, none of whom had any experience in counterinsurgency warfare, had tried and failed to beat the Taliban guerrillas using the same "search and destroy" tactics that the U.S. Army had used in Vietnam forty years earlier, and that the Soviets had repeated during the 1980s with the same disastrous results. Some American officers serving in Afghanistan who had studied military history at West Point or in college wondered how the generals in Kabul could be so stupid as to repeat the mistakes of the past. Marine Corps Lt. Colonel Chris Nash, who served a tour of duty as an adviser with the Afghan National Army in 2007 and 2008, later caustically wrote that the U.S. military in Afghanistan was "stealing pages from the Russian playbook one by one."

The parallels with the Soviet military's disastrous experience in Afghanistan in the 1980s were striking. The U.S. and NATO troops in Afghanistan, under strict orders from the risk-averse ISAF command staff in Kabul to keep casualties to a minimum, had reverted to what a U.S. Marine Corps After Action Report not meant for release to the public described as a "forward operating base mindset." Just like the Soviet military twenty years earlier, 90 percent of all U.S. and allied troops in Afghanistan were holed up behind the walls of 150 heavily fortified forward operating bases and smaller outposts trying to protect the country's cities and towns. In Helmand Province in southwestern Afghanistan, which the Taliban had controlled since 2006, British commanders admitted to American vice-president-elect Joe Biden in January 2009 that their four thousand troops were essentially being held captive inside their firebases by the Taliban, who roamed at will outside the gates of the bases.

In the summer of 2008, the British Army garrison in the town of Sangin in Helmand Province found itself surrounded by hundreds of Taliban fighters and cut off from the rest of the British forces in the province. The garrison in Sangin, belonging to Lt. Colonel Ed Freely's 1st Battalion of the 1 Royal Irish Regiment, was unable to move more than a mile or two beyond the town's outskirts without coming under attack by the Taliban. When Freely's troops opened an outpost south of Sangin called Patrol Base Armagh, the Taliban immediately cut it off, blocked the only road between the base and Sangin with dozens of IEDs (improvised explosive devices), and tied down the outpost's garrison with relentless RPG and AK-47 fire. Fearing that the Taliban might overrun the isolated and lightly manned outpost, the British evacuated it less than a month after it was established.

When the U.S. and NATO troops did venture out of their bases, they tended not to stray far from the beaten track, staying close to the roads because their heavy armored vehicles had very limited off-road capacity. For example, the six-ton MRAP mine-resistant vehicles used by the U.S. Army and Marines, which broke down frequently, were so heavy that they could not be used off road.

At nightfall, following the protocol laid down by the generals in Kabul, the patrols retired to the safety of their firebases, relinquishing control of the countryside to the Taliban. In the morning, the process repeated itself all over again, with one Marine Corps officer sarcastically characterizing this practice as "Clear . . . go back to FOB. Clear . . . go back to FOB," a repeat of what the U.S. military in Vietnam had done more than forty years earlier. Over time the U.S. and NATO troops wearied of their Catch-22 predicament and abandoned to the enemy's control the rural towns and villages around their bases that they were unable to protect, which is also exactly what the Russian military had done in Afghanistan in the 1980s.

The situation maps in the heavily guarded joint operations center at Kandahar International Airport, from where the military activities of all NATO forces in southern Afghanistan were controlled, looked like a post-Surrealist painting, consisting of dozens of blue inkblots, representing the firebases manned by NATO forces, surrounded by a sea of red, which represented the areas that were controlled or contested by the Taliban. Major Fred Tanner, who was the military assistant to Brigadier General John W. Nicholson, the American deputy commander of forces in southern Afghanistan, recalled that "there were areas where we had absolutely no presence, that we had ceded control to the Taliban. That was shocking to me."

There was near unanimity among intelligence analysts that the U.S.-NATO strategy of depending on air power to make up for lack of "boots on the ground" was also not working. According to declassified data, in 2008 U.S. and NATO warplanes were flying ninety bombing missions a day in Afghanistan. More bombs were being dropped in Afghanistan than in Iraq. U.S. and NATO commanders in Afghanistan wasted no opportunity to publicly crow about the staggering body count that these air strikes inevitably produced, forgetting the lesson learned the hard way in Vietnam that in a guerrilla war, the body count means absolutely nothing.

Classified U.S. Army and Marine Corps intelligence assessments confirmed that the bombing attacks in Afghanistan were having little, if any, effect on the Taliban's ability or willingness to fight. A restricted-access Marine Corps intelligence briefing revealed that while the air strikes were indeed killing hundreds of Taliban field commanders and thousands of their fighters, the attacks were not disrupting the Taliban's military operations in any meaningful way.

The air strikes were actually helping the Taliban by indiscriminately killing thousands of innocent Afghan civilians. Every errant air strike that ended up killing civilians handed the Taliban propaganda machine a victory and led to dozens of angry young Pashtun men flocking to join the Taliban's banner. U.S. and NATO intelligence analysts at the time estimated that for every civilian killed by an air strike, the Taliban got as many as twenty new recruits seeking revenge for the death of their relatives.

On April 13, 2010, General Stanley A. McChrystal, former commander of U.S. and NATO forces in Afghanistan, admitted something that the intelligence analysts had been saying for years—dependence on air strikes was self-defeating: "Because of civilian casualties I think we have just about eroded our credibility here in Afghanistan. The constant repeat of civilian casualties is now so dangerous that it threatens the mission."

The Taliban, on the other hand, have never aspired to win the war in Afghanistan by force of arms. Borrowing a page from the playbook utilized by the Viet Cong during the early stages of the Vietnam War, the Taliban's strategy has always been to outlast the U.S. and NATO forces, trading the lives of their fighters for time while wearing down their larger and better-armed opponents with a ceaseless campaign of ambushes, suicide bombings, and IED attacks.

According to a senior Pakistani intelligence official, Mullah Baradar, the Taliban's military chief who was captured in Karachi, Pakistan, in February 2010, told his interrogators that the Taliban's strategy was predicated on the belief that if they could hold on long enough, eventually public support in the West for the war would dissipate and force the United States and allied governments to pull their troops out of Afghanistan, just as the Russians had done in February 1989. In short, the Taliban viewed the war in Afghanistan as a battle of wills.

There was no questioning that the Taliban's commitment to their cause was very real. They had demonstrated their determination to win by the willingness of their mostly illiterate fighters to absorb massive numbers of casualties and endure extreme hunger and privation over a span of ten long years. According to a restricted-access Marine Corps intelligence study, the Taliban guerrillas are "simply the ones committed enough to live in misery in order to win."

The Taliban's strategy was prevailing. Despite having lost every battle since the U.S.-led invasion in October 2001, and suffering casualties so severe that they would have crippled a Western army, the Taliban had not only survived the best shots that the U.S. and NATO forces could dish out, but they had emerged stronger, smarter, and more resilient than before. In the process, they had succeeded in bringing reconstruction in southern Afghanistan to a near-complete halt, driven a wedge between coalition forces and the populace of southern Afghanistan, and further weakened the credibility of Hamid Karzai's government.

According to Major Jim Grant, a Green Beret officer who served multiple tours of duty in Afghanistan, "We have killed thousands and thousands of the 'enemy' in Afghanistan and it clearly has not brought us closer to our objectives there. Just as important is the fact that we could kill thousands more and still not be any closer five years from now."

By 2008, Mullah Omar's guerrilla fighters had morphed from what Donald Rumsfeld had while secretary of defense sarcastically described in one of his periodic fits of bravado as a motley collection of "religious zealots, criminals, narco-traffickers, and social malcontents" into a cohesive and surprisingly sophisticated guerrilla force that was, in almost all respects, a tougher, smarter, and more disciplined foe than the local insurgents and al Qaeda fighters that the American troops had faced in Iraq.

American and European politicians may have had only contempt for the Taliban, but field commanders and intelligence officers in Afghanistan had developed a grudging respect for them as soldiers. For instance, a 2009 study prepared for the U.S. Marine Corps Intelligence Activity that was never released to the public had this to say about the Taliban:

> Afghan insurgents tend to be brave and tenacious, with a gift for small unit tactics . . . They have launched hundreds of attacks on

fortified bases and raised the costs of maintaining these positions by targeting Coalition supply lines with IEDs and ambushes. When attacked, Afghan insurgents often counter-attack, and maintain contact even when faced with vastly superior firepower. On many occasions, they have fought through air strikes and intense artillery bombardment. Taliban fighters protecting high-level commanders have been known to stand their ground in the face of certain death. They almost never surrender.

As was the case with the Viet Cong in Vietnam forty years earlier, the Taliban had all the advantages that came with fighting on their home turf. The guerrillas knew the terrain that they were fighting on. They spoke the languages and were intimately familiar with all of the intricacies of local tribal politics and culture, which allowed them to seamlessly blend into the local population and move freely without being detected. They had family and friends scattered throughout southern Afghanistan who provided them with food, shelter, and hiding places. Their vast network of spies closely monitored every aspect of U.S. and NATO military activities in southern and eastern Afghanistan in order to discern the strengths and limitations of the U.S. and NATO forces. They had unimpeded access to sanctuaries across the border in northern Pakistan, where they could rest and refit, recruit, train, and raise money without fear of interference from U.S. and NATO forces. Hardened from birth to Afghanistan's brutal climate, they traveled light and lived off the land, allowing them to move farther and strike faster than their road-bound American and NATO counterparts, who according to a September 2008 Marine Corps report had "long forgotten how to live off the land and sustain themselves in challenging situations."

Thanks to generous donations from wealthy Arab businessmen in Saudi Arabia and Pakistan, as well as the vast sums of money being collected from Afghan opium farmers and narcotics traffickers, the Taliban were cash rich. The Taliban had so much cash on hand that the monthly salary of the average Taliban guerrilla was $200, more than double the amount made by the average Afghan government soldier or policeman. A burgeoning war chest also meant that the Taliban had a plentiful supply of weapons and ammunition, much of which they surreptitiously bought from corrupt Afghan army and police commanders.

Even the lowliest Taliban fighters believed implicitly in their cause. According to Colonel Donald C. Bolduc, who today commands all U.S. and NATO

Special Forces in Afghanistan, the "Taliban fighters truly believe in their cause. Their strength of commitment compensates for their lack of military capability. They are waging total war, not the limited war of their enemy. Coalition soldiers await the end of their tours; Taliban tours only end in death, which the Taliban believe is [their] entry into paradise."

They also believed that time was on their side. A number of mid-level Taliban commanders captured in 2008 told their interrogators at the Joint Interrogation Facility at Bagram Air Base north of Kabul that the longer the war lasted, the better their chances of prevailing, with one quoting Mullah Omar's now famous line "The Americans have the wristwatches, but we have the time."

The event that finally shattered the last remaining vestiges of complacency in Washington and Kabul about how bad the military situation in Afghanistan had become occurred early on the morning of July 13, 2008, when a force of two hundred Taliban guerrillas came within a hair's-breadth of overrunning an isolated U.S. Army outpost called Vehicle Patrol Base Kahler, which was situated outside a tiny village in southeastern Afghanistan called Wanat. The attack was beaten back only because of the heroism of the base's defenders, but nine American soldiers lost their lives and another twenty-seven were wounded in the engagement. A week later, the U.S. Army abandoned the outpost and the Taliban marched in without any opposition, giving Wanat the dubious distinction of being the first defeat suffered by the U.S. military in Afghanistan since the war began in 2001.

A number of army officers who held command positions in Afghanistan at the time now wonder if Wanat was worth fighting for in the first place. Wanat is situated in the heart of the desolate Waygal Valley in the southernmost part of Nuristan Province, just a short distance from the Pakistani border. Known until 1896 as Kafiristan (Land of the Infidels), Nuristan was the setting for Rudyard Kipling's short story "The Man Who Would Be King" and the 1975 film of the same name starring Sean Connery and Michael Caine.

Nuristan is remote, mountainous, impoverished, and sparsely populated, with most of the provinces's few towns and villages being located in isolated valleys surrounded by steep mountains. The village of Wanat itself was a tiny, wretchedly poor, and entirely unremarkable place, so small in fact that it did not appear on even the most detailed maps of Afghanistan.

Wanat had no strategic importance other than the fact that it was a district seat, which meant that it had a mayor's office, a run-down police station, and a decrepit, flea-ridden building that had the effrontery to call itself a hotel. But because it was a district seat, albeit an insignificant one with no overall importance to the war effort, the U.S. Army felt obligated to defend it; to lose it would be perceived in Washington and Kabul as a political disaster of the first magnitude.

According to U.S. Army intelligence officials, the Taliban commander who led the assault on Kahler, Mullah Osman, knew in advance virtually everything about the layout of the base's defenses and the size of its garrison, which consisted of a platoon of forty-eight soldiers from the 2nd Battalion, 503rd Infantry Regiment (Airborne) of the 173rd Airborne Brigade Combat Team, commanded by twenty-four-year-old 1st Lieutenant Jonathan P. Brostrom, as well as a detachment of twenty-four Afghan soldiers who had never seen combat before.

From the day that the Kahler outpost had been established—July 9, four days before the attack—Taliban sympathizers in Wanat had carefully monitored the progress of the construction work on the base's defensive positions, reporting any changes to Mullah Osman by messenger. This was not particularly difficult to do, since Kahler was built on the valley floor next to the village of Wanat, allowing the Taliban's local spies to sit on the slopes of the surrounding hills and mountainsides and follow every move inside the base without being detected.

Lieutenant Brostrom had no way of knowing it, but according to numerous government sources he was also being betrayed by the two local Afghan government officials that he was supposed to defend, District Governor Ziaul Rahman and Afghan National Police district chief Hazrat Ali. Both men were corrupt, using their positions to line their pockets with U.S. aid money; they were also secretly collaborating with the local Taliban in a marriage of convenience to force the Americans out of their valley. A U.S. Army postmortem review of the battle found that Rahman and Ali had not only helped the Taliban by providing the insurgents with information about the layout and strength of the base, but the night before the attack they warned local villagers that an attack was about to happen and told them to flee to the hills before the first shots were fired.

While the villagers were leaving the village in droves, Mullah Osman then did what the U.S. Army intelligence analysts said the Taliban could not do. He and his subordinate commanders secretly gathered a force estimated at two hundred men, most of them local villagers armed only with AK-47s and RPGs, and moved them in the middle of the night to their attack positions in the mountains and hills surrounding the base, all without being detected.

The fact that Mullah Osman was able to execute this maneuver without any trace being picked up by the U.S. Army's array of intelligence sensors is not surprising.

There was little SIGINT collection against local Taliban radio traffic because the area's mountainous terrain inhibited the ability of American SIGINT intercept teams to hear the insurgents' short-range signals. Even when the signals could be heard, they could not be interpreted, because the local Taliban communicated in the local Nuristani dialect, which none of the U.S. Army linguists could understand.

Intelligence from foot patrols and human intelligence sources was not available because the hostile Nuristani villagers refused to cooperate with local U.S. Army intelligence officers. This left unmanned reconnaissance drones as the sole remaining intelligence asset that could have provided any warning of the impending attack. The problem was there were only two U.S. Air Force Predators and a slightly larger number of U.S. Army unmanned drones available for all of Afghanistan. With few resources available, Nuristan rarely got any drone coverage because the province was not rated as being particularly important, nor was the Taliban presence there deemed to be sufficiently high risk to warrant additional intelligence coverage.

There had been some desultory airborne reconnaissance and unmanned drone coverage of the area around the village of Wanat after the base was established on July 9. But four days later, on July 12, the day before the Taliban assault on Wanat, Lt. Colonel Pierre D. Gervais, the 101st Airborne Division's chief of intelligence at Bagram Air Base, ordered that all drone and airborne reconnaissance coverage of the area around Wanat be withdrawn because, according to a postmortem study of the battle, in four days of monitoring the area around the town "nothing of consequence was detected," and Gervais needed the drones that had been orbiting over Wanat to cover a major combat operation scheduled that day around the city of Jalalabad to the south.

Colonel Gervais's decision to pull all drone coverage from the area around Wanat effectively left Lieutenant Brostrom's platoon deaf, dumb, and blind. They did not know that several hundred Taliban fighters were dug in all around them ready to attack until literally the first volley of machine-gun fire and Russian-made rocket-propelled grenades began impacting on their positions just as the sun was coming up.

As relatively insignificant as Wanat may have been when compared with the other great battles in history, its impact reverberated far beyond the Waygul

Valley, earning it the nickname among Washington intelligence analysts "the mouse that roared."

In the aftermath of Wanat, Dr. Peter R. Lavoy, the DNI's national intelligence officer for South Asia, began preparing a new National Intelligence Estimate on the security situation in Afghanistan. By late September 2008, a draft of the NIE was being circulated to high-level policymakers in Washington for their review and comment. According to several former Bush administration officials who read it, the estimate confirmed what almost everyone suspected—that the war in Afghanistan was not going well. The final version of the top secret study was not issued until two weeks after Barack Obama was elected president of the United States on November 4, 2008, which meant that most senior Bush administration officials never read it because they were busy packing up their offices and looking for new jobs.

So it fell to the career Pentagon and State Department officials who remained at their posts to pass on the bad news contained in the report to America's friends and allies. According to a leaked State Department cable, NATO officials who were briefed on the contents of the estimate described it as "unrelentingly gloomy."

The estimate for the first time gave the Taliban guerrillas passing grades as a military force. Up until this point in time, the U.S. intelligence community believed that the lightly armed Taliban were incapable of taking on, much less beating, the much more heavily armed U.S. and NATO forces in Afghanistan. Wanat proved this theory to be wrong. The U.S. and NATO intelligence communities had also believed that the Taliban guerrillas could not mount sophisticated large-scale attacks on heavily defended targets. This theory too was proven to be illusory when on the evening of June 13, 2008, a large force of Taliban guerrillas managed to infiltrate the city of Kandahar and blow up the walls of the notorious Sarposa Prison, freeing almost a thousand prisoners, including four hundred hardcore Taliban militants. The attack showed that the Taliban were not only capable of conducting a coordinated battalion-sized attack, but they could assemble their forces without being detected, accurately reconnoiter coalition defensive positions, effectively use massed RPG fire to provide fire support for the attack, and press their attacks despite suffering heavy losses.

According to some current-serving intelligence analysts, where the Lavoy report fell flat on its face was that it placed the onus of responsibility for most of Afghanistan's problems squarely on the shoulders of President Karzai and his government, concluding that the resurgence of the Taliban would not have been possible except for the breakdown in the authority of the Afghan government. According to Lavoy, "The Afghan government has failed to consistently deliver services in rural areas. This has created a void that the Taliban and other insurgent groups have begun to fill . . . The Taliban have effectively manipulated the grievances of disgruntled, disenfranchised tribes to win over anti-government recruits."

As venal as the Afghan government was, making Karzai the scapegoat for all that was going wrong with the war in Afghanistan was not only simplistic, but it missed the mark completely. No mention was made in the estimate of the U.S. and NATO government officials who had allowed Afghanistan to become a bleeding sore by ignoring the problem for years. Nor did it ascribe any blame to the American generals who were doggedly continuing to pursue a badly flawed military strategy in Afghanistan well after it was painfully obvious to everyone that it was not working. It was to take a change of occupants in the Oval Office and a major shakeup of the military command structure in Afghanistan before General David H. Petraeus, the commander of U.S. Central Command, would publicly admit that the "situation [in Afghanistan] has deteriorated over the last two years," and that the military strategy then being employed was not working.

The tenor and tone of the Lavoy estimate also smacks of the "blame game" tactics that were employed forty years earlier, when the U.S. government began to publicly allege that the war in Vietnam would be going better if not for the rampant corruption of Ngyuen Van Thieu's South Vietnamese government that American soldiers were fighting and dying to defend. For example, in October 1966 Secretary of Defense Robert McNamara wrote a blistering top secret memorandum to President Lyndon Johnson wherein he admitted that the U.S.-led pacification program against the Viet Cong guerrillas in South Vietnam was stalled. But McNamara did not ascribe any blame to the Americans running the program. Instead, he rather disingenuously laid the blame for the lack of progress on the fact that "the GVN [government of South Vietnam] was ridden with corruption."

According to Harold P. Ford, a thirty-year CIA veteran who wrote many of the high-level National Intelligence Estimates in the 1960s warning that the war in Vietnam was not going well, "It has always been politically expedient in Washington to blame someone else for your own mistakes."

CHAPTER 2

Liberty Crossing

Uneasy lies the head that wears a crown.
—WILLIAM SHAKESPEARE, *HENRY IV, PART 2*

Within days of winning the November 2008 presidential election, Barack Obama surprised many in Washington by naming a sixty-one-year-old retired U.S. Navy admiral, Dennis C. Blair ("Denny" to his friends), to be the director of national intelligence, and as such the head of the entire U.S. intelligence community. What follows is a portrait of the massive enterprise that he inherited.

When it came to intellect, Denny Blair was no slouch. A native of Kittery, Maine, he had graduated near the top of his class at the U.S. Naval Academy in 1968, where his classmates included the current chairman of the Joint Chiefs of Staff, Admiral Mike Mullen; Senator Jim Webb of Virginia; and Colonel Oliver North of Iran-Contra infamy. Blair went on to study Russian at Oxford University in England as a Rhodes Scholar, where his classmates included a future president of the United States, Bill Clinton.

Blair spent thirty-four years in the navy before retiring as commander in chief, Pacific Command (CINCPAC), one of the top field command slots in the U.S. military. His only substantive exposure to the intelligence community during his career had been a brief posting to CIA headquarters in the 1990s as the agency's associate director of operations for military support, which meant it was his job to make sure that the brass at the Pentagon got the intelligence they needed from the clandestine operators at Langley.

Since his retirement in 2002, Blair had been biding his time waiting for something better to come along. He had spent four years as the president of an influential think tank, the Institute for Defense Analysis, in Alexandria, Virginia; then moved to Honolulu, Hawaii, to chair a department at the National Bureau of Asian Research, a lesser-known foreign policy research institute that former colleagues joked was created especially for retired generals and admirals who wanted to get paid to play golf.

Within hours of Blair being nominated for the DNI post, a security officer arrived at his house in suburban Alexandria, Virginia, bringing with him a thick file of security clearance forms and financial disclosure statements that Blair was required to fill out immediately so that the FBI could begin the process of investigating his background for the plethora of security clearances he would need to perform his job.

A few hours later, a team of workers arrived to install a huge safe and encrypted telephones and fax machines in Blair's study so that he could communicate with his staff from home. They also installed cipher locks on the door to the room, completely soundproofed it and clad it with a special material called "TEMPEST shielding" that was resistant to eavesdropping devices, and put in a new alarm system to make sure that burglars could not get at the sensitive materials in the house.

But Blair was not to be alone at the top. On January 5, 2009, president-elect Obama surprised many in Washington by naming President Bill Clinton's former chief of staff, seventy-year-old Leon E. Panetta, to be the next director of the CIA.

Panetta's nomination upset the incumbent CIA director, Michael V. Hayden, who had made no secret of wanting to keep his job. Hayden's press spokesman at Langley had been calling Washington reporters since Obama's election in November to float the idea that Hayden should remain at the helm of the CIA in the new administration.

However, Obama's advisers rejected keeping Hayden on because he was tainted by his involvement in a number of the Bush administration's more controversial intelligence activities, such as the National Security Agency's post-9/11 domestic eavesdropping programs and his defense of the CIA's use of waterboarding on captured al Qaeda operatives. "We couldn't keep him even if we had wanted to," one of Obama's advisers recalled in a 2009 interview. "He was just too toxic."

Blair's first day on the job was January 29, 2009. Before sunrise an armored town car and a security escort picked him up at his home and drove him twenty miles through the abysmal D.C. rush hour traffic to the DNI headquarters compound known as Liberty Crossing in McLean, Virginia, located just a few miles up Route 123 from CIA headquarters at Langley.

Blair's nationally televised confirmation hearing a week earlier before the

Senate Select Committee on Intelligence had been so banal and anticlimactic that one of his aides caustically referred to it as "puff pastry." The carefully orchestrated and stage-managed hearing lasted just a little more than two hours, and Blair did not have to field a single tough question from the committee members. The only thing the committee was really interested in was eliciting from Blair a promise to keep them informed of what he was doing once he took office, something which Blair's predecessors as DNI had pointedly failed to do on more than one occasion.

Sadly, the fact that no one on the committee asked any hard questions of Blair came as no surprise. Increasingly divided by rancorous partisan politics, in the opinion of many longtime congressional staffers the House and Senate intelligence committees had ceased being effective overseers of the U.S. intelligence community a decade ago. No less a figure than Senator Jay Rockefeller (D-WV), a former chairman of the Senate intelligence committee, found himself "dismayed about the work of the intelligence committees." In his opinion, the committees were "not conducting hearings in any meaningful sense, much less oversight hearings," and they were "swamped in backward-looking investigations and spending almost no time on future questions or the organization of the Intelligence Community."

What the House and Senate intelligence committees excelled in was giving the intelligence community money, lots of it, a fact that became apparent on Blair's first day on the job. The DNI headquarters building at Liberty Crossing was brand spanking new. For the first three years of its existence (2005–8), the DNI staff had worked out of a suite of offices on the top two floors of the Defense Intelligence Analysis Center building at Bolling Air Force Base in Washington, D.C. Although the facility was spacious and ultramodern, the DNI staff made no bones about the fact that they didn't like working at Bolling because it was located in a crime-ridden neighborhood where at night the crackle of gunfire could clearly be heard inside the base's high-security perimeter.

Ambassador John D. Negroponte, the first director of national intelligence, hated Bolling so much that he gave serious thought to moving his office to the location of the post–World War II headquarters of the CIA on the corner of 24th and E streets across the street from the State Department in downtown Washington. According to one of his aides, he was only dissuaded from following through on the idea by the decrepit state of the buildings on the site and the massive expense that would have been required to bring them up to code.

In 2008, the DNI staff quietly moved out of Bolling to their newly constructed headquarters at Liberty Crossing, a heavily guarded 51-acre parcel of
land situated on the north side of Highway 267 across from the massive Tysons
Corner shopping mall complex. If you take a taxi from downtown Washington to catch a flight at Dulles International Airport, you drive right by the
innocuous-looking office complex.

In the middle of the Liberty Crossing complex sit two office buildings that
house 1,700 DNI staffers and 1,200 private contractors, most of whom are
technical specialists, like computer network operators and software specialists, who keep the place up and running. The newer building, a six-story edi-
fice called LX-2, was the home of Blair's staff. Just to the west of it, the somewhat
older seven-story X-shaped building called LX-1 held the offices of the National
Counterterrorism Center (NCTC) and the National Counterproliferation Center (NCPC), which collected intelligence on those countries that were covertly
trying to develop nuclear, chemical, or biological weapons.

Once settled in his spacious office suite on the top floor of LX-2, Blair took
stock of the vast empire that he now commanded. Eight years earlier on 9/11,
the intelligence community was a rudderless ship, a massive and fractious
conglomeration of sixteen competing agencies, which, because of a combination of poor leadership and inattention from high-level policymakers, was
short of funds, burdened with a bloated and stifling bureaucracy, and struggling to operate in an organizational framework left over from the Cold War
that was entirely unsuited for the twenty-first century. Even senior intelligence
officials like Carl Ford, at the time the head of intelligence at the State Department, thought that the intelligence community was "too big . . . an almost
unworkable bureaucracy."

The intelligence community that Blair inherited in January 2009 was far
larger, better funded, and, at least on paper, far more capable than what had existed eight years earlier. Thanks to the almost $500 billion that had been
pumped into it by the Bush administration, the U.S. intelligence community
had rapidly become the largest and most powerful conglomeration of intelligence agencies anywhere in the world, consisting of 208,000 civilians and
military men, including about 30,000 private contractors, stationed in almost
170 countries around the world at a cost to the U.S. taxpayers of more than $75
billion a year.

By comparison, Great Britain's intelligence community consisted of about
11,000 intelligence officers and support staff with an annual budget of only

$3.5 billion, according to the latest annual report of Parliament's Intelligence and Security Committee. "I wish we had just a fraction of the money that Washington puts into intelligence," a now retired senior British intelligence official said in a 2008 interview.

But bigger was not necessarily better. The growth of the U.S. intelligence community during the Bush administration had been unregulated, with dozens of secret units being created after 9/11, mostly by the Pentagon, which were allowed to operate freely outside the community's formal command structure.

For example, in early 2009 a Pentagon official named Michael D. Furlong established an off-the-books intelligence-gathering operation run by the defense contracting giant Lockheed Martin with $22 million in secret contingency funds to collect intelligence inside Pakistan on al Qaeda. Although the operation was approved by the head of U.S. Central Command, General David Petraeus, a senior intelligence official confirmed that Blair and Leon Panetta, the director of the CIA, were not told about the operation until shortly before it was publicly disclosed by the *New York Times* in March 2010, which reflected an alarming lack of transparency inside the intelligence community itself.

Moreover, the House and Senate intelligence committees asked few questions about how the tens of billions of dollars they were giving the nation's spies was being spent; and the internal checks and balances that had been put in place within the intelligence community to prevent abuses were pushed aside in the rush to respond to 9/11.

Contrary to what one reads in the newspapers, there were two separate and quite distinct American intelligence communities. The first, which Blair personally commanded, comprised the 2,900 men and women who directly worked for him in the office of the DNI at Liberty Crossing and the more than 100,000 civilians, soldiers, and private contractors who made up the nation's sixteen intelligence agencies, which together had an annual budget of $49.8 billion. Then there was a second, more secretive intelligence community, consisting of more than 100,000 soldiers, sailors, and airmen, who worked exclusively for the Pentagon and who had their own boss, retired U.S. Air Force Lt. General James R. Clapper Jr., who held the unprepossessing title of Undersecretary of Defense for Intelligence.

The Pentagon's burgeoning intelligence empire had always been a prickly thorn in the side of the Director of National Intelligence. Not only did Blair have no control over the activities of the more than 100,000 military personnel performing intelligence functions around the world, such as in Iraq and Afghanistan, his staff at Liberty Crossing did not have much say about how Jim Clapper spent his $25 billion budget.

"I wish to hell I knew what the hell they were doing over there [at the Pentagon]," a senior DNI official complained in a 2010 interview. "It would be nice if once in a while they would let us know what they are doing."

THE U.S. INTELLIGENCE COMMUNITY (ALL FIGURES ESTIMATES)

Organization	*Employees*
Office of the Director of National Intelligence (ODNI)	2,900
Central Intelligence Agency (CIA)	25,000
Defense Intelligence Agency (DIA)	16,500
Federal Bureau of Investigation (FBI)	34,000
National Geospatial-Intelligence Agency (NGA)	16,000
National Reconnaissance Office (NRO)	4,500
National Security Agency (NSA)	35,000+
Drug Enforcement Administration (DEA)	250
Department of Energy (DOE), Office of Intelligence and Counterintelligence	300
Department of Homeland Security (DHS), Office of Intelligence and Analysis	700*
Department of State (DOS), Bureau of Intelligence and Research (INR)	330
Department of the Treasury, Office of Intelligence and Analysis	200
U.S. Army	54,000
U.S. Navy	11,000
U.S. Air Force	32,000
U.S. Marine Corps	3,000
U.S. Coast Guard	300

---

* DHS figures include personnel assigned not only to the Office of Intelligence and Analysis but also to the other intelligence components controlled by DHS, such as the Transportation Security Agency (TSA).

Admiral Blair's new command included the venerable Central Intelligence Agency. While no longer the top dog of the U.S. intelligence community, the CIA had still grown from 17,000 people on its payroll on 9/11 to 25,000 in January 2009.

The CIA's 5,000-person National Clandestine Service (NCS), headed by Michael J. Sulick, was still the lead U.S. government agency collecting intelligence overseas using secret agents (in government jargon, this is known as human intelligence, or HUMINT). The NCS had come a long way from the dark days of 9/11, when it had fewer than 2,500 case officers deployed around the world. Pat Hanback, the CIA's former assistant deputy director of operations, recalled that when she transferred to the agency in 2001, the Clandestine Service was a pale shadow of what it had been during the Cold War; it had "a depleted capability, was very lean, and faced draconian cutbacks because its budget had been decreased." As a result, Hanback recalled, the CIA's spies were "hard-pressed to meet its priorities."

The Clandestine Service's performance prior to 9/11 had left something to be desired. General Montgomery C. Meigs, former commander of U.S. Army forces in Europe, recalled that during the wars in Bosnia and Kosovo in the 1990s, the CIA's clandestine intelligence gathering efforts were, in his opinion, "amateurish."

By 2009, the dark days were behind the Clandestine Service. Its budget had been dramatically augmented, and its personnel were now operating from stations in 250 U.S. embassies and consulates in almost 170 countries. These CIA stations varied in size from over 700 officers in Afghanistan to a single officer and a secretary in the smaller Pacific Island republics. And the NCS was still growing rapidly. Hundreds of newly minted case officers were being churned out at the agency's 10,000-acre training center, colloquially known as "the Farm," outside Williamsburg, Virginia, and sent to overseas stations as fast as orders could be drawn up.

A small but growing number of these newly minted agents were NOCs, which stands for nonofficial cover. These agents are posted overseas without any diplomatic cover, pretending to be businessmen, financial analysts, technical translators, and the like. According to former NCS head Mike Sulick, these NOCs are becoming increasingly important because "diplomatic cover isn't going to get you access to the targets you need to reach in today's war on terrorism."

Senior intelligence officials are fond of repeating the truism that the CIA's failures are well known, but its successes are not. Behind the scenes, the CIA was enjoying an unprecedented level of success not seen since the halcyon days of the Cold War. According to information contained in a number of leaked State Department cables placed online by WikiLeaks, as of 2009 the CIA was providing valuable intelligence reporting from inside the governments of a number of America's allies. For instance, in the Middle East and South Asia, the CIA had a plethora of high-level sources in countries such as Afghanistan, Saudi Arabia, and Yemen, while in Latin America, the agency was operating high-level penetration agents inside the governments and security forces of countries such as Colombia, Ecuador, El Salvador, Paraguay, and Venezuela.

Occasionally news about the agency's major successes leaks out. Prior to the killing of Osama bin Laden in Pakistan on May 1, 2011, the CIA's biggest public success had occurred in June 2010, when the FBI arrested ten Russian sleeper agents the bureau had been watching for almost a decade. All ten of the agents and their families were sent back to Russia as part of a swap for a Russian scientist named Igor V. Sutyagin, who had been imprisoned for allegedly spying for the United States.

Five months later, on November 11, 2010, the Russian newspaper *Kommersant* published an article alleging that the sleeper agents had been betrayed by a Russian intelligence official identified only as "Colonel Shcherbakov," who had been the head of the North American illegals branch of the Russian foreign intelligence service (Sluzhba Vneshney Razvedki, or SVR). "Shcherbakov" was in fact Colonel Alexander Poteyev, who had been recruited by the CIA more than a decade earlier when he was posted to the United States. According to a senior U.S. intelligence official, Poteyev had provided the agency with "extremely valuable" information about Soviet spying activities in the United States before he was exfiltrated from Russia by the CIA in June 2010.

The CIA was only one of twenty-one different government agencies or military commands engaged in conducting clandestine human intelligence. Virtually every major U.S. military overseas command had its own clandestine human intelligence gathering units, which operated largely independent of the CIA. For example, the Joint Special Operations Command based out of Fort Bragg, North Carolina, was operating small agent networks in support of its highly classified commando operations in Iraq, Afghanistan, and Pakistan. Even the electronic eavesdroppers at the National Security Agency (NSA) had their own secret HUMINT collection teams called Target Exploitation (TAREX) detachments, which interrogated prisoners and examined captured codes, communications equipment, and documents to try to help NSA's codebreakers solve enemy code and cipher systems, or conversely, protect U.S. communications and codes from being broken and exploited by the other side.

The CIA's military counterpart, the Defense Intelligence Agency (DIA), was the intelligence arm of the Department of Defense, producing intelligence reporting for the secretary of defense's office, the Joint Chiefs of Staff, and senior U.S. military commanders around the world. Long considered by intelligence insiders as the "lightweight" of the intelligence community because of the historically poor quality of the material that it produced, the DIA had grown dramatically since 9/11 from 7,500 military and civilian personnel to over 16,500 in 2009, reflecting a surge in the importance of military intelligence.

Even before 9/11, the Federal Bureau of Investigation had become a veritable powerhouse inside the U.S. intelligence community, investigating potential terrorist threats at home and abroad, as well as its more usual work of monitoring the activities of foreign intelligence agencies and their operatives in the United States and investigating violations of federal criminal and civil statutes. Since 9/11, the bureau has continued to grow in both size and power. With 33,925 employees, including 13,492 special agents who did the investigative work, by 2009 the FBI had become one of the largest intelligence agencies in the world, operating fifty-six field offices and four hundred resident agency offices throughout the United States. There were also a couple of hundred FBI agents assigned to more than sixty "Legal Attaché" offices in U.S. embassies overseas who not only liaised with their foreign counterparts but also actively collected intelligence on a wide range of foreign terrorist and organized crime groups, such as the Pakistani Taliban and the Russian mafia.

The FBI even had its own air force. As of 2009, the FBI's Aviation and Surveillance Branch, headed by Special Agent James F. "Jim" Yacone, was flying 132 surveillance aircraft and helicopters from more than two dozen medium-sized regional airports throughout the United States, making the FBI's fleet larger than most European air forces. According to Federal Aviation Administration (FAA) records, all of the FBI's aircraft are owned by six Delaware front companies, while the bureau's fleet of helicopters is owned by another dummy corporation in Manassas, Virginia.

From its modern headquarters complex a few miles south of Dulles International Airport in Chantilly, Virginia, since 1961 the National Reconnaissance Office (NRO) has designed, built, and operated all of the American reconnaissance satellites that are currently in orbit over the earth. Although its headquarters staff is, by Washington standards, very small and compact, with only 3,000 government employees, NRO has by far the largest budget of any agency in the intelligence community and a reputation for wasteful spending to go with it.

Unlike its larger cousins, the CIA and NSA, the NRO does not produce any intelligence information itself. Rather, according to declassified NRO documents, all of the vast amount of photo and radar imagery and intercepted signals collected by its spy satellites are beamed down to earth in near realtime to a series of heavily guarded NRO facilities called mission ground stations located at Buckley Air Force Base, Colorado; Las Cruces, New Mexico; and Fort Belvoir, Virginia, in the United States; and RAF Menwith Hill Station in England and the Joint Defence Facility Pine Gap outside Alice Springs, Australia. The data is then forwarded to the other branches of the U.S. intelligence community responsible for analysis.

One of the agencies responsible for analyzing NRO's satellite data is the National Geospatial-Intelligence Agency (NGA), whose headquarters is located in a complex of buildings on Sangamore Road in Bethesda, Maryland, across from a shopping mall. The principal mission of NGA's 16,000 employees is to review and analyze all of the imagery that NRO's satellites generate, as well as make thousands of detailed maps of the entire globe for use by the U.S. government and military.

During every Washington Nationals home game, tens of thousands of baseball fans unknowingly walk right by one of NGA's most sensitive facilities. Located on the corner of M and 1st streets in southeast Washington, D.C., is a multistory, windowless structure called Building 213, which houses the National Photographic Interpretation Center (NPIC), where all imagery taken by American photo reconnaissance satellites is processed, analyzed, and reported on. By the end of September 2011, NPIC and all other NGA facilities in suburban Maryland and Virginia, as well as the District of Columbia, will have moved to a new headquarters complex currently under construction at Fort Belvoir, Virginia.

As it was during the Cold War, satellite imagery remains an important source for the U.S. intelligence community. For example, in 2009 the Ukrainian government denied that it had shipped T-72 medium tanks to Sudan in violation of U.S. economic sanctions that barred the shipment of weapons to the regime in Khartoum. At a meeting with their Ukrainian counterparts, State Department officials pulled out sanitized satellite photos showing the T-72 tanks being offloaded at the port of Mombasa in Kenya from a Ukrainian merchant ship, then loaded onto rail flatcars, and finally being delivered to a military garrison in southern Sudan. According to a leaked State Department cable summarizing the meeting, the production of the satellite photos led to "a commotion on the Ukrainian side" of the negotiating table.

However, the U.S. intelligence community's heavy reliance on these spy satellites to see what was taking place deep inside hostile territory has over time eroded as America's enemies learned how to hide their most sensitive military facilities from the cameras on the satellites. Countries like Iran and North Korea, for example, had become quite adept at burying their sensitive nuclear weapons and ballistic missile production facilities underground, thereby denying the satellites access to what was going on inside the plants.

With more than 60,000 military and civilian employees eavesdropping on all forms of electronic communications around the world, the National Security Agency was the nation's largest and most powerful intelligence agency. Like the rest of the intelligence community, NSA had completely reengineered itself since 9/11, when the agency was so fraught with problems that its deputy director for operations at the time, Richard Taylor, admitted that "NSA was a shambles." SIGINT had been in rapid decline throughout the 1990s because new telecommunications technologies, like fiber-optic cables and cellular telephones, were being introduced faster than NSA's ability to design and field equipment to monitor them. According to General Montgomery Meigs, during the wars in Bosnia and Kosovo in the late 1990s, the ability of the NSA to intercept enemy radio traffic became increasingly difficult because in 1998 the Bosnian Serbs moved their most sensitive communications to a secure fiber-optic cable system that NSA could not intercept, and in Kosovo in 1999 the Yugoslav military used cell phones to direct their military operations, which NSA was not equipped at the time to monitor.

By 2009, though, NSA had changed dramatically. The agency still had about a dozen large listening posts in the United States and overseas, like the massive intercept site at Menwith Hill in northern England, which today sucks up thousands of radio messages and telephone calls every day from throughout the Middle East and Near East, including Israel and Iran.* But the majority of NSA's SIGINT effort remained focused on Iraq, Afghanistan, and the surrounding area. At Balad Air Base in Iraq, and Bagram and Kandahar airfields in Afghanistan, SIGINT aircraft took off around the clock to monitor insurgent radio and cell phone communications. On the ground there were dozens of small but very secretive SIGINT units manned by military personnel running around the countryside with oblique names like Joint Expeditionary SIGINT Terminal Response Unit, Cryptologic Support Teams, SIGINT Terminal Guidance Units, and Signal Survey Teams.

In the American zone in southeastern Afghanistan there were almost a dozen tiny military SIGINT units called Low-Level Voice Intercept (LLVI) Teams, made up of four linguists who were trained to listen to the walkie-talkie chatter of Taliban fighters. In a 2010 interview at his home in Texas, an army SIGINT intercept operator just returned from a one-year tour of duty in Afghanistan recalled that his classified technical training was straightforward. "I just had to learn all the words and phrases used by the Taliban for 'IED,' 'bomb,' 'gun,' 'open fire,' and 'kill the infidels,'" he said. The work of these LLVI teams was extremely dangerous because, in some cases, the enemy fighters they were listening to were hiding only a few hundred yards away, requiring that the intercept operators perform their missions while firing on the enemy they were monitoring at the same time.

With eighty-seven offices in sixty-three countries around the world, the Drug Enforcement Administration (DEA) ran a surprisingly large and diverse series of clandestine intelligence collection programs in places like Mexico, Colombia, and Afghanistan. The DEA station in Afghanistan was running networks of informants in Helmand and Kandahar provinces trying to uncover links between the Taliban guerrillas and Afghan narcotics kingpins, all independent of the CIA's intelligence-gathering efforts. The DEA even had its own sophisticated SIGINT collection system for listening to the telephone calls of narco-traffickers, including a state-of-the-art cell phone intercept system called Matador. In 2009, the president of Panama, Ricardo Alberto

---

* According to intelligence sources, much of the best realtime intelligence reporting on the events leading up to the downfall of Egyptian president Hosni Mubarak in February 2011 came from intercepts emanating from Menwith Hill. The station is currently heavily engaged in monitoring efforts by the Syrian military to suppress popular demonstrations in the northwestern part of the country, as well as the ongoing fighting between Libyan military forces loyal to Muammar Qaddafi and rebel forces.

Martinelli, threatened to expel the entire DEA station unless the Americans agreed to his demand that they use Matador to tap the phones of his domestic political opponents.

The Department of Homeland Security's (DHS) small Office of Intelligence and Analysis in Washington was not a collection agency. Rather, it acted as a central clearinghouse for intelligence information about potential terrorist threats to the United States.* DHS's intelligence organization was deeply troubled. General Patrick M. Hughes recalled that when he took over the organization in November 2003, it consisted of only "27 people, no capability—a total mess." By April 2004, things were somewhat better, but not much. According to Hughes, the DHS intelligence database had "nothing in it," and DHS officials could not be given the best intelligence available to the U.S. intelligence community because the department was not yet authorized to receive SIGINT from NSA. As will be seen in chapter 6, by 2009 the DHS intelligence organization had made significant strides in rectifying these and a host of other problems, but it was still not fully functional.

The U.S. State Department itself has become increasingly active as an intelligence collector since 9/11. Since Barack Obama became president in 2009, Secretary of State Hillary Rodham Clinton has ordered her diplomats to step up their intelligence collection efforts by laying hands on any kind of personal information about the foreign government officials that they come into contact with, such as business cards; telephone, cell phone, pager, and fax numbers; e-mail addresses; credit card numbers; and even frequent flyer miles accounts.

Unlike Denny Blair's alphabet soup of sixteen national spy agencies, which focus primarily on strategic geopolitical issues of interest to the president and his cabinet members, the Pentagon's 100,000 soldier-spies focus almost exclusively on the kind of arcane intelligence information that only soldiers are typically interested in, such as the organizational structure and deployment of enemy military forces opposing them, how many ships the opposing fleet has, how large their air defense radar network is, how many fighter interceptor aircraft they have and where their bases are located, how much fuel is stored in enemy supply depots, and so on.

Since 9/11 the Pentagon's intelligence community—if it could be called

---

* DHS also controlled the intelligence offices of the U.S. Citizenship and Immigration Services (USCIS), U.S. Coast Guard (USCG), U.S. Customs and Border Protection (CBP), U.S. Immigration and Customs Enforcement (ICE), and Transportation Security Administration (TSA).

such, because it is not a truly cohesive entity—has sprawled into a massive, labyrinthine, and chaotic polyglot of hundreds of individual commands, staffs, and intelligence collection units deployed in the United States and around the world.

As of 2009, the U.S. Army had a staggering 54,000 men and women doing intelligence work at home and abroad, twice as many people as the CIA. Almost half of these personnel, more than 19,000 men and women, were assigned as collectors and analysts with army corps, division, brigade, and battalion intelligence staffs, mostly in Iraq and Afghanistan.

The U.S. Navy's intelligence organization, the Office of Naval Intelligence, was much smaller than army intelligence but was performing some very dangerous missions. The navy was running several dozen top secret submarine reconnaissance missions, code-named Aquador, off the coasts of a number of hostile countries. Some missions covertly monitored Iranian naval activities in the Gulf of Hormuz to ensure the safety of international shipping through these vital sea lanes. Other missions involved tracking foreign merchant shipping believed to have been involved in transporting nuclear weapons and ballistic missile technology. For instance, one naval intelligence officer recalled a series of submarine reconnaissance missions conducted a few years back that surreptitiously tracked the movements of North Korean merchant ships the analysts in Washington believed were carrying ballistic missiles and support equipment, from their home ports to Syria and Iran.

Thanks to massive infusions of cash after 9/11, the size and scope of the U.S. Air Force's intelligence mission had rebounded dramatically since the end of the Cold War. Air Force RC-135 and U-2 reconnaissance aircraft still were producing vast amounts of intelligence information about the military activities of countries such as Syria, Iran, and North Korea.

The air force also controlled a small intelligence organization called the Air Force Technical Applications Center (AFTAC) located at Patrick Air Force Base, Florida, which was responsible for detecting foreign nuclear weapons tests. During the Cold War, AFTAC's activities were among the least sensitive in the U.S. intelligence community, but that changed immediately after 9/11, when the air force decided that AFTAC deserved the same degree of secrecy as the CIA and NSA. Between 2001 and 2006, a team of defense contractors belonging to the Raytheon Company working for the air force reclassified over eight thousand documents relating to AFTAC's work held by the National Archives. Among the mundane items that were reclassified were dozens of twenty- and thirty-year-old unclassified State Department press releases about Soviet and Chinese nuclear weapons tests, which the air force security personnel thought revealed the ability of the U.S. intelligence community to monitor foreign nuclear weapons tests, even if the material was fifty years old and available online.

Since 9/11, the U.S. Coast Guard had built up a robust intelligence mission. All of the Coast Guard cutters operating in the Caribbean and Pacific carried small teams of SIGINT operators, who tracked the movements of ships and planes suspected of being used by narcotics traffickers to move cocaine from Latin America to the United States.

But it was the unmanned reconnaissance drone that had become the superstar of the U.S. military intelligence effort by the time Barack Obama became president. In a span of only seven years, the drone had replaced manned aircraft like the U-2 spy plane as the sensor of choice for reconnaissance in Iraq and Afghanistan. For the CIA, the drone had become the weapon of choice for killing insurgents and terrorists around the world.

The growth of the military's drone fleet since 9/11 had been nothing short of spectacular. In 2002, the military had only 167 drones. By 2009, there were more than 6,000 of the unmanned aircraft flying missions around the world, 2,000 in Iraq and Afghanistan alone. The CIA had its own much smaller and more secretive unit of six Reaper drones that operated from Shamsi and Tarbela airbases in Pakistan, which the agency used to attack al Qaeda and Taliban targets in their sanctuaries in the northern part of the country. Later in 2009, the CIA was forced to move the drones to Jalalabad airfield in southeastern Afghanistan after the London *Times* revealed on February 19 the locations of the airbases in Pakistan from which the drones were flying.

The darling of the American news media, the drones are technological marvels. Powered by little more than a souped-up snowmobile engine, the air force's 118 Predator drones can hit targets with the two Hellfire missiles each carries with pinpoint accuracy from an altitude of 25,000 feet—the equivalent of pitching a strike at Yankee Stadium from a commercial airliner flying high overhead. Its successor, the Reaper, is twice as fast and can fly twice as high, and is far more lethal, carrying six times more bombs and missiles than the Predator.

Then there are the air force's thirteen huge and very secretive RQ-4 Global Hawk strategic reconnaissance drones, whose wings are twenty-one feet longer than a Boeing 737 airliner. Operating from forward operating sites at Sigonella Air Base on the island of Sicily, Al Dhafra Air Base in the United Arab

Emirates, and Andersen Air Force Base on the Pacific island of Guam, the Global Hawk can take detailed photographs of an entire continent in a single twenty-eight-hour mission. For example, the Global Hawk drones in Sicily, which are housed in a massive new hanger on the east side of Sigonella Air Base, can photograph all of western Iran, the entire Middle East, and the entire North African coastline in a single mission. But air force officials confirm that the Global Hawk drones still suffer from mechanical problems and frequent equipment failures, as has been the case during the ongoing crisis in Libya.

The U.S. Army and Marine Corps fly a much larger number of smaller drones that were designed specifically for the intelligence needs of battalion and company commanders on the battlefields in Iraq and Afghanistan. One such drone is the Raven, which is so small that it resembles the balsa-wood toy aircraft that children across America used to fly when they were growing up. Soldiers can carry the four-pound Raven, equipped with a tiny gas-powered engine and an even smaller digital video camera, into the field in a backpack and launch it by just turning on its motor and chucking it into the air like a football.

As important as they have been on the battlefields in Iraq and Afghanistan, the drones have proven to be difficult to fly and very expensive to operate. According to intelligence officials, by the end of 2009 the unmanned drone program had become the single most expensive component of the U.S. military's intelligence budget. Today there are more than 20,000 military personnel and civilian contractors operating and maintaining drones around the world, accounting for 20 percent of all military personnel engaged in intelligence work; and it requires roughly $5 billion annually both to operate the drones currently in service and build the new systems just coming off the drawing boards.

One of the reasons the drones are so expensive is that they require a huge number of pilots to fly them remotely, and an even larger number of maintenance people to keep them operational. According to a June 2010 U.S. Air Force briefing paper, it takes 174 pilots, sensor operators, analysts, and maintenance and support personnel to fly a single Predator drone mission, far more than what is needed to fly a comparable mission by a U-2 spy plane. The air force alone has 1,100 airmen in the Middle East and South Asia maintaining the drones that fly daily strike and reconnaissance missions over Iraq, Pakistan, and Afghanistan, plus another 5,000 pilots and support personnel back at Creech Air Force Base outside Las Vegas, Nevada, who actually fly the drones by remote control via satellite.

But the biggest problem with the drone program was that the military was building drones faster than it could process the materials the crafts were producing. The amount of raw video footage and SIGINT data that each drone mission generates is so massive that the air force's swamped intelligence analysts have coined a phrase to describe it—"data crush."

According to a current-serving U.S. Air Force intelligence officer, the unmanned drone programs are a classic case of "bureaucracy run amok." According to the officer, the air force "pushed into operation a sexy new piece of high-tech spy gear without giving much thought to the human dimension . . . how much data these new machines were going to produce and how many people were going to be needed to process and analyze the data . . . We put the cart before the horse once again."

Whatever one may think about the profession of spying, one has to admit that the men and women who serve in the intelligence community are, and have always been, a very talented and dedicated group of people.

The late General William E. Odom, the director of the NSA from 1985 to 1988, liked to tell the story of bringing a group of visitors down to the basement of the NSA headquarters building at Fort George G. Meade, Maryland, to see the agency's massive complex of computers. As they were passing through the area that contained a number of glass-enclosed Cray supercomputers, the general noticed a partially clothed man fast asleep on top of one of the cooling coils that surrounded the computer. According to the general, the man, who was one of NSA's "computer nerds" responsible for keeping the enormously expensive Crays up and running, had been babysitting the computer all night because it had been malfunctioning the day before. Rather than go home at the end of his shift, the technician had decided to camp out inside the computer's glass enclosure so that he could be there in case the system malfunctioned during the night. General Odom was so impressed that he gave the man a cash reward for his dedication to duty, as well as a fierce dressing-down for embarrassing him in front of the visiting dignitaries.

The list of famous personalities who have at one time or another served in the intelligence community is long and distinguished. Three former U.S. Supreme Court justices were spies during World War II. Justice John Paul Stevens was a Navy codebreaker. Justice Lewis F. Powell Jr. analyzed German ULTRA radio intercepts. And Justice Byron "Whizzer" White was a naval intelligence officer in the Pacific who wrote the report on the sinking of PT-109, whose captain was future president Lieutenant John F. Kennedy. Country music star Johnny Cash was a Morse intercept operator in the U.S. Air Force in the 1950s. Comedian David Brenner served as a cryptologist in the U.S. Army in Germany in the 1960s. Former television talk show host Montel Williams was a linguist and cryptologic officer in the U.S. Navy who conducted a number of top secret submarine reconnaissance missions off the Soviet coastline during the 1980s. Wanda Sykes worked as a procurement officer at NSA headquarters from 1986 to 1992 before leaving the agency to work full-time as a stand-up comic.

There are literally thousands of equally talented and dedicated men and women who work today for the U.S. intelligence community. One U.S. Army Pashto linguist interviewed for this book was in civilian life a computer software designer who studied languages as a form of recreation. He enlisted in the Texas Army National Guard and served a tour of duty in Afghanistan because, as he put it, "someone has to do it. It might as well be me."

There is no fast and firm rule for what a typical American spy looks like. Generally speaking, they tend to be young (according to statistics provided by the DNI's office, half of all the employees of the intelligence community—100,000 people—have been hired since 9/11), computer literate, and well educated (the number of individuals holding advanced university degrees is higher in the intelligence community than in just about any other branch of the U.S. government). Most have traveled or studied abroad, the majority of the operations officers and analysts speak at least one foreign language, and they have all passed some of the most rigorous psychological tests (a stable personality is of paramount importance) and background investigations ever devised before being allowed to handle classified information.

The National Security Agency, the nation's eavesdropping giant, is the largest employer of linguists, mathematicians, computer scientists, software designers, and electronic engineers in the U.S. government. As was the case during the Cold War, both NSA and the U.S. military still like to recruit many of their linguists from among the Mormon population in Utah because the Church of Jesus Christ of Latter-day Saints encourages all young men to serve two years as missionaries, giving those who serve abroad invaluable exposure to foreign cultures and language skills that are hard to find in the general U.S. population. The fact that Mormons do not, as a rule, smoke or drink alcohol also makes them easier to clear for access to classified information than many of their fellow Americans.

The Central Intelligence Agency's intelligence analysis component, the

Directorate of Intelligence, likes skeptics and contrarian thinkers hired out of academia, while the agency's cloak-and-dagger component, the National Clandestine Service, tends to be more eclectic in who it hires. It takes a special sort of person to do this job given that one must lie for a living, be willing to take chances that would get one fired in any other civilian job, and be willing to make deals with individuals so disreputable that one would never invite them home for dinner with the family. During the Cold War era, one of the groups of people the CIA's clandestine service liked to recruit was former college football players because they were physically and mentally tough and enjoyed a good fight. Since 9/11, the CIA has hired hundreds of former prosecutors and defense lawyers, policemen, and detectives because, as a group, these men and women are mentally tough, can think on their feet, are used to dealing with professional liars, cheats, and thieves, and have a Type A personality willing to take risks and a desire to win, even if it means occasionally bending the truth.

But hidden from view, thousands of these talented individuals are leaving the intelligence community every year. During George W. Bush's second term in office, the number of employees resigning or taking early retirement exceeded the number of new recruits being brought into the intelligence community. The departure of so many of the intelligence community's best and brightest people was causing incalculable damage because they took with them their institutional knowledge and unique skills learned during decades of service.

While many of the departing staffers said that they were leaving to seek better economic opportunities in the private sector, many left because they could no longer accept the enormous hardship and sacrifices that the job required. The stress and strain associated with working in the intelligence community, combined with long workdays, poor pay, lack of recognition, frequent overseas deployments, and the depersonalized and secretive nature of the job, took a terrible physical and mental toll on many intelligence officers.

NSA medical studies have shown that the agency's workforce is prone to a higher occurrence of ulcers, digestive tract problems, and sleeping and eating disorders than civilians who work ordinary nine-to-five jobs. A study of the health of military intercept operators at four NSA listening posts in the mid-1990s revealed that these personnel suffered from a host of maladies and ailments, such as high rates of diarrhea, constipation, gastritis, respiratory problems, back pain, forgetfulness, nervousness, and irritability.

Excessive drinking remains commonplace in the intelligence community;

so do fatigue and a host of other stress-related illnesses. The divorce rate among workers in the intelligence community is one of the highest in the nation, and the suicide rate is also well above the national average. Mental disorder and breakdown statistics for intelligence workers are well above virtually any other government job.

One result is that the number of intelligence officers resigning before they reach retirement age because of stress and overwork is increasing. Many have left because they had to make a choice—their families or their country. Nine times out of ten, family won out. In the fall of 2008, I was forced to watch as a friend, a career military intelligence officer, was told in no uncertain terms by his wife to either get out of the service or agree to a divorce. He submitted his retirement papers that same week.

As amply demonstrated by the May 1, 2011, killing of Osama bin Laden by U.S. Navy commandos, there have been marked improvements inside the U.S. intelligence community since 9/11. According to interviews with over a dozen senior intelligence officials over the past three years, dramatic strides have been made since 9/11 in knocking down the security firewalls that prevented the sharing of information among the agencies that now make up the intelligence community. There is also better coordination of effort within the intelligence community; the quality of the intelligence analysis that is being produced has improved significantly; and there are signs that the intelligence community's relations with Congress are on a much better footing than they were during the Bush administration, when the White House deliberately withheld crucial information from the House and Senate oversight committees.

Monumental efforts have been made over the past decade to make the vast amount of information being generated by the intelligence community available to those who need it. The 100,000 intelligence reports, memos, briefs, and cables that the intelligence community produces every month are fed into a new centralized computer database called the Library of National Intelligence, roughly patterned on the massive Library of Congress collection of books and magazines, which all analysts with the appropriate security clearances can access.

However, the intelligence community failed to effectively address the fundamental underlying problem, which was that it was collecting far more data than its analysts and computers could conceivably process. Throughout the Bush administration, U.S. intelligence officials struggled to try to rectify the problem, but with little success as spending on new high-tech collection systems, like unmanned aerial drones, exploded but no new funds were allocated to hire and train the personnel to analyze the data. As Secretary of Defense Donald Rumsfeld put it in a declassified memo, the intelligence community was producing "more data than we can translate into useable knowledge."

Moreover, according to intelligence insiders, the intelligence community still lacked the technical tools to sift and search through this data in a timely fashion so that analysts can spot potential threats. According to a congressional source, the available data was proliferating faster than the search tools needed to analyze what was in the databases. According to the source, "It was as if someone was paid to paint a picture and they never painted the picture but continued to argue that they had made gallant efforts to buy as much paint as they possibly could . . . Paint is still paint . . . it ain't a picture."

Beyond the data avalanche, interagency turf battles over access to information were still taking place. According to Colonel Barry Harris, who commanded a U.S. Army intelligence unit in Iraq, the U.S. Air Force refused to allow reconnaissance data from their unmanned drones to be given to his unit because they would not countenance army personnel controlling one of their intelligence assets. "This is parochialism at its worst," Harris said, "and it deprived soldiers . . . of intelligence that could have given them a significant advantage."

The quality of the analysis coming out of the intelligence community has also improved since 9/11, thanks in part to the efforts of former deputy director of national intelligence for analysis Dr. Thomas Fingar, who now teaches at Stanford University in California. Still, some of the intelligence community's consumers remain highly critical of the quality of the intelligence reporting. According to a senior State Department intelligence official, much of the intelligence reporting he saw coming out of DNI headquarters resembled "the fast food my kids eat at McDonald's."

This is an age-old problem that has never been fixed to anyone's satisfaction. Forty years earlier at the height of the Vietnam War, Henry A. Kissinger, President Richard Nixon's sometimes acerbic national security adviser, famously compared the authors of what he was reading coming out of the intelligence community to "a hysterical group of Talmudic scholars doing an exegesis of abstruse passages." In plain English, Kissinger was saying that America's spies were, in his opinion, producing a lot of incomprehensible and irrelevant crap.

The intelligence community has also done a commendable job in recent years of pushing pertinent information to military field commanders in Iraq

and Afghanistan as far down the chain of command as battalion and company level. Today, lowly intelligence analysts in Baghdad and Kabul can look
at the same agent reports, satellite imagery, and SIGINT intercepts on their
laptop computers that are being shown that same day to President Obama
and the National Security Council (NSC) in Washington.

For example, in 2007 NSA deployed to Iraq an electronic system called
Real-Time Regional Gateway (RT-RG), which for the first time gave field commanders access to the agency's SIGINT databases. Now deployed in southern
Afghanistan, RT-RG has revolutionized the ability of intelligence analysts at
isolated firebases far from major military installations to instantaneously access SIGINT about what is going on in their "neck of the woods." It has also
dramatically speeded up the ability of the analysts to process the raw intelligence. According to a restricted-access Pentagon briefing, thanks to RT-RG,
"analysis that used to take 16 hours or more now can be done in less than one
minute."

While everyone celebrates the fact that Washington is now pumping vast
amounts of intelligence information to the field, the result has been that
the material is drowning the intelligence analysts in Iraq and Afghanistan.
By 2009, the situation had become so acute that the head of the Kandahar
Intelligence Fusion Center in southern Afghanistan wrote in a memo, "Information is like confetti; it is everywhere, but no one will turn off the fan!"

While it is certainly true that things have changed for the better within the
U.S. intelligence community since 9/11, many of the most serious problems
that had directly contributed to the 9/11 and Iraqi weapons of mass destruction intelligence failures remained unfixed. Many of the fundamental
intelligence-community reforms and structural changes that the 9/11 Commission had recommended in its final report in 2004 were never acted upon
by the Bush administration, like the recommendation calling for the creation
of a domestic intelligence and security agency roughly comparable to Great
Britain's MI5. And as we shall see, some of the changes that were made actually made the situation worse rather than better, according to intelligence officials. The result was that when Barack Obama entered the White House, the
intelligence community remained "fundamentally unreformed," according
to Patrick C. Neary, who was the DNI's chief planner from 2005 to 2010.

The problems started at the top with Blair's own position as head of the
intelligence community. In its July 2004 final report, the 9/11 Commission
had strongly urged the Bush administration to create a new position called

the director of national intelligence to provide strong and effective leadership for the fractious and strife-ridden U.S. intelligence community. The fervent hope of the commissioners was that by creating the position, the intelligence community would finally get a real leader, America's first true "intelligence czar," who would bring order out of the chaos and make the gigantic American intelligence apparatus work the way it should.

But the commission's findings, while immensely popular with the American public and the families of the victims of the 9/11 attacks, were treated by the U.S. government like "a flaming bag of dog poo," according to a retired CIA official. No one in Washington wanted intelligence reform. Not the Bush White House, nor the Pentagon, Congress, or the leadership of the intelligence community. The fiercest opposition to intelligence reform came from the Pentagon. On September 11, 2004, Secretary of Defense Donald Rumsfeld wrote a memo to President Bush strongly opposing intelligence reform, telling the president that "there is a risk that legislation could be drafted in a way that is damaging to our intelligence capabilities." In particular, Rumsfeld opposed a proposal to give the director of national intelligence control over the budgets of all the agencies comprising the intelligence community, warning the president that to do so would "be a train wreck."

Inside the intelligence community, according to Pat Neary, senior officials "looked at the reform brouhaha with detached bemusement, believing reform would result in no meaningful change." Sadly, they were right. The White House and the intelligence community's supporters on Capitol Hill watered down the legislation creating the position of DNI, stripping it of its control over the budgets of the sixteen intelligence agencies that it was supposed to govern, crippling the organization before it was born. Then the chairman of the House Armed Services Committee, Representative Duncan L. Hunter (R-CA), and Representative Jim Sensenbrenner (R-WI), got language added to the bill that exempted the Pentagon's vast intelligence empire from the DNI's jurisdiction. And the FBI's supporters in Congress piled on, successfully lobbying to keep the bureau's autonomy intact.

By the time the legislation was passed in December 2004, the DNI had been reduced to a figurehead position with little authority. Like his predecessors, Blair was going to have a sword hanging over his head every day he was in office. If the intelligence community made a mistake, however trivial, he was going to get the blame, even if he had no power to rectify the problem in the first place. It was, in the words of one of Blair's deputies, "an impossible job."

Blair's predecessors had shown themselves to be reluctant to use the limited powers that Congress had given them to try to seize the reins of the U.S. intelligence community and provide it with the forceful leadership that it so desperately needed.

The first DNI, John D. Negroponte, who held the post from February 2005 until January 2007, is credited with canceling a controversial National Reconnaissance Office reconnaissance satellite that was five years behind schedule and massively over budget, and creating DNI mission managers to coordinate the U.S. intelligence community's collection and analytic efforts against a number of high-priority targets, such as Iran, North Korea, Cuba, and Venezuela, as well as terrorism, nuclear proliferation, and counterintelligence.

In the opinion of a number of past and present DNI officials, however, Negroponte saw himself as a facilitator rather than a chief, and as such he did not forcefully make his office the command nexus for the entire intelligence community. For example, shortly after taking the helm of DNI in 2005, Negroponte proposed naming a National Security Agency official as the new chief of station in New Zealand, a position that in the past had always been held by a CIA official. When a number of senior CIA officials threatened to resign in protest, Negroponte backed down and rescinded the order.

His successor, retired U.S. Navy Admiral John M. "Mike" McConnell, who held the position of DNI from February 2007 to January 2009, is best known for pushing through Congress a controversial revision to the Foreign Intelligence Surveillance Act (FISA). He also authored a number of modest reforms, which did not fundamentally change the way the intelligence community did its job. Like Negroponte, he too did little to impose the authority of his office over the fractious U.S. intelligence community.

So what Denny Blair inherited when he moved into the director's office suite at Liberty Crossing in January 2009 was a vast and still-growing intelligence empire that lacked a real leader. This reality was summarized succinctly by a classified 2010 study by the President's Foreign Intelligence Advisory Board, which concluded, "For the IC [intelligence community] to function effectively and deliver credible and timely intelligence, it needs an acknowledged leader. This should be the DNI." But the report added that "this has not yet happened."

With no leadership coming from the top, the office of the DNI had become just another layer in the intelligence community's already massive bureaucracy. A November 2008 report by the DNI inspector general, Edward Maguire, found that mismanagement and the failure of the DNI's office to provide

effective leadership was "undermining ODNI's credibility and fueling asser-
tions that the ODNI is just another layer of bureaucracy."

Despite the plethora of problems remaining to be addressed, it now seems
unlikely that reform will ever come from within the intelligence community's
risk-averse bureaucracy because instinctive and reactive resistance to change
of any sort is so deeply ingrained in the insular culture of the U.S. intelligence community, where conformity and loyalty are deemed to be far more
important qualities than innovation and creativity. According to Patrick G.
Eddington, a former CIA satellite imagery analyst, the U.S. intelligence community has become "a system that values consensus over creativity, conformity
over conscience."

Senior intelligence and congressional officials point to the host of problems they have experienced over the past decade trying to get the FBI to modernize and change the way it does business because of the deeply ingrained
cultural resistance to reform among senior bureau officials. Efforts to bring
in outside talent after 9/11 to build an intelligence analysis program for the
bureau were met with resistance by the bureau's insular bureaucracy. Admiral David Jeremiah, formerly vice chairman of the Joint Chiefs of Staff and a
member of the President's Foreign Intelligence Advisory Board during the
Bush administration, recalled that FBI director Robert S. Mueller III tried to
implement these reforms but ultimately gave up because he "received a lot of
resistance from [within] the FBI." The cultural resistance to any meaningful
reform within the bureau was so fierce that the former chairman of the Senate
intelligence committee, Senator Jay Rockefeller (D-WV), admitted that he had
"doubts whether the FBI can carry out reform."

This sort of obstructionist behavior was an unwanted legacy from the intelligence community's Cold War past. All of the agencies who comprised the
intelligence community traced their origins to the post–World War II era,
when the Soviet Union was the main threat to the survival of the United States.
The Cold War intelligence community had been constructed using Henry
Ford's automotive assembly lines in Detroit as its model. Sheer size and massive output were the standards of the day. Raw materials went in on one end,
and finished products destined for consumers came out the other.

The system remains essentially the same today, even though the targets
have changed completely. But the big difference between then and now is that
sixty years ago when the intelligence community was young, quality was job
one. The men and women who then ran the institution were first and foremost

practitioners of the art of intelligence who had started at the bottom of the heap and worked their way up through the ranks.

Eventually, though, the bureaucrats took over. The emphasis on product quality was replaced by a focus, just as in the struggling American automotive industry, on the mass production of products that were flashier but not as well built as in the past. The professional spies at the top of the intelligence community were over time replaced by professional managers, staffers who had been kicked upstairs because they could handle paperwork and manage personnel and resources, even though they were not necessarily the best spies. Promotion no longer was decided by skill or subject matter expertise but rather by being a "team player" and not "rocking the boat."

In this kind of environment, more often than not, mistakes are covered up, mediocrity tends to get rewarded, and unconventional thinkers are viewed, according to a current-serving CIA intelligence analyst, as "heretics." As a result, it is very difficult for eccentrics, iconoclasts, and freethinkers to survive, much less prosper, in today's intelligence community, since the natural tendency of all bureaucracies is to demand conformity, stifle dissent, and squelch personal initiative. A number of senior intelligence officials reluctantly admit that in this oppressive atmosphere, real and fundamental reform of the intelligence community stands little chance of ever seeing the light of day.

Take the example of Thomas A. Drake, a bright mid-level NSA official who tried to bring to his superiors' attention the fact that a number of the agency's modernization programs were being mismanaged but was ignored at every turn. He tried to take his concerns to Congress but ran into the same set of roadblocks. Angry and not knowing where to turn (intelligence community employees have no protection under the federal whistleblower statutes), in 2005 Drake began leaking information about these programs, which he has claimed was entirely unclassified, to a reporter from the *Baltimore Sun*. For his sins, in April 2010 he was indicted in federal court in Baltimore, Maryland, and charged not with leaking information but rather with five counts of retaining classified information in his home, obstruction of justice, and four counts of making false statements to the FBI.

On June 9, 2011, three days before his trial was due to begin, Drake accepted a deal offered by the U.S. attorney's office in Baltimore. The U.S. government dropped all of the felony charges, and Drake agreed to plead guilty to a single count of misusing government computers, but got no jail time.

Two weeks later, on June 22, 2011, the Department of Defense released to the Project on Government Oversight in Washington, D.C., a heavily redacted version of a December 2004 DOD inspector general's report that corroborated many of the complaints that Drake had made about NSA's mismanagement of a number of high-tech collection systems.

The inability or unwillingness of the intelligence community to reform itself is immensely frustrating for many of the younger members of the community's workforce. The prevailing sentiment is that no matter how bright or talented you may be, or how vitally important the information you produce is, you are still a small and insignificant cog in a massive bureaucracy that is not only parochial and inefficient but obsessed with secrecy, focused on protecting its prerogatives, and inherently suspicious of, and resistant to, change of any sort.

In the opinion of many intelligence professionals, the community's priorities are misplaced. Instead of obsessing about how to keep its secrets, the community should do a better job collecting intelligence, producing better products, and getting the material to the people who need it in a form that they can use. According to Major General Mike Flynn, the former chief of military intelligence in Afghanistan, the intelligence community has "a culture that is emphatic about secrecy but regrettably less concerned about mission effectiveness."

The most striking example showing that intelligence reform had not yet taken hold was to be found in Afghanistan. The U.S. military's intelligence operations in Afghanistan were a disjointed and dysfunctional spit-and-paste conglomeration of more than twenty major intelligence organizations and at least double that number of smaller units lacking any centralized command structure. If one added to the mix the larger number of NATO and Afghan intelligence organizations, you ended up with a nightmarish Macedonian fruit salad, where waste and duplication of effort were so pervasive that, in many cases, these intelligence organizations were working at cross-purposes with one another.

The duplication of effort in Afghanistan had an almost surreal quality. In Kabul there were not one but four large intelligence fusion centers, servicing the intelligence needs of U.S. and NATO forces in Afghanistan. There was the multinational Joint Intelligence Center at ISAF headquarters, which supported U.S. and NATO forces in Afghanistan. Then there was the Joint Intelligence Operations Center–Afghanistan, 90 percent of whose intelligence product could only be seen by American military commanders. The CIA station in the U.S. embassy had its own independent fusion center, whose material the agency refused to share with either the U.S. or NATO military commanders in Afghanistan. And the fusion center supporting the joint U.S.-NATO special operations task force at Bagram Air Base outside Kabul produced intelligence reports that nobody could see except a Green Beret or Navy SEAL team member.

Also in Kabul there were two competing signals intelligence fusion centers—an American one at Bagram and one comprised of NATO personnel at ISAF headquarters in Kabul—plus three organizations engaged in counter-IED intelligence analysis and three performing counternarcotics intelligence.

Outside of Kabul, each of the five U.S.-NATO division staffs in Afghanistan, called regional commands, had its own large intelligence staff; as did each of the seven American and NATO brigades and twenty battalions or armored cavalry squadrons, each of whom was producing its own separate series of intelligence reports tailored specifically for its commanders. On top of that, dozens of smaller American, NATO, and Afghan intelligence fusion centers were sprinkled throughout every province and district because, according to a British intelligence officer stationed at ISAF headquarters in 2008, "you had to have one to have any standing."

Intelligence operations in Afghanistan were hamstrung by layers of bureaucratic red tape. A U.S. Army officer who served a tour of duty with a brigade intelligence staff at Jalalabad in eastern Afghanistan complained that his superiors at Bagram were "trying to run things out of a field manual. Everything had to be done by the book. Every op we ran, no matter how small, had to be written up in triplicate and endorsed three times before they would let us do it . . . These guys had no clue what it was like trying to run realtime intel ops downrange in a war zone."

How did the intelligence situation in Afghanistan become such a mess? The answer is that the Pentagon, jealous of its bureaucratic prerogatives, told Blair's predecessors, John Negroponte and Mike McConnell, to stay out of Iraq and Afghanistan because they were military theaters of operation, and thus outside the DNI's jurisdiction. This has been a recurring problem in U.S. intelligence history, which clearly the creation of the office of the DNI has not resolved. During the Korean War, successive U.S. military commanders in the Far East demanded that the CIA subordinate its behind-the-line activities to those being run by the military. The same thing happened during the Vietnam War; the Pentagon insisted that the CIA subordinate its clandestine activities in North Vietnam to those of the U.S. Army. It was not until Barack Obama became president that the DNI hired a former CIA official whose name cannot be mentioned here to be the organization's first mission manager for Afghanistan and Pakistan.

Despite the staggering number of tiny intelligence fiefdoms in Afghanistan, there were desperate shortages of just about everything that the intelligence operators needed—reconnaissance aircraft, unmanned drones, advanced SIGINT collection systems, clandestine intelligence case officers, Special Forces personnel, interrogators, translators, and analysts. According to two U.S. intelligence officials, the equipment and personnel that should have been going to Afghanistan were being co-opted and sent instead to Iraq, which left only hand-me-downs for Afghanistan. When one intelligence officer cabled Washington to inquire why the increasingly quiescent Iraq was still getting first pick of all intelligence resources, he was told that the reconnaissance platforms he wanted had been "programmed" years earlier by the Pentagon for Iraq, and once the decision had been made there was no way to alter or change the order.

In effect, Iraq was sucking the life out of the U.S. intelligence effort in Afghanistan by starving it of desperately needed resources. Statistics provided by a former military intelligence officer tell the story in stark terms. There were fifty SIGINT intercept operators and analysts in Iraq for every one in Afghanistan. For every CIA case officer in Afghanistan, there were almost ten in Iraq. For every reconnaissance aircraft in Afghanistan, there were ten in Iraq. And for every unmanned drone in Afghanistan, the U.S. military in Iraq had almost five. For example, the U.S. Air Force had 34 Predator drones assigned to Iraq but only two in Afghanistan, while the U.S. Army had 256 drones in Iraq versus only 62 in Afghanistan.

The meager intelligence resources that were available in Afghanistan were being misused. Nearly a quarter of all American and NATO intelligence collection systems in Afghanistan were exclusively dedicated to trying to find Taliban commanders to hit with air strikes, despite reams of intelligence data showing that this effort was not working. According to Lt. Colonel Shane B. Schreiber, a Canadian officer who served a tour of duty in southern Afghanistan, "We also spent a lot of time, money, blood and treasure going after MVTs [medium-value targets] and HVTs [high-value targets] . . . and I don't think it had a great deal of effect on the Taliban . . . If we killed one guy, they just replaced him in about 10 minutes."

There were few attempts to use the Green Berets or Navy SEALS to capture or kill these Taliban commanders because American Special Forces commanders had to get written permission from Kabul in order to conduct even the smallest commando raid. One Green Beret commander in Afghanistan, whose staff at Bagram Air Base had to draw up these bulky documents, called CONOPs (Concept of Operations), likened them to the massive Environmental Impact Statements that all U.S. government agencies are required to submit anytime they want to build something back home. By the time the CONOP had been written and all the necessary endorsements obtained, the target had usually vanished.

Another 25 percent of all intelligence collection resources in Afghanistan were tied up trying to protect U.S. and NATO troops from Taliban IED attacks. According to a declassified document, in some months 80 percent of the time flown by American unmanned drones in Afghanistan was spent flying ceaselessly up and down roads and dirt tracks looking for Taliban IED teams surreptitiously placing their devices. According to Captain Kyle Greenberg, who commanded an army drone platoon in Iraq in 2008, the results of such missions were "lackluster" at best.

When the drones did find Taliban IED teams, the restrictive rules of engagement then in place inhibited their ability to attack the targets. Unlike in Pakistan, where the CIA was free to attack targets whenever and wherever they were found, in Afghanistan every drone missile strike required a half-dozen endorsements from officers all the way up the chain of command to the ISAF chief of operations before they could be executed. According to a 2008 U.S. Army postmortem report, it typically took "a minimum of 72 hours [three days] to gain all necessary approvals to action targets [i.e., fire a missile at a target]." By then, the target of opportunity had almost always disappeared.

A regulation entitled ISAF Standard Operating Procedure 362 contained strict guidelines on how captured Taliban fighters were to be handled, including a requirement that U.S. and NATO forces transfer all detainees to the Afghan government within ninety-six hours of being captured or release them. Time and time again, SOP 362 proved to be unworkable on the battlefield because frontline American and NATO troops were not trained cops. They had no training in how to secure and mark evidence, and in the heat of battle, there was no time to complete the reams of paperwork required by the regulation for each prisoner. As a result, according to a restricted-access Marine Corps report, "over 90% [of all detainees were] released due to insufficient evidence" or because the ISAF authorities deemed that the evidence was "contaminated or improperly handled/documented."

Those few Taliban detainees who were turned over to the Afghan authorities often paid a small bribe and were back on the streets in less than seventy-two hours. Some frustrated American field commanders went to extraordinary lengths to avoid turning prisoners over to the Afghan authorities, even going so far as doctoring detention reports and hiding prisoners.

There was no shortage of intelligence reporting for the analysts to read. Every American and NATO intelligence unit in Afghanistan was producing its own daily, weekly, and monthly intelligence summaries, assessments, estimates, and studies. According to several former ISAF intelligence analysts, they had to read on average about three hundred intelligence reports every day.

Another problem was that they had to wade through over a dozen computer databases in order to find the material they needed to do their job because very few of the databases were compatible with one another. The ISAF officer responsible for trying to knit together all of the intelligence databases admitted that "all the information we need is available in ISAF. We just don't know where it is or how to access it."

CHAPTER 3

The Sword of Damocles

The Continuing Travails in Afghanistan

Afghanistan is a place where the land fashions the people, rather than the people fashioning the land.

—SIR OLAF KIRKPATRICK CAROE

(1892–1981)

In an interview conducted several months before his death in December 2010, Ambassador Richard C. Holbrooke, President Obama's special adviser for Afghanistan and Pakistan, opined that "we should have done things differently in Afghanistan."

According to Holbrooke, "We made the same mistake the Russians made in the 1980s. We walked into a situation which we were not prepared for." He was referring to the Soviet military's disastrous ten-year war in Afghanistan between 1979 and 1989, where despite committing 620,000 soldiers to the war, the Russians were soundly defeated, in the process suffering almost 15,000 dead and 55,000 wounded.

In Holbrooke's opinion, the Pentagon had failed to candidly tell President Obama just how bad the situation was in Afghanistan and how poor the short-term prospects were for turning the situation around: "We did not know how bad the situation on the ground had become . . . We couldn't hold the ground we took because of a lack of troops."

What Ambassador Holbrooke was describing was remarkably similar to a decision made by President Lyndon Johnson more than forty years earlier in the summer of 1965: Against the advice of some of his advisers, including CIA director John McCone, he committed U.S. ground troops to the war in Vietnam when, if due consideration had been given to all the facts on hand, it might have been more statesmanlike to go back on the promises he made on the campaign trail and just walk away from the problem, as President Bill Clinton did in 1993 in Somalia.

If he had had a better understanding of the situation in Afghanistan, Obama could have told the American people after he was inaugurated that the Bush administration had ignored the problems in Afghanistan for seven years and had prosecuted the war with a flawed military strategy, allowing what had been a fixable problem in 2002 to metastasize into a full-blown and perhaps inoperable cancer by the time he took office in January 2009. But he didn't. For better or for worse, Obama decided to stick by the promises that he had made on the campaign trail and stay the course with the Bush administration's flawed Afghan military strategy, all because he was not given the information that he needed to make a more informed judgement.

But Holbrooke reserved his harshest criticism for the U.S. intelligence community, whose knowledge of the political, economic, and social dynamics of Afghanistan was grossly inadequate despite the fact that the U.S. had been at war in the country for more than seven years. President Obama's 2009 decision to double the size of American forces in Afghanistan, according to Holbrooke, was made in an information vacuum. He recalled attending an intelligence briefing on the Taliban held in the White House Situation Room in early 2009, where a senior Obama National Security Council staffer, frustrated by the lack of specifics contained in the presentation, pointedly asked the CIA briefer, "What the hell have you guys been doing for the past seven years?"

Holbrooke was particularly shocked by how poor the intelligence was on the Taliban. "We did not know who we were up against. We did not know how many [Taliban] we were fighting, where they came from, or why they were against us . . . We knew nothing about the men leading them. Intel did not even have a good bio for Mullah Omar . . . and we did not even know who was on our side and who was on theirs."

What Ambassador Holbrooke was describing was eerily similar to the Russian experience in Afghanistan in the 1980s. Compare Holbrooke's views with a secret May 1988 report to the Central Committee of the Communist Party of the Soviet Union, which admitted that "the decision [to invade Afghanistan] was made where there was a lot of uncertainty as to the balance of forces in Afghan society. Our picture of the real social and economic situation in the country was also insufficiently clear . . . We did not even have a correct assessment of the unique geographical features of the country."

In other words, the Soviets got themselves bogged down in a quagmire because, in large part, they did not have a good understanding of the country they were trying to tame. In Richard Holbrooke's opinion, the Obama administration made the same mistake in 2009 when it decided to expand the number of U.S. troops in Afghanistan.

If anyone at the Pentagon had bothered to read any of the well-researched books written about the Soviet war in Afghanistan during the 1980s, they would have quickly discerned that one of the principal reasons the Soviets lost the war was that they did not use their vast intelligence resources to drive their military operations until it literally was too late.

Sadly, the U.S. military made exactly the same mistake as the Soviets, and it was not until recently that American commanders finally came to the sober realization that the strategy and tactics employed by the U.S. military since the U.S. invasion in 2001 were not working. For five years, counterinsurgency experts in the Pentagon and the U.S. intelligence community have argued in vain that the Vietnam-era big-battalion search-and-destroy tactics used against the resilient and elusive Taliban guerrillas have been an utter failure. The problem has been that for the past five years, the White House and the Pentagon have not listened to what the experts were saying.

In June 2006, the top Pentagon official responsible for special operations, Michael G. Vickers, wrote a memorandum to President Bush harshly critical of the way the U.S. military was handling the wars in Iraq and Afghanistan. Vickers, who is now the undersecretary of defense for intelligence in the Obama administration, told Bush that the U.S. military had to stop using the failed Vietnam-era search-and-destroy tactics and shift the military's focus to getting away from the protection of their firebases and attacking the enemy using intelligence information to drive the operations.

Unfortunately, neither President Bush nor Secretary of Defense Donald Rumsfeld heeded Vickers's advice. Only in the past year or two has the realization sunk in at the Pentagon that the strategy employed in Afghanistan was wrong, and that the only way the war can be won is by harnessing the power of our nation's intelligence collectors and analysts so that they can give our soldiers the information they need to fight the Taliban. The change in strategy is a risky one. If the intelligence operators fail to do their job, then the chances for success on the Afghan battlefield dim to a very low order of probability.

Winning the intelligence war against the Taliban will not be an easy task. According to American military intelligence officials who have served there,

Afghanistan is probably the most complex environment that they have ever worked in. Everyone agrees that Afghanistan is not really a country in the conventional sense of the word. Rather, it is an impoverished eighteenth-century landlocked feudal state roughly the size of the state of Texas, a loosely knit patchwork of seven major ethnic groups, 400 major tribal networks, and 32 million people, 80 percent of whom live in 40,000 poor rural villages. When you probe down to the village or rural farming community level, Afghanistan becomes even more complex; there loyalties are dictated not by who is in power in Kabul but rather by local tribal and clan politics and family ties. How previous rulers of the country managed to keep even a modicum of order in this chaos flummoxes many longtime Afghan observers, most of whom believe that the country is essentially ungovernable in its present form.

According to intelligence analysts who have served in Afghanistan, the problem has always been trying to get the succession of American and NATO generals who have held command positions in Kabul to understand that Afghanistan is much more than just a name on a map and a bunch of statistics on powerpoint slides. Without understanding the country and what makes it tick, victory is impossible.

Perhaps the first senior commander to fully appreciate how complex the Afghan battlefield really was, and how critically important it was to understand every facet and nuance of the country, was Major General Michael T. Flynn, who arrived in Kabul on June 15, 2009, as the new ISAF director of intelligence. Flynn was a protégé of General Stanley A. McChrystal, the new commander of U.S. and NATO forces in Afghanistan, who had been brought in to replace General David D. McKiernan, who had been fired by Secretary of Defense Robert M. Gates on May 11, 2009.

Flynn was no stranger to Afghanistan. He had served as the chief of intelligence for U.S. forces in Afghanistan in 2002, departing in July of that year when the country was still relatively peaceful. But much had changed in the intervening seven years. Flynn and his aides did a whirlwind tour of Afghanistan and quickly learned that the military situation was worse than he expected. His grim findings were incorporated into General McChrystal's August 2009 classified report to Secretary Gates, which bluntly concluded that "many indicators suggest the overall situation [in Afghanistan] is deteriorating despite considerable effort by ISAF. The threat has grown steadily but subtly, and unchecked by commensurate counter-action, its severity now surpasses the capabilities of the current strategy."

According to one of Flynn's aides, the general was profoundly disturbed by the discombobulated state of the organization that he inherited. Not only was U.S. intelligence in Afghanistan poorly organized and desperately short of resources, it was not producing the kind of information that American field commanders urgently needed. According to the aide, "Our intelligence system was failing us."

Flynn wasted no time demanding more intelligence manpower and equipment for Afghanistan, and he quickly got them. In a matter of only six months the size of the ISAF intelligence staff in Kabul doubled from 125 to 300 American and NATO officers, including a contingent of top-flight civilian and military intelligence officers plucked from domestic assignments. By the end of 2009, there were almost 10,000 intelligence collectors, sensor operators, linguists, analysts, communicators, and the like in Afghanistan, about 5,000 of whom were Afghan nationals performing intelligence-related duties on the U.S. payroll. Dozens of new intelligence collection systems had arrived in Afghanistan, including more unmanned drones, reconnaissance aircraft, and a new family of ground-based SIGINT collection systems that were far better suited for the harsh and unforgiving Afghan environment than the systems they replaced.

Flynn also changed the way that intelligence worked in Afghanistan. The separate American and NATO intelligence infrastructures were merged together into a single coherent unit under the command of Rear Admiral Paul Becker. The old classification stovepipes that had prevented the sharing of intelligence between U.S. and NATO forces were dismantled; and all intelligence reports coming out of the ISAF intelligence staff were now written at a classification level low enough so that everyone down to platoon commanders could read them. Previous restrictions on how money could be spent on intelligence projects, like rentals of safe houses and cash payments to informants, were relaxed; and the bureaucratic red tape and prohibitive rules of engagement that had been inhibiting the use of drones and commando raids were done away with almost completely, with the number of intelligence-driven commando raids shooting up from about a hundred a month during General McKiernan's tenure to more than five hundred a month by the end of 2009.

Serious problems remained, however. So many secret American intelligence organizations were running around Afghanistan with little or no supervision from Kabul that they sometimes tripped over one another. Matthew P. Hoh, then the State Department's political adviser in Zabul Province and now a senior fellow at the Center for International Policy in Washington, recalled an incident in August 2009 when he was informed that Joint Special

Operations Command commandos belonging to the special counternarcotics task force at Bagram Air Base were about to conduct a raid on the bazaar in downtown Qalat, the provincial capital of Zabul Province, based on a single unverified piece of human intelligence that some of the sellers in the bazaar were dealing in illegal narcotics. But according to Hoh, nobody at Bagram had bothered to verify the intelligence, much less consult with U.S. government officials in Zabul to see if the planned raid was feasible, or if the intelligence was deemed credible by independent sources on the ground. The commando raid was canceled because of insufficient credible intelligence to warrant going ahead with the operation, but according to Hoh, "The damage to our standing in Qalat that the raid could have done was massive."

Flynn ordered his analysts to start paying attention to the Afghan towns and villages coalition troops were fighting to hold on to and the people who lived in them. During his initial orientation tour, one field commander after another had told him that they knew very little about the environment they were fighting in or the people they were trying to defend. One battalion operations officer told Flynn, "I don't want to say we're clueless, but we are. We're no more than fingernail deep in our understanding of the environment."

The problem was not an academic one. At the tactical level, army field commanders knew very little about the battlefield they were operating on. One battalion commander with the 4th Brigade Combat Team of the 4th Infantry Division recalled in a recent interview that when his troops arrived in eastern Afghanistan in June 2009, he had only the vaguest notion of which villages in his sector were friendly, unfriendly, or sitting on the fence. The intelligence staff of the battalion he had replaced did not seem to have thought such information important. There was no database with the names and backgrounds of the local major landowners or village chiefs, what their tribal affiliation was, or even how many people lived in each village and what their politics were. "How was I expected to win their hearts and minds," the commander wondered, "if I knew nothing about them?"

If there is a nerve center for the Afghan intelligence war, it is Bagram Air Base, a sprawling 5,000-acre military complex thirty miles north of Kabul that is populated by almost 18,000 U.S. and NATO troops and civilian contractors.

The flightline and hangars at Bagram are jammed with a host of publicity-shy intelligence-gathering aircraft and unmanned drones. There is a U.S. Army unit called Task Force ODIN-A (Observe, Detect, Identify, Neutralize–Afghanistan), which flies both unmanned drones and some very secretive

C-12 King Air aircraft that are equipped with reconnaissance cameras and sensitive SIGINT collection gear. This unit's planes hunt for Taliban IED teams. Next to them on the flightline is a U.S. Air Force squadron that flies a dozen or so MC-12W aircraft that are equipped with high-resolution video cameras and SIGINT collection equipment to track the movements of Taliban commanders in southern Afghanistan.

Keeping these mission-critical drones and aircraft flying in Afghanistan has always been a major challenge. Depending on the time of the year, these drones and reconnaissance aircraft spend more time idling on the tarmac than flying missions because of bad weather. During the summer months, winds aloft of fifty knots or more are not uncommon, and massive dust storms can cause brownouts that last days at a time. Army and air force drone maintenance crews at Bagram and Kandahar complain that they have had difficulty keeping their systems flying because of the massive amount of windblown sand and dust that gets ingested into the engines of their aircraft.

The west side of the Bagram base is honeycombed with over a dozen barbed-wire-enclosed compounds housing a plethora of secretive intelligence units. On one corner of the base is a heavily guarded building with a sign posted out front that identifies it as the home of the Remote Operations Cryptologic Center, where Taliban and al Qaeda cell phone calls are intercepted and translated. Just down the road is another compound, which houses the Joint Document Exploitation Center, where all captured Taliban documents go to be translated and analyzed.

And in a remote corner of the base is Parwan, the new military prison built in 2009, which currently houses about eight hundred Taliban prisoners. Most of the prisoners are undergoing reeducation classes, which it is hoped will eventually lead to their release back into Afghan society. There is also a maximum security wing of the prison, which houses about forty hardcore Taliban commanders who probably will be held indefinitely.

Everything about the Afghan capital of Kabul, population 1.5 million, has a surreal quality to it. Just as in Saigon at the height of the Vietnam War, you would never know that there was a war going on just outside the city gates. Kabul has become a boomtown, thanks to the billions of dollars of U.S. and foreign reconstruction aid that have been pumped into the city since 2001. The city's streets teem with life. There are so many cars, SUVs, motorcycles, and mopeds that snarling traffic jams are the norm downtown. Every inch of sidewalk space is crammed with hawkers selling their wares, and the city's bazaars are packed full of every conceivable type of goods for sale, including one stall that the author found selling U.S. military computers with their classified hard drives still in them.

Despite the vast poverty of the city's population, Kabul has a vibrant night-life complete with coffee bars, teahouses, discos, and hundreds of restaurants and cafés, many of which cater to foreigners, all doing a booming trade. According to an Australian aid official stationed in Kabul in 2009, the prevailing sentiment is "Live for today because there may be no tomorrow."

Over the past decade Kabul has become a spy's paradise, surpassing Berlin and Vienna during the Cold War era in the pantheon of great spy meccas of history. According to an Afghan security official interviewed in 2010, today there are more spies working the streets and the diplomatic cocktail circuit in Kabul than anywhere else in the world.

The embassy of virtually every major foreign power in Kabul has a contingent of intelligence officers on staff who openly trawl the city looking for any tidbits of information that they can report to their capitals, as well as SIGINT listening posts hidden inside the chanceries, which intercept the cell phone calls of Afghan government officials, foreign diplomats, United Nations officials, private security contractors, aid workers, and just about anyone else of importance in Kabul.

The two top luxury hotels, the Hotel InterContinental in the northern part of the city, and the Serena Hotel in downtown Kabul, are veritable dens of spies. The Serena's four restaurants, especially the chic Café Zarnegar, are favorite meeting places for Afghan government officials, diplomats, spies, and a smattering of underpaid journalists, foreign aid workers, and UN officials. You figuratively cannot turn around without accidentally hitting someone trying to eavesdrop on your conversation. And for a modest gratuity, the business-savvy hotel porters will tell you which of the suites they believe have electronic surveillance devices installed inside, although they claim they have no idea who is listening in on the conversations or what other nefarious activities may be taking place in these rooms.

The Taverna du Liban, a popular Lebanese restaurant in downtown Kabul, is another favorite watering hole for the legion of spies and diplomats who now call Kabul home. So is Kabul's only golf club, where, weather permitting, one can almost always find some American, French, or Russian intelligence officer trying to extract secrets from a gaggle of Afghan government officials who, from the look of things, are just trying to learn how to putt.

The largest contingent of spies in the Afghan capital belongs to the CIA's

Kabul station, which occupies the entire top floor of the new $736 million U.S. embassy on Great Massoud Road in the heart of the Green Zone in downtown Kabul. The CIA station chief, whose cover position is Counselor for Regional Affairs works here, as do his top deputies, a sizable group of case officers from the National Clandestine Service, and most of the station's intelligence analysts. Also on the top floor of the U.S. embassy is an ultrasophisticated NSA-CIA listening post, which monitors cell phone calls and radio traffic throughout Kabul. Access to the various sections of the station is protected by armed U.S. Marine guards, surveillance cameras, and the latest security devices.

The CIA's massive presence is an open secret. It seems that virtually every foreign diplomat and Afghan government official in Kabul knows the names of the CIA station chief and his top deputies. One Afghan security official gave me the private office telephone number at the U.S. embassy for the agency's station chief in the hope that I might say a good word about him if the occasion ever arose. It never did.

The Kabul station has grown dramatically since President Obama was inaugurated. In early 2009, DNI Denny Blair ordered the immediate transfer from Iraq to Afghanistan of many of the CIA's best case officers and intelligence analysts. By the end of the year, the size of the CIA station in Afghanistan doubled from three hundred people to almost seven hundred agency officers and contract employees, instantly becoming the agency's largest station in the world. The station has become so large that one agency analyst who served in Kabul referred to it as "the Archipelago."

Up at Bagram Air Base is a large contingent of paramilitary operatives assigned to the CIA base on the west side of the airfield. These operatives, in conjunction with the thousand-plus Green Berets and Navy SEALs stationed just a few hundred yards away at a separate compound called Camp Vance, conduct what are referred to as "direct action" operations, which is a polite way of referring to commando raids designed to capture or kill Taliban commanders. The main CIA resource for these operations is three thousand Afghan mercenaries known as the Counterterrorist Pursuit Teams (CTPT), who were first publicly identified in Bob Woodward's 2010 book *Obama's Wars*. The CTPT teams, which are deployed at twenty-six firebases in southern and eastern Afghanistan, are rated as some of the most effective combat units in Afghanistan because, unlike their Afghan army and police counterparts, they are well armed, well trained, and combat tested, and their loyalty is not an issue because they are paid four times the monthly salary of an average Afghan soldier or policeman.

Besides the station in Kabul and the paramilitary base at Bagram, the CIA has three large bases along the Afghan-Pakistani border at Kandahar, Khost, and Jalalabad, which recruit and operate agent networks inside northern Pakistan. Small CIA bases have recently been established inside the new U.S. consulates in Herat in western Afghanistan, which monitor activities in eastern Iran; and at Mazar-e-Sharif in the northern part of the country, from which the CIA monitors Muslim extremist activities in neighboring Uzbekistan. There are also a host of smaller CIA bases along the Afghan-Pakistani border, like the small agency-run listening post called Cardinal, which is located directly adjacent to the Pakistani border above the Ghaki Pass in Kunar Province.

The CIA maintains very close relations with the Afghan intelligence service, the National Directorate for Security (NDS), which it completely subsidized until 2008, when the Afghan government assumed responsibility for funding the organization. Despite the NDS's well-deserved reputation for abusing prisoners, American officials interviewed for this book admitted that they depended heavily on the Afghan intelligence agency.

For example, the CIA and the NDS jointly ran a number of important surveillance operations targeting the movements and activities of all Pakistani and Iranian intelligence officers based in Kabul and elsewhere inside Afghanistan. In the summer of 2008, surveillance of the movements of Pakistani intelligence officers assigned to their embassy in Kabul revealed that these individuals were closely monitoring the Indian embassy and the activities of Indian diplomats and businessmen in Kabul just weeks before a car bomb destroyed the embassy on July 7, 2008, killing more than forty people.

While the level of cooperation between the CIA and the NDS is close, the CIA deliberately keeps the details of its most sensitive operations away from its Afghan counterparts. In particular, there is no sharing of information about the CIA station's top target, Afghan president Hamid Karzai, whom the agency had been carefully watching since he first came to power after the U.S. invasion in 2001.

Spying on Karzai has proven to be relatively easy, thanks to the array of sources the CIA has recruited inside the Afghan government over the past decade. Published newspaper reports have disclosed that President Karzai's brother, Mahmoud Karzai, and his half brother, Ahmed Wali Karzai, who was assassinated in July 2011, were at one time or another on the CIA's payroll. In addition to members of Karzai's family, the CIA also has dozens of paid informants within the Afghan Ministries of Defense, Interior, and Foreign Affairs, the office of the Afghan national security adviser, and even the NDS.

The files are stuffed with thousands of intelligence reports about virtually every aspect of Karzai's personal and professional life. Reading through the Karzai files, several recurring themes emerge. Beset from all sides, Karzai worries constantly about maintaining his independence while at the same time resisting what he views as the increasingly pervasive influence of the United States in the conduct of his government's affairs. Karzai makes no secret that he detests Vice President Joe Biden and the former U.S. ambassador in Kabul Karl W. Eikenberry. He takes as a personal affront the repeated efforts by the Obama administration to push him to be more aggressive in countering corruption inside his own government, and he has taken to resisting attempts by the U.S. embassy in Kabul to influence key government appointments. He complains constantly that the economic aid that he has been promised by the United States and European countries has never been delivered. Karzai is also convinced that the Pakistani government is actively seeking to overthrow his government.

If you want to find the real war in Afghanistan, not the "feel good" version of the conflict that you usually see on the nightly news across America, drive thirty minutes southwest of Kabul on the nation's only fully paved road, Highway 1, into Wardak Province. The moment you cross the line into Wardak, you leave behind the twenty-first century and enter a rough-and-tumble, inhospitable world that has not changed appreciably since the birth of Christ.

Time has stood still in the 383 poor and isolated villages of Wardak for centuries. Village life continues to revolve around the *qalah* (pronounced *kala)*, the picturesque whitewashed compounds that have been the homes of the same families going back generations. The villages have none of the basic services that even the smallest and most impoverished town in America would take for granted: no town hall, police station, fire house, post office, hospital, school, stores, or telephones. Basic infrastructure is nonexistent. Absent are paved roads, running water, electricity, or even cars. The venerable donkey is still the preferred means of transport in the province.

For years after the U.S. invasion, Wardak was a sleepy, peaceful provincial backwater, its 540,000 inhabitants largely untouched by the war raging to the south. The U.S. military's public relations people in Kabul routinely directed reporters to Wardak if they wanted to see what a peaceful Afghan province looked like. Cut off from the rest of the world, the average Wardaki knew little about the war going on all around them. In their lifetime, average Afghan villagers rarely venture any farther than ten to twenty miles from the village where they were born. With no newspapers (80 percent of all Afghans cannot read), radio, or television, their knowledge of the world outside their village or valley is largely limited to what they hear on the local grapevine.

But behind its peaceful façade, Wardak was seething with discontent, and nobody on the ISAF intelligence staff in Kabul seems to have noticed. In 2007, the Taliban infiltrated into Wardak from Pakistan some young field commanders and recruiters whose mission was to organize a guerrilla force from among the local Pashtun villages. Once the Taliban recruiters reached Wardak, they found the province ripe for recruiting. The local Pashtun tribesmen, who made up 70 percent of the province's population, were angry. Since the U.S. invasion in 2001, they had been treated as second-class citizens by their own government and had been forsaken by the American military, who had promised both to protect them and lift them out of poverty but did neither. Their economic lot in life had deteriorated sharply because little reconstruction money had ever made it to their impoverished villages, and what money had gotten through was promptly stolen by venal local Afghan government officials and police commanders.

So when the Taliban recruiters arrived, almost one thousand Pashtun tribesmen flocked to their banner. According to U.S. Army intelligence reports from this period, the fact that the Taliban were able to successfully recruit such a large number of fighters in Wardak in such a short time indicated that the insurgency had become almost entirely homegrown and self-sustaining and was no longer dependent on Pakistan for safe haven, recruits, and supplies.

In the spring of 2008, these guerrillas came down from the hills and overran one district after another against feeble resistance from the few poorly trained and equipped Afghan National Police units in Wardak. By the time the fighting season came to an end in November, the Afghan government had lost control of the province. The Taliban not only controlled most of six of the province's eight districts, but they had also established their own provincial "shadow government" to administer the territory that they controlled, complete with their own governor, military commander, court system, and religious leaders.

In January 2009, the U.S. Army was forced to divert the 3,500-strong 3rd Brigade Combat Team of the 10th Mountain Division to Wardak and neighboring Logar Province to try to stem the tide. The brigade was almost completely unprepared for the rigors of Afghanistan. It was supposed to have been deployed to Iraq, but because of the deteriorating security situation the brigade was diverted at the last moment to Afghanistan. In the haste to get them to the battlefield, the brigade's troops were given virtually no cultural or language training about Afghanistan prior to deployment. One of the brigade's company commanders admitted that there was no time to teach his soldiers even the rudiments of the Pashtun dialect, except for the phrase that all GI's in Afghanistan eventually learn, *"Dresh! Ka na daz kawam!"* which means "Halt! Or I will shoot!"

Upon arrival in Afghanistan, the brigade's commander, Colonel David Haight, was told that he had to make do with whatever resources he had brought with him from the U.S. There were no reserves available, and the 31,000 American and Afghan forces in eastern Afghanistan were stretched to the breaking point just trying to hold on to 43,000 square miles of mostly mountainous terrain that they were responsible for, which was equal in size to the states of Georgia and South Carolina combined, including 450 miles of border with Pakistan. Wardak was but one of fourteen provinces that the U.S. Army was responsible for, and the security situation in many of the other provinces was far worse than was the case in Wardak.

Just as in Vietnam forty years before, there were no clearly defined front lines separating the U.S. forces from the Taliban. The plastic-covered situation maps on the walls of the Tactical Operations Center at the 3rd Brigade's headquarters at Forward Operating Base Airborne outside the provincial capital of Maydan Shar reflected the tenuous and complicated nature of the Afghan battlefield. The U.S. Army held Maydan Shar and all of the district seats, which appeared on the situation map as blue "inkblots"; these were surrounded by a sea of red, which was the area the Taliban controlled or contested. There were hundreds of villages spread across the province. Some rated as "friendly" by the brigade's intelligence staff; some were classified as "sitting on the fence." Others were overtly hostile and made no secret of their loyalty to the Taliban.

The friendliest villages in Wardak were those inhabited by the Hazara people, an ancient tribe of Shiites who speak a version of Farsi (the national language of Iran), not the Pashto dialect of their Pashtun neighbors. The Hazaras, who comprise 30 percent of the province's population, have traditionally been the sworn enemies of the Taliban. Because they are Shiites, they were labeled "infidels" by Mullah Omar's Taliban regime and treated brutally. Because of their natural antipathy for the Taliban, the Hazaras have probably done more than anyone else to help the U.S. Army hold Wardak Province over the past three years. They have also been a continual gold mine for the U.S. Army intelligence collectors in the region.

According to a U.S. Army platoon commander who served with the 10th Mountain Division in Wardak in 2009, "The Hazaras were wonderful people and fantastic sources of intel about the Taliban. When we visited their villages up in the hills, everyone came out to meet us. We had to sit down for tea with the village chief and all the old men, followed by a meal. We were there for hours. And when we finally said our good-byes and got out of the village, my intelligence NCO had a notepad full of juicy tidbits about local Taliban activities."

These informal sit-down *shuras* (meetings) over tea with the Hazara village elders invariably produced a plethora of hard, and sometimes actionable, intelligence information about what the Taliban were up to. Two U.S. Army intelligence officers who served in Wardak in 2009 and 2010 conservatively estimated that they got about 75 percent of their best intelligence information about the Taliban from the Hazaras.

But the relationship with the Hazaras took a painfully long time to develop, in part because the U.S. Army and the Afghan government had largely ignored the Hazaras and their needs since the U.S. invasion in 2001. The harmonious relationship that the U.S. military once had with the Hazara villagers immediately after the 2001 invasion was gone, replaced by wariness, and sometimes outright hostility, because the promises that had been made a decade earlier in return for their support against the Taliban had never been honored.

So shortly after arriving in Wardak in January 2009, several of the brigade's company and platoon commanders began asking local landowners (*khans*) and village chiefs (*maliks*) in their sectors for any information about the Taliban, in return for which they promised to build schools or dig water wells. The village elders politely rejected the requests, telling the American officers that their predecessors had made similar promises but had never delivered. And they were not about to get fooled again.

There are literally hundreds of stories just like this, where in remote villages across Afghanistan young American field commanders were being denied access to basic ground-level intelligence about the Taliban because of the broken promises made by their predecessors. Because of our own obduracy, the American soldiers in Afghanistan had become, in the words of the current commander of U.S. forces in Afghanistan, General David H. Petraeus, "an army of strangers in the midst of strangers."

So Colonel Haight's brigade had to start from scratch to build a sense of trust amongst the local Hazara tribesmen. Seemingly small acts of kindness went a long way toward building up a sense of goodwill among the villagers. Taking a page from the Green Berets' toolkit, U.S. Army commanders in Wardak found that offering free medical checkups was a very effective way to build goodwill and trust. Showing a degree of concern for the welfare of the village's all-important livestock herds was another. One army lieutenant, who grew up in sheep-herding country in central California, proved to be an effective intelligence collector because he took the time to sit down with village elders to discuss the diseases that were afflicting the local goat and sheep herds. The officer arranged for a veterinarian to visit the village and inoculate the village's sheep herds. Within a matter of weeks, the village elders were feeding the lieutenant's platoon with tidbits of information about what the Taliban were up to around the village.

The field commanders found that the most effective way to build trust and generate intelligence information at the same time was to spoil the village children, who invariably ran out to greet the troops because they had learned long ago that the soldiers brought gifts. The rule of thumb was that every child got a toy, usually a soccer ball, as well as whatever chocolate or other candy the soldiers had received from home.

Army commanders refer to this as "Hershey Bar Diplomacy," because spoiling the village children is an incredibly effective icebreaker. Villagers who were overtly hostile or suspicious when an American patrol entered their village relaxed and became friendlier in a matter of minutes when they saw the smiles on the faces of their children. Almost always, a village elder came out to exchange greetings with the troops, and if everything went right, the patrol commander was invited to sit down for tea to discuss local issues. If all went well after that, the intelligence began to flow.

As gratifying as the Wardak experience may have been, there were parts of Afghanistan that were far more hostile environments than Wardak Province.

Fifty years ago, French historian Bernard Fall described the doomed French military stronghold of Dien Bien Phu in North Vietnam as "Hell in a very small place." This moniker aptly describes the Korengal Valley in southeastern Afghanistan, which a number of American field commanders have said was by far the worst place they ever served in.

Located in the heart of Kunar Province, the desolate Korengal Valley, dubbed the "Valley of Death" or alternatively the "Valley of Fire" by the American troops, does not even appear on most maps of Afghanistan. It is only a fly-speck, only a half mile wide and six miles long, the equivalent of the length of the boardwalk in Atlantic City, New Jersey.

The valley's 4,500 inhabitants, known colloquially as Korengalis, are not Pashtuns. Like the Hazaras to the north, the Korengalis are a separate ethnic group who speak their own language and have a distinct culture, reinforced by centuries of self-imposed isolation from the outside world.

According to Afghan government officials, Korengalis are the Afghan equivalent of hillbillies. They live in a dozen or so impoverished villages set high up on the walls of the valley's steep and bare mountainsides, eking out a living through subsistence farming and by smuggling timber out of the valley to Pakistan. Intensely clannish, they make no secret of the fact that they dislike outsiders, so much so that even their kinsmen from neighboring valleys know better than to visit.

The outright hostility of the Korengalis to whichever government happens to be in power in Kabul is legendary. The Soviets never dared enter the valley during their nine-year occupation of Afghanistan in the 1980s. Even the Taliban had the good sense to leave them alone when they ruled Afghanistan between 1996 and 2001. Since the American invasion, the Korengalis have resisted all attempts by the U.S. Army to bring them into line and refused to accept the legitimacy of Hamid Karzai's government in Kabul. In short, the Korengalis wanted nothing to do with the outside world. When the U.S. Army established a permanent presence in the Korengal Valley in 2004, many Korengalis joined the Taliban overnight.

The fierceness of the Korengali resistance to the U.S. military was intense. Many of the American officers and enlisted men who served in the Korengal Valley honestly believed at the beginning of their tours that these illiterate peasants, armed with nothing more sophisticated than their family's vintage AK-47 assault rifle, would turn tail and run when they came face-to-face with American superiority in numbers and firepower.

But between 2004 and 2010, six different U.S. Army and Marine Corps battalions tried and failed to quash the Korengali Taliban, despite the fact that they never numbered more than a couple of hundred fighters at any one time. During this six-year period, forty-two American soldiers were killed in the Korengal. To give an idea of the fierceness of the fighting: One U.S. Army unit, the thousand-man 1st Battalion, 26th Infantry Regiment, lost eighteen men killed and over one hundred men wounded in the Korengal between June 2008 and June 2009.

U.S. Army intelligence officers now admit that they failed to fully compre-
hend the enemy they were fighting because they were never able to penetrate
the veil of secrecy surrounding what the Taliban were up to in the valley. Unmanned drones were not of much use except when the Taliban came out into
the open to slug it out with an American patrol. SIGINT was a vitally important tool to warn American commanders of impending attacks but next to
worthless on high-level Taliban plans and intentions because the Korengalis
usually sent this type of information by a sophisticated courier network that
ran down the full length of the valley, which of course the SIGINT intercept
operators could not access.

Four former or current-serving army intelligence officers who served in
the valley confirm that they never got any viable intelligence information
about the Taliban from the valley's inhabitants because, as it turned out, the
Korengali villagers *were* the Taliban. A series of classified reports written in
2008 and 2009 by army intelligence officers at Forward Operating Base Blessing, the headquarters of the U.S. Army battalion responsible for guarding the
Korengal Valley, revealed that virtually every family in the valley was involved
with the Taliban to one degree or another.

Entire villages in the Korengal were known to be completely "bad." Sergeant Major Dwight Utley, a Green Beret who served four tours of duty in
Afghanistan with the 3rd Special Forces Group, recalled a particular sweep
that his "A team" conducted in the village of Korengal at the southern end of the
valley. Utley's team searched all the houses in the village, only to discover that
all the men had mysteriously disappeared. As the Green Berets were leaving
the village on the only road through the valley, they were ambushed by Taliban guerrillas. It was the villagers showing what they thought of the U.S.
Army. According to Utley, "We now knew where all of the males in the village
were, 400 meters away from us on the other side of the valley engaging us with
machine guns and RPGs."

And those Korengali elders who were not active Talibs steadfastly refused
to provide any intelligence information to the Americans, abiding by a strict
code of silence that would have impressed even the fiercest of American Mafia dons. According to Captain Mike Moretti, who commanded a company of
the 2nd Battalion, 12th Infantry Regiment in the Korengal Valley in 2009–
10, "The people here have an incestuous relationship with the Taliban. I may
be speaking to an elder whose brother or son is a fighter. He's not going to
give me information that is going to enable me to kill his family member."

The experience in the Korengal raises a fundamental question for American commanders and intelligence officers. The problem was succinctly put by Matthew Hoh, a former State Department political adviser in Zabul Province: "How do you separate the insurgency from the population, when the population is the insurgency?" The short answer is: you can't. That fact, more than anything else, explains why the U.S. military failed to subjugate the Korengal over a span of six years. As it turns out, the people we were trying to save did not want to be saved. They just wanted us to go away.

With virtually all of the valley's inhabitants actively or passively assisting the Taliban, it should come as no surprise that the Taliban had a better intelligence network in the Korengal than the U.S. military did. The Taliban had spies everywhere, including many of the villagers who did manual labor on the four American bases in the valley, who routinely provided insurgent commanders with advance notice of all U.S. Army patrols and combat sweeps through the valley.

This became apparent in 2008, when the army low-level voice intercept team at the Korengal Combat Outpost at the head of the valley intercepted Taliban walkie-talkie transmissions warning a village farther down the valley that an American patrol was on its way. The Taliban commander ordered the immediate evacuation of all of the village's women and children, and the village's men were to "prepare for battle." According to an army intelligence officer stationed in the Korengal at the time, "My battalion's intelligence officer said that if there were women and children in the village, the Taliban almost always would not attack. These were their wives and children. But if ICOM [walkie-talkie] chatter indicated that the women and children were running into the hills, then we knew that an attack was imminent."

Not only did the Taliban's spy network make surprising the insurgents next to impossible, it also meant that the Taliban usually surprised the U.S. troops. According to an intelligence officer with the 173rd Airborne Brigade Combat Team, "Finding the Taliban in the valley wasn't hard. Eight times out of ten, they found you before you found them."

Within days of General McChrystal taking command in Afghanistan in June 2009, the Pentagon began putting pressure on the general to provide a clear-cut victory to show that President Obama's Afghan surge was working.

The problem was that the understrength and badly overextended U.S. forces in Afghanistan were having difficulty defending the territory they were responsible for, much less going on the offensive against the 27,000 Taliban guerrilla fighters they were now up against.

In fact, all over Afghanistan, the Taliban had the momentum. On September 8, 2009, several hundred Taliban guerrillas ambushed a hundred-man patrol of Afghan troops and U.S. Marine advisers outside the village of Gangjal in Kunar Province, killing five marines, eight Afghan troops, and an interpreter. Less than a month later, on October 3, 2009, three hundred Taliban fighters attacked an exposed army base in Nuristan Province called Combat Outpost Keating, killing eight U.S. troops and wounding twenty-two others. On October 24, 2009, the *Wall Street Journal* reported that Khost Province, located just to the south of Kunar Province, which the Pentagon only a few months earlier had heralded as "an American success story," was now largely controlled by the Taliban despite the presence of 2,400 American troops in the province.

The attack on the Keating outpost was the last straw. In late October 2009, McChrystal decided to cut his losses and pull U.S. troops out of all the isolated outpost areas in Nuristan and Kunar provinces in eastern Afghanistan that, in his staff's opinion, were not worth fighting for. The hardest decision that General McChrystal had to make was whether to abandon the Korengal Valley or not. It took several months, but in the end McChrystal concluded that the valley was a lost cause. The Taliban were too deeply embedded among the valley's inhabitants, and the cost of rooting them out had proven far higher than what the bleak valley was worth in terms of blood and treasure.

On April 14, 2010, the U.S. Army pulled all of its troops out of the Korengal as part of what General McChrystal described as a "strategic redeployment of forces." Many army commanders vehemently disagreed with McChrystal's decision to abandon the Korengal. An angry U.S. Army officer, who served two tours of duty in the Korengal with the 173rd Airborne Brigade, voiced an opinion shared by many of his fellow officers: "For years we were told that the Korengal was the anchor of our defense, and that it had to be held at all costs. Then one day, we get a directive telling us that we had to abandon it because some shithead in Kabul decided that holding the valley was no longer essential to the war effort. What a load of bullshit!"

For all the anger felt at abandoning the Korengal, there was also some relief. An army helicopter pilot from the 3rd Combat Aviation Brigade involved in the evacuation of the army's main firebase in the valley, known as the Korengal Outpost, recalled that as his Black Hawk helicopter took off from the base, the troops onboard his chopper took up the iconic 1965 rock anthem made famous by the English band the Animals, singing at the top of their voices, "We gotta get out of this place, if it's the last thing we ever do."

Within hours of the U.S. Army pulling out of the Korengal, the Taliban emerged from the shadows. In an act designed to embarrass the U.S. military, the Taliban smuggled in an Al Jazeera film crew from Pakistan to document their victory. U.S. commanders in Kabul were crestfallen when the Al Jazeera videotape was posted a few days later on YouTube for all to see. It was a suitably bitter end to the U.S. Army's experience in the Korengal.

For the past decade, Helmand Province has been a cancer that the U.S. and NATO forces have never been able to cure. Located in southwestern Afghanistan, Helmand is the largest of Afghanistan's thirty-four provinces, roughly equal in size to Ireland, with a population estimated at 1.4 million people. Lawless and unruly even in the best of times, Helmand has a well-deserved reputation as one of the most dangerous places in all of Afghanistan. Even Afghan government officials in Kabul dread going there, with one senior official indelicately referring to the Helmandis as "brigands and outcasts" during a 2009 interview.

Today, more than twenty-five thousand U.S., British, and Afghan troops hold the area around provincial capital Lashkar Gah, all of the major towns, and a few large firebases scattered around the province. The Taliban control virtually everything else. The Taliban remain so omnipresent in the province's rural areas away from the populated areas that soldiers have taken to calling the hostile and desolate countryside outside the gates of their firebases "Talibanland" or "Hajiville"—"Haji" being one of the many derogatory terms that U.S. soldiers use to refer to the Taliban.

A common theme heard from American and British soldiers who have served tours of duty there is that Helmand was far rougher than anything they had previously experienced in Iraq. The statistics back them up. Since 2006, more Taliban attacks have occurred in Helmand than in all other Afghan provinces combined. More American and British soldiers have died or been wounded in Helmand Province since 2001 than in any other province in Afghanistan.

A morbid sense of humor has cropped up among soldiers who have served there. One sharp-witted Marine Corps infantryman who pulled a tour of duty in Helmand in 2008 had a T-shirt made up when he got back to the United States that read "I visited Helmand Province, and all I brought back was a case of PTSD," a reference to post-traumatic stress disorder.

Just as in the Korengal Valley, the hostility to the presence of American and British troops in Helmand is palpable. Part of the reason for the hostility is that, like in the Korengal Valley, virtually every family in the province is connected in one way, shape, or form with the Taliban. When U.S. Marine Corps combat units first arrived in the Garmsir District in the southern part of the province in the spring of 2008, they discovered that all fifty Pashtun tribes in the district were connected to the Taliban to varying degrees, with a declassified Marine Corps report admitting that "everyone is somewhat associated [with the Taliban] if they live here."

But perhaps more than anything else, what allowed the Taliban to thrive in Helmand was that corruption was more pervasive there than in Kabul, and opium poppy cultivation, heroin trafficking, smuggling, and organized crime dominated the province's political and economic landscape. The bazaars and teahouses of Lashkar Gah were filled with Taliban operatives, drug lords, crime bosses, smugglers, corrupt government and police officials, spies, gunmen for hire, arms merchants, thieves, and confidence artists of every sort and variety. In 2009, the province's governor, Gulabuddin Mangal, one of the very few Afghan governors with a reputation for honesty, told the U.S. ambassador to Afghanistan, Karl W. Eikenberry, that there was a "complete lack of security in the provincial capital," admitting that "narcotics traffickers operating with impunity lived within 100 meters of the police station in the capital."

Outside the city limits of Lashkar Gah, the Taliban guerrillas operated openly, periodically attacking Afghan army or police checkpoints just to remind everyone that they were still there. To make the point, my guide took me to the bank of the Helmand River and told me matter-of-factly that if I wanted to find the Taliban, all I had to do was cross the bridge to the other side. "You will not have to look long. They will find you," he said ominously. Afghan intelligence officers told me that they knew that dozens of Taliban agents kept close tabs on everything that went on in the city of Lashkar Gah. "There are no secrets from the Talibs," one officer told me.

The opium poppy, the main ingredient in the manufacture of heroin, still dominates Helmand's political, economic, and social landscape. Virtually everybody who lives in the province is tied into the illegal narcotics business. According to British intelligence reports reviewed by the author, virtually every family in Helmand has its hand in the illegal narcotics trade, either growing opium poppies, processing them into heroin, or moving the finished product out of Afghanistan. And according to Elizabeth Lee Walker, the ISAF Rule of Law adviser in Kabul, "Almost all officials [in Helmand Province] are assessed to be in some way involved in, or dependent on, narcotics trafficking."

Take any road out of Lashkar Gah and within minutes you are driving through thousands of acres of hauntingly beautiful fields of green, pink, and white opium poppies stretching as far as the eye can see. Local farmers freely admit that the local Afghan police will not touch the fields because the owners are variously Afghan government ministers in Kabul, some of the country's most powerful warlords, and a host of local government or police officials in Lashkar Gah, all of whom earn enormous sums of money from the illegal opium trade. Army Lt. Colonel Michael Slusher recalled that in 2006 during Operation River Dance, the first large-scale opium eradication effort in Helmand Province, the Afghan contractors hired for the project refused to plow under the opium poppy fields owned by the province's then governor, Mohammad "Engineer" Daud. According to Colonel Slusher, "When they got into the area that Daud controlled, they just went around his fields."

In this incredibly hostile and chaotic environment, a number of senior American and British civilian and military intelligence officials admitted that they were continually frustrated trying to figure out just who was the enemy in Helmand. According to Major Stuart Farris, who commanded a Green Beret "A team" in Helmand, "It was hard to determine if folks were actually no-joke Taliban or just criminals . . . We had to figure out who the bad guys were, whether they were [Taliban] versus just being criminals and thugs. Sometimes, though, they're tied together. It was a very complex environment and was difficult at times to determine who the enemy was."

Intelligence was only marginally useful in terms of separating the good guys from the bad because reliable sources in Helmand were few and far between. Unlike in Wardak Province, where the Hazara tribesmen were willing to cooperate and provide intelligence on the Taliban, the Helmandi villagers were reluctant to provide intelligence on the Taliban, going to extraordinary lengths in some cases to avoid even the perception that they were cooperating with U.S. and NATO forces. The village chiefs knew from long and bitter experience that the Taliban would exact terrible reprisals on anyone who collaborated with the U.S. military.

The U.S. military's problems with collecting intelligence from Afghan civilians date back nearly a decade to the early days of the Taliban insurgency, when U.S. Army intelligence personnel were restricted to their firebases in order to hold down casualties. Barred from leaving their bases, the army intelligence personnel typically set up a shack outside the main gate of their firebase to meet with local villagers who wanted to pass on information about the Taliban. The Taliban quickly figured out what was going on, put the "safe house" under surveillance, noted which villagers went in and out, and then killed them or blackmailed them into passing false information.

As a result, gathering intelligence about the Taliban has become progressively more difficult as the insurgents have expanded and tightened their control over the remote villages in the rural areas of Helmand. A marine platoon commander who served a tour of duty in the Garmsir District in southern Helmand Province in 2009 described a patrol to reconnoiter a village located not far from his battalion's firebase that was assessed by the battalion's intelligence staff as "sitting on the fence" in terms of where its loyalties lay. The purpose of the patrol was to "show the flag" by reminding the villagers of the presence of American forces in their neighborhood, demonstrate goodwill, and pick up any intelligence on Taliban activities in the sector.

But the patrol revealed that in the two months since the village had last been visited, the Taliban had taken control of the village. There had been no pitched battle. As best the Americans could figure out, one day the Taliban had arrived and the loyalties of the village had changed overnight without any apparent bloodshed.

According to the lieutenant, "When you enter a Taliban village, the first thing you notice is the silence. There is no music playing. Maybe dogs barking. No children run out to try to get candy off us . . . never a good sign. Then you notice that all the young men are gone. No one comes out of their homes. All that was left were the old, the sick, the women, and maybe a few stray dogs. That's it . . . We knew things were bad when the village chief was sent out to politely encourage us to get out of the village . . . No invitation to sit and chat or have a cup of tea. Just leave please!"

If the Obama administration and General McChrystal had seriously hoped that they could turn the tide in Afghanistan in 2009, they were sorely disappointed. Classified intelligence assessments produced by the DNI, the CIA, and the ISAF all said basically the same thing—that despite the doubling of the size of U.S. forces in Afghanistan from 34,000 to 68,000 troops, the United States and its allies had failed to arrest the Taliban's momentum. The size of the Taliban guerrilla forces inside Afghanistan had grown; the insurgents had expanded their military presence into 160 of Afghanistan's 364 districts; the tempo of Taliban attacks against U.S. and NATO forces jumped by a staggering 75 percent in 2009; and U.S. combat deaths in Afghanistan doubled from 151 in 2008 to 304 in 2009, making it the single bloodiest year since the U.S. invasion of the country. According to a senior American intelligence officer in Kabul, "The metrics were definitely against us."

With few tangible results to show for all the effort, the Obama administration was forced to go back to the drawing board. After a sobering meeting of the National Security Council in the White House Situation Room on September 30, 2009, National Security Adviser Jim Jones and his Afghan "war czar," General Doug Lute, quietly began a ten-week review of the U.S. military effort in Afghanistan. When the review was completed in late November 2009, its conclusion was simple. More American troops—a lot more troops—were needed to stave off defeat in Afghanistan.

On Tuesday night, December 1, 2009, President Obama gave a speech at the U.S. Military Academy at West Point to announce that he had signed a directive ordering an additional 30,000 U.S. combat troops be sent to Afghanistan on top of the 68,000 troops already there. All of these troops were expected to be on the ground by the end of the summer of 2010, with all troops to be withdrawn by the end of 2011.

Back in Washington, not everyone on the president's staff was confident that more troops was the answer. Richard Holbrooke remembered thinking that the speech was comparable to what Spartan commanders were told before they marched off to battle, "Come back victorious or come back on your shield."

Going into 2010, all the top U.S. and NATO generals in Afghanistan, from General McChrystal on down, promised Washington a quick, decisive victory that would publicly demonstrate that the tide was indeed turning in Afghanistan. The place chosen by the generals in Kabul for the decisive battle was Marjah, the sole town of any size still held by the Taliban in Helmand Province.

Early on the morning of February 13, 2010, the combined U.S., British, and Afghan offensive to take Marjah began. About 5,000 British and Afghan troops seized the neighboring town of Nad Ali, while 5,000 U.S. Marines and Afghan troops seized Marjah and the surrounding area. The operation was supposed to have been a cakewalk. It did not turn out that way. It took two weeks of intense fighting before the marines announced that Marjah was secure.

If one were to believe all of the pronouncements from ISAF headquarters in Kabul, Marjah was a strategic victory of the first order. But as it turned out, Marjah was nothing close to being the kind of victory that the generals claimed it was. If the purpose of the operation was to draw the Taliban forces into a major battle and destroy them, then it was a complete failure. The Taliban had known for months that the attack was coming. According to a British military intelligence officer, intercepted Taliban radio traffic revealed that the insurgents knew as early as November 2009, more than three months before the offensive began, that the U.S. was planning to attack Marjah.

The Taliban got their advance warning directly from us. Not only were White House and Pentagon officials, like Joint Chiefs chairman Admiral Mike Mullen, telling reporters that they were going to take Marjah, but several Afghan newspapers and TV networks actually broadcast the outlines of the attack plan in December 2009, two months before the offensive kicked off. The commander of Marine Corps forces in Helmand Province, Brigadier General Larry Nicholson, even told a reporter for the *New York Times* that "the overt message we're putting out is, Marjah is next." A U.S. Army intelligence officer stationed in Kabul at the time later stated, "We might as well have just broadcast the date and time of the attack. The element of surprise had already gone straight to the crapper."

Going into the Marjah offensive, U.S. intelligence knew very little about the number of Taliban forces they were facing, or what their dispositions were. U.S. Marine Corps intelligence officers estimated that there were roughly a thousand Taliban fighters situated in and around Marjah, but this was only a guesstimate, with a British report confirming that "little was known by ISAF about the human terrain and insurgent dispositions in Marjah."

The reason was that every November, after the Afghan fighting season officially came to an end, most Taliban fighters in Helmand Province quietly slipped away from the battlefield and returned to their villages and farms to plant a new crop of opium poppies and rest up during the long winter. So no matter how hard the U.S. military's HUMINT collection teams, unmanned drones, and SIGINT teams scoured the countryside looking for their elusive enemy, the fact is that over the winter months it is virtually impossible to find the enemy. Come the spring and the beginning of the fighting season, the U.S. military typically knows very little about the enemy they are facing.

Once the attack on Marjah began, the Taliban refused to engage the superior U.S. and British forces arrayed against them, with the vast majority of the Taliban fighters managing to escape because the U.S. Marines for some reason made no effort to cut off their escape routes. So ninety days after the fall of Marjah, the Taliban had managed to reinfiltrate the town. Sniper fire and IED attacks on marine patrols around Marjah resumed. Local villagers suddenly became uncooperative, with some elders going to extraordinary lengths not to be seen talking with the marines for fear that it would prompt Taliban retaliation against them and their families.

Attempts to get the Afghan government to take over responsibility for administering Marjah stalled because the administrators and police officials who were supposed to restore the Afghan government's presence in the town refused to take up their posts. From the elaborate excuses given by the officials, it was clear that Marjah was seen as a life-ending rather than a career-enhancing assignment.

In a move that shocked American military and intelligence officials, the Afghan government announced that Abdul Rahman Jan, a notoriously corrupt official who formerly served as police chief of Helmand Province from 2003 to 2006, was to be the new police chief in Marjah. Jan was infamous for making his private militia and his police available to guard opium and heroin shipments in return for a cut of the profits, according to CIA and U.S. Army intelligence reports. The announcement brought immediate howls of protest from Marjah's village elders, who told marine commanders that they would refuse to acknowledge the authority of the Afghan government if Jan was to be their police chief. Under immense pressure from the U.S. embassy in Kabul, Karzai withdrew Jan's name from consideration, but the incident showed U.S. officials that, according to a senior ISAF intelligence officer, "Karzai doesn't get it."

Panic over Marjah set in at ISAF headquarters in Kabul. Bombarded by negative press reporting, on May 24, 2010, General McChrystal flew down to Marjah to make his own assessment of the situation. With time running out on his mandate to reverse the course of events in Afghanistan, McChrystal did not like hearing that the Taliban were creeping back into Marjah. He wanted results and he wanted them soon. "This is a bleeding ulcer right now," McChrystal told his commanders, according to an account of the meeting published in the *Miami Herald*. "You don't feel it here, but I'll tell you, it's a bleeding ulcer outside."

The marines quickly staged a photo op three days later for a visiting CBS News film crew to try to demonstrate that all was normal in Marjah by erecting a tent that was to be a new school. Everything about the event bordered on the farcical. Lt. Colonel Brian S. Christmas, the commander of the 3rd Battalion, 6th Marines, which was responsible for guarding Marjah, half-dragged the white-turbaned village chief out of the crowd, put a shovel in his hand, and encouraged him to break ground on the foundation for the new school while the CBS crew filmed the scene. The mortified village chief, perhaps thinking that he had just been involuntarily drafted into a work gang, looked like he was going to have a heart attack.

Off to the side, a bemused group of marine intelligence officers videotaped the event, paying special attention to a cluster of black-turbaned men who were intently watching. The marines' interest in these men was heightened when they suddenly became camera shy when video cameras were pointed at them, covering their faces with the edges of their turbans. One of the marine intelligence officers present muttered to his sergeant, "They're back"—meaning the Taliban.

While officials continued to put on a brave face for the public, by the spring of 2010 deep concern about the situation in Afghanistan had begun to creep into the highest levels of the U.S. government and its NATO allies. Public opinion polls showed that support for the war in Afghanistan was slipping among the American people. In Western Europe and Canada, support for the Afghan war, which had never been very high to begin with, plummeted. In March 2010, after a lengthy public debate, the Dutch government had collapsed because of the vast unpopularity of the war in that country, which according to a confidential CIA report "demonstrates the fragility of European support for the NATO-led ISAF mission" in Afghanistan. The Canadian, Dutch, and Polish governments all announced that they were pulling their troops out of Afghanistan at a time when the Obama administration was pressing the NATO governments to increase their troop levels there.

The situation on the ground was increasingly grim, with the April 2010 ISAF intelligence staff's assessment of the security situation showing that in the NATO zone in southern Afghanistan, only one district, the city of Kandahar, was rated as "sympathizing with the Government of Afghanistan," while thirteen districts were assessed as actively supporting or sympathizing with the Taliban. In the American zone in eastern Afghanistan, the situation was better, with fifteen districts rated as being supportive of the Afghan government and twelve as actively supporting or sympathizing with the insurgents. All of the remaining districts were "on the fence," waiting to see who would come out on top.

Despite all of the bad news, a small but determined group of officers at ISAF headquarters in Kabul, snidely referred to by their colleagues as "Team Victory," continued to resolutely believe in eventual victory in Afghanistan. One of the leading members of "Team Victory" was Major General Bill Mayville, General McChrystal's operations chief, who confidently predicted in a March 17, 2010, blog posting that "there are growing fissures between [the Taliban] groups and we believe they are starting to experience considerable stress due to the increased operational tempo on both sides of the Afghanistan and Pakistan border."

This statement was met with disbelief by a number of ISAF intelligence officers. Not only was there no tangible support for the general's statement in any of the intelligence reporting they were reading, but it actually ran contrary to all of the official internal estimates they had been sending to Mayville and General McChrystal. Even the Pentagon's April 2010 assessment on Afghanistan sent to Congress admitted that the security situation was "far from satisfactory."

Speaking at a closed-door NATO defense ministers' meeting in Brussels in June 2010, General McChrystal admitted that only 5 of the 121 districts in Afghanistan that he deemed to be essential if the war in Afghanistan was to be won were rated as "secure," while 40 of these key districts were rated as "dangerous." Moreover, a document prepared by his staff admitted that ISAF did not expect any major improvement in the military situation in Afghanistan for the rest of the year.

A number of American, Canadian, and European defense and intelligence officials attending the meeting left the briefing believing that General McChrystal's "protect the populace" strategy in Afghanistan was not working. Not only had the new strategy failed in its primary objective of securing the most heavily populated areas of the country, but the officials feared that by ceding the rural areas of Afghanistan to the Taliban, McChrystal was tacitly admitting that the U.S. and NATO forces would never be strong enough to take on the Taliban in their backyard.

A senior British military official summarized the sentiments of many of his colleagues during a coffee break: "McChrystal's counterinsurgency strategy is predicated on the belief that in the time allotted to him by the White House, it was impossible to take back the countryside from the Taliban. So the only alternative was we had to save what we could of the country if we were going to try to negotiate from a position of strength at a peace conference with the Taliban."

The British general was right, of course. President Obama had put General McChrystal in an untenable situation when he announced on December 1, 2009, at West Point that he had ordered that an additional 30,000 troops be sent to Afghanistan on top of the 68,000 troops already there, but that the first of these troops were to be withdrawn by July 2011. Even if they did not say so publicly, everyone at the NATO summit meeting knew that McChrystal had been saddled with an impossible task. In essence, the president had given the general only a year and a half to turn the battlefield situation around before he had to begin drawing down the size of U.S. forces in Afghanistan. In the time allotted and with the forces at his disposal, McChrystal could not militarily defeat the Taliban, given the amount of territory that the guerrillas then controlled. The best McChrystal could reasonably be expected to do was to degrade the strength of the Taliban's guerrilla forces and try to secure the major cities and towns of Afghanistan. And now, McChrystal was admitting to NATO's top commanders that he might not be able to accomplish even this very limited goal.

But a few weeks later, General McChrystal was gone. On June 21, 2010, news broke that *Rolling Stone* magazine was about to publish an article containing disparaging remarks made by General McChrystal and his senior staff about President Obama and other members of the administration. Two days later, McChrystal flew back to Washington to be relieved of his command by President Obama and sent unceremoniously into retirement.

CHAPTER 4

The Root of All Evil

The Pakistani Problem

If you do not know your enemies nor yourself,
you will be imperiled in every single battle.
—SUN TZU

Anybody who has watched any of the Sunday morning political talk shows on the major television networks since 9/11 has probably heard at one time or another some senior U.S. government official intone with great seriousness and gravity something along the lines of "Pakistan is a valued partner in the fight against terrorism."

In the aftermath of 9/11, these words actually had some resonance and meaning. When the Taliban regime in Afghanistan collapsed in December 2001, Mullah Omar and all of the Taliban's leadership and hardcore fighters escaped across the border into Pakistan. A few weeks later, Osama bin Laden and several hundred of his al Qaeda fighters also fled across the border into Pakistan after the Battle of Tora Bora. In an instant, Pakistan became a front-line state in the war on terrorism, where for a time U.S. and Pakistani intelligence operatives worked together to try to find and destroy what was left of the militants hiding in the desolate northern part of the country.

Ten years later, many of the U.S. government officials who agreed to be interviewed for this book believe that the phrase "Pakistan is a valued partner in the fight against terrorism" is now empty, cynical rhetoric. Anger and frustration with the Pakistani government in Washington is now so overt that Ambassador Richard Holbrooke described Pakistan in a 2010 interview as "the root of all evil."

American officials now firmly believe that the Pakistani government has, as a matter of national policy, given aid and comfort to our enemies, costing the lives of American soldiers fighting next door in Afghanistan. This widely held view was enunciated in a secret cable sent by Secretary of State Hillary Rodham Clinton to U.S. embassies in the Persian Gulf in December 2009, which stated unequivocally that "Pakistan's intermittent support to terrorist groups and militant organizations threatens to undermine regional security and endanger U.S. national security objectives in Afghanistan and Pakistan."

Even within the U.S. intelligence community, which still depends to some degree on Pakistani cooperation in its continuing efforts to ferret out al Qaeda, the majority view among senior officials is surprisingly negative, with a former DNI official taking the view, "How can any country that hides our enemies and obstructs our efforts to find them be an ally?"

Interviews with a dozen American and Pakistani intelligence officials have revealed that since 9/11, the CIA and the rest of the U.S. intelligence community have had what can only be described as a tempestuous, love-hate relationship with Pakistan's powerful intelligence service, the Inter-Services Intelligence Directorate, which virtually everyone refers to by its initials, ISI.

It is not an exaggeration to say that many of the CIA's greatest intelligence successes and failures since 9/11 stem directly from its inordinately convoluted relationship with the ISI. Even in the best of times, the U.S.-Pakistani intelligence relationship has been dogged by mutual suspicion and even open animosity, fueled to a certain degree by the strong undercurrent of anti-Americanism that pervades the ranks of the Pakistani military and intelligence services. This should come as no surprise, since the U.S. government and its policies in the Muslim world are extremely unpopular in Pakistan, with recent State Department polling data showing that 68 percent of all Pakistanis have a decidedly unfavorable view of the United States.

This has meant that every CIA chief of station in Pakistan since 9/11 has worked hard to improve their personal relationships with the director of ISI and his senior staff. The CIA chief of station spends much of his time during the workweek commuting back and forth between the fortresslike U.S. embassy in Islamabad's diplomatic enclave (one former CIA staff officer sarcastically referred to the heavily protected area as the "ghetto of the damned") to ISI's headquarters, located just four miles away at the intersection of Khayaban-e-Suhrawardy Road and Service Road East.

In keeping with its penchant for secrecy, everything about the ISI is hidden from public view. The ISI's 40-acre headquarters complex is surrounded by a ten-foot-high wall and guarded twenty-four hours a day by a contingent of elite Pakistani Army troops who not only shoo away unwanted visitors but have orders to shoot anyone foolish enough to try to enter the compound without authorization. Beyond the main gate is a circular driveway, which leads to a white multistory office building where most of ISI's senior officials have their offices. Most of ISI's staff work in a series of drab multistory office buildings that extend back several hundred yards from the ISI headquarters building.

But according to a Western European intelligence source, most of the ISI's really sensitive intelligence-gathering and covert action activities, including all activities relating to Afghanistan, are run from two military bases eight miles to the south called the Hamza Camp and the Ojri Camp, both of which are hidden away behind high walls and guard towers in the city of Rawalpindi. "We've been trying to find out what goes on in those camps for years," a former CIA case officer revealed in a 2010 interview, "but without much success. Everything they [the ISI] did not want us to see or hear about they hid in 'Pindi."

The chief of ISI on 9/11, Lt. General Mahmood Ahmed, had been the bête noire of the U.S. intelligence community for years because of his overtly pro-Taliban views. At the request of the U.S. government, after 9/11 Ahmed went to Afghanistan and met with Taliban leader Mullah Mohammed Omar in Kandahar to try to stave off the U.S. invasion of Afghanistan. But evidence suggests that Ahmed instead urged the Taliban to fight. After his return from Afghanistan, CIA officials privately told Pakistani president Pervez Musharaf in no uncertain terms that they did not trust Ahmed, and that the general had to go as part of the price tag for Pakistan joining the U.S.-led war on terror. It came as no surprise to intelligence insiders when General Ahmed was abruptly and unceremoniously forced to take early retirement on October 7, 2001, only three weeks before the U.S. invasion of Afghanistan began.

His replacement, Lt. General Ehsan ul Haq, ran the ISI for three years from October 2001 until he was promoted to the position of chief of staff of the Pakistani armed forces in October 2004. General ul Haq was handpicked for the post not because he was an intelligence professional but rather because he was a close personal friend and confidant of President Musharaf.

During General ul Huq's tenure, the top task for the CIA and ISI was to hunt down and capture or kill the remnants of al Qaeda that had fled into the wilds of northern Pakistan after the Battle of Tora Bora in December 2001. According to a half-dozen retired and current-serving CIA officials, the ISI aggressively collaborated with the CIA in going after the remnants of al Qaeda. Almost all of the senior al Qaeda officials captured since 9/11 and now biding their time behind bars at the military-run Guantánamo Bay detention facility in Cuba were captured in Pakistan during General ul Haq's tenure in office, including Abu Zubaydah (captured March 28, 2002), Sheikh Ahmed Salim Swedan (July 11, 2002), Ramzi Bin al-Shibh (September 11, 2002), Abu Umar and Abu Hamza (January 9, 2003), and the biggest capture of them all, al Qaeda's operations chief, Khalid Sheikh Mohammed, on March 1, 2003. "We would not have gotten any of these guys without the help of ISI," a former senior CIA official said in an interview.

As a reward for this assistance, the CIA has secretly funneled hundreds of millions of dollars every year since 2002 to the ISI, with senior American intelligence officials confirming media reports that until 2009 the agency was directly subsidizing about one third of ISI's annual budget, which did not include the tens of millions of dollars of training, equipment, and logistical support that the agency also provided to Pakistan. According to author Bob Woodward, in 2008 the annual CIA subsidy to the ISI amounted to a staggering $2 billion.

But for all the successes, there were some glaring failures. Until al Qaeda's leader, Osama bin Laden, was finally found and killed by U.S. Navy SEAL commandos in Abbottabad, Pakistan, on May 1, 2011, American and Pakistani intelligence officials interviewed for this book agreed that the failure to find him was the single most important failure in the war on terror.

Since bin Laden and his adherents had fled to Pakistan after the Battle of Tora Bora almost a decade earlier in December 2001, the belief within the U.S. intelligence community had been that bin Laden and his Egyptian-born deputy, Ayman al-Zawahiri, continued to run al Qaeda from their hiding places somewhere in the lawless 10,000-square-mile area of northern Pakistan bordering Afghanistan called the Federally Administered Tribal Areas, or FATA, which is roughly the size of the state of Massachusetts.

But senior Pentagon officials, including Secretary of Defense Donald Rumsfeld and his deputy, Paul Wolfowitz, believed that bin Laden had been killed at Tora Bora, and steadfastly refused to admit that the terrorist leader was still alive until the Arab news organization Al Jazeera began broadcasting bin Laden's videotaped pronouncements in late 2002. Rumsfeld and Wolfowitz were angered by U.S. intelligence community assessments that bin Laden was still alive because there were no indications appearing in intercepted al Qaeda communications traffic that he was dead. Rumsfeld and Wolfowitz believed that al Qaeda was keeping the fact that bin Laden was dead a secret by keeping the news of the terrorist leader's demise out of their electronic communications that NSA was intercepting. A clearly angry Wolfowitz wrote in a classified July 2002 internal memo that "I fear we are so mesmerized [by signals intelligence] that we find it impossible to adequately account for the fact that the terrorists know that we do this. We are a bit like a drunk looking for our keys under the lamppost because that is the only place where there is light."

Fortunately, the intelligence community ignored Rumsfeld and Wolfowitz and kept looking for the elusive al Qaeda leader. After the Battle of Tora Bora in December 2001, the U.S. intelligence community's top priority remained finding bin Laden and his top deputies, with the Bush administration believing that if we managed to neutralize the top leadership of al Qaeda, then the whole organization would collapse from within. So Washington ordered the CIA station in Islamabad and its subordinate bases in Pakistan to do "whatever is needed to bring bin Laden to justice." In the years that followed, the Islamabad station expended vast amounts of time, money, personnel, and equipment on the effort, but bin Laden and Zawahiri somehow eluded the massive dragnet for a decade despite having $25 million bounties on their heads. An army intelligence briefing described the problem as "looking for a silver needle in a stack of 6 million needles."

During the early stages of the search, from 2002 through 2004, there were occasional fragmentary references to bin Laden in CIA clandestine agent reports and in intercepted al Qaeda communications traffic emanating from northern Pakistan. But none of the leads panned out. The last hard information about bin Laden was in 2004, when the National Security Agency intercepted a reference to "the Sheikh," referring to bin Laden, in an intercepted al Qaeda transmission emanating from North Waziristan in the lawless tribal areas of northern Pakistan. But since then, the trail had gone stone cold.

According to a senior Pakistani intelligence official, in desperation, the CIA surreptitiously tapped the phones of the Islamabad bureau of the Arab news organization Al Jazeera in the hope that the intercepted calls might lead them to the clandestine couriers who periodically gave the network CDs containing the latest videotaped pronouncements by Osama bin Laden and Zawahiri. But these taps never produced any viable intelligence other than to confirm in the minds of the CIA officers who listened to the recordings that many of the network's reporters had a clear anti-American bias.

The inability of the CIA to find bin Laden and Zawahiri was not the end of the problems, either. U.S. intelligence officials have confirmed that, try as they might, the CIA and its foreign partners have had little sustained success penetrating al Qaeda over the past decade. Getting inside al Qaeda proved to be nigh on impossible, with Secretary of Defense Donald Rumsfeld admitting in a 2001 classified memo that "some terrorist groups use family and communal relationships that make them extraordinarily difficult to penetrate." As reported by the Associated Press on November 5, 2010, the CIA and the British foreign intelligence service, MI6, managed to recruit a small number of former al Qaeda and Taliban detainees held at Guantánamo and sent them back to Pakistan to spy on their former masters under the direction of the ISI. However, al Qaeda and Taliban counterintelligence operatives quickly identified them as spies, possibly with the help of pro-Taliban ISI officers in Islamabad. They were immediately arrested, tortured, and, once every ounce of information had been extracted from them, publicly executed.

One American intelligence official interviewed for this book admitted that the extreme paranoia of al Qaeda's top leaders about the presence of spies in their midst made it next to impossible to insert agents into the organization. According to a former head of the CIA's National Clandestine Service, Michael J. Sulick, these terrorist groups "screen their recruits probably better than the U.S. government does."

The loss rate among the few agents that were recruited was extraordinarily high. For example, on Sunday, November 8, 2010, a Pakistani Taliban drumhead court in the al Qaeda and Taliban stronghold of Miram Shah in North Waziristan found three local tribesmen guilty of spying for the United States after a trial that lasted less than an hour. Taliban gunmen immediately blindfolded the three men, tied their hands behind their backs, and led them to a nearby gas station, where they were shot to death in front of a crowd of several hundred men who had gathered for the occasion. The identities of the three men were never made public.

The glory days of U.S.-Pakistani intelligence cooperation came to an abrupt end in the fall of 2004, when ISI chief General Ehsan ul Haq was promoted to the position of chief of staff of the Pakistani armed forces. U.S.-Pakistani intelligence relations took a decided turn for the worse when Lt. General Ashfaq Parvez Kayani, now the Pakistani Army's chief of staff, took over as director-general of the ISI in October 2004. A chainsmoker and golfing fanatic, Kayani is a shrewd if not brilliant officer whose long experience in the upper echelons of the Pakistani military and high-level exposure to Pakistani politics (he had been the military assistant to Prime Minister Benazir Bhutto from 1988 to 1990) made him a gifted practitioner of the Machiavellian art of getting what he wanted by whatever means necessary.

Kayani quickly made his imprint on ISI. According to U.S. intelligence officials, beginning in 2004 the quality and reliability of the intelligence information that Washington received from the ISI, which was never very good to begin with, began to decline markedly. Shortly thereafter, sensitive intelligence sources confirmed that ISI was deliberately withholding from the United States increasing amounts of the intelligence that it had in its possession on al Qaeda activities in the FATA. A retired Pakistani intelligence official confirmed in an interview that Pakistan had, in his words, "dialed down" the amount of intelligence it gave the CIA because Washington was deliberately withholding from it equally important intelligence information.

U.S. intelligence officials confirm that there is truth in this allegation. CIA officials admit that the security regulations in effect at the time prevented them from giving the Pakistani government any intelligence information above the "secret" classification level, such as signals intelligence intercepts and sensitive human intelligence reports, all of which were classified at the "top secret" level.

But what galled the Pakistanis the most was that the CIA and U.S. military repeatedly refused to give the Pakistani military access to the live video feeds from CIA Predator and Reaper unmanned drones, which were flying reconnaissance and missile strike missions over northern Pakistan. In 2004, the Pakistani Air Force secretly made available for CIA Predator drones, real estate on two of its airfields, from which the agency flew armed combat missions attacking al Qaeda and Pakistani Taliban targets in the tribal areas of northern Pakistan. But the Pakistanis imposed very strict limitations on the drone flights. From 2004 to 2010, CIA drone missions over North and South Waziristan in northern Pakistan were permitted without any restrictions, but no flights over the neighboring province of Baluchistan and the Taliban command center of Quetta have ever been approved by the Pakistani government. The first missile strike by a Pakistani-based Predator drone occurred on June 18, 2004, near the town of Wana in South Waziristan, killing the leader of the local Pakistani Taliban, Nek Mohammed. Over the next four years (2004–8), CIA Predator drones conducted forty-six missile strikes on targets in the FATA, with the vast majority of the drone attacks taking place in the last year of the Bush presidency, 2008.

Pakistani military officials thought that since the drones were based at their airbases, and flying combat and reconnaissance missions in which Pakistani militants and civilians were being killed, then the very least that the CIA could do was let them know what intelligence was being derived from these missions that might assist their forces. They were doomed to be disappointed. Senior Pakistani military officials asked for access to Predator imagery at virtually every high-level meeting they had with their American counterparts, only to be politely but firmly rebuffed every time.

In recent interviews, Pakistani intelligence officials made clear that they have been aware for some time that the CIA station in Islamabad spent as much time spying on the activities of the Pakistani government and military as it did trying to find Osama bin Laden and his followers in northern Pakistan. According to Pakistani officials, they know that the CIA station has been operating a network of agents inside the Pakistani government and military since well before 9/11. A senior Pakistani official related how a few years ago a newly arrived U.S. Army intelligence officer, whose cover was as a military attaché at the U.S. embassy in Islamabad, approached a member of his paramilitary security unit and tried to recruit him by offering him a briefcase full of brand-new one-hundred-dollar bills. ISI officials were also certain that the CIA had installed highly sophisticated communications intercept gear inside the U.S. embassy in Islamabad and the American consulates in Peshawar, Lahore, and Karachi to intercept Pakistani government radio and telephone communications traffic.

So at some point after 2004, the ISI decided to treat the CIA station in Pakistan just like any other hostile intelligence presence operating in their country. The CIA's intelligence-gathering efforts inside Pakistan suddenly became much more challenging. CIA counterintelligence officers noticed that all U.S. diplomatic establishments in Pakistan were under twenty-four-hour-a-day video and electronic surveillance, and ISI surveillance teams were keeping close tabs on the movements of all CIA operatives in Pakistan. The home phones and personal cell phones of U.S. diplomats and CIA operatives in Pakistan were being tapped, their mail was opened, and their movements were closely watched. Even their personal cooks, maids, and porters were widely believed to be on the ISI payroll. Pakistani government and security officials who had cooperated with the United States were harassed, some even receiving anonymous death threats. The U.S. embassy in Islamabad complained about the hostile and obstructive behavior of Pakistani intelligence and security officials, but no remedial action was ever taken by the Pakistani government.

One CIA case officer just returned from a tour of duty in Pakistan recalled going with his family for a weekend drive in the hills outside Islamabad to escape the oppressive heat in the city. For the entirety of their day-long excursion they were followed by a black SUV with two ISI operatives inside watching their every move. When they stopped at a roadside stop to take in a scenic vista, the ISI surveillance vehicle parked a short distance behind them. The CIA man looked over, and both of the ISI agents were sitting inside their vehicle scanning the horizon with their binoculars trying to figure out what the Americans were looking at. The CIA officer and his wife laughed themselves silly all the way back to Islamabad.

In addition, ISI counterintelligence officers began systematically detaining the CIA's agents inside Pakistan, especially those individuals who were passing the CIA information from the al Qaeda and Taliban stronghold of the FATA in northern Pakistan. With the liberal application of less than gentle forms of persuasion, these individuals were coaxed, prodded, or cajoled into becoming double agents, feeding the CIA's Islamabad station with whatever material the ISI counterintelligence officers gave them.

It was not until late 2009 that the CIA became suspicious of the material they were getting from these agents and began an internal investigation. CIA counterintelligence officers discovered that at least fifteen of the agency's agents in the FATA were almost certainly under the "positive control" of the ISI, and that the reporting from another dozen or so operatives was sufficiently suspicious that the assets were "put on ice" for fear that they too were being controlled by ISI.

By the end of General Kayani's tenure at the helm of the ISI in the fall of 2007, the relationship between the Pakistani intelligence service and the CIA had deteriorated to the point that senior CIA officials were convinced that the ISI was penetrated by pro-Taliban sympathizers at all levels of command, leading Michael J. Sulick, then the head of the National Clandestine Service, to comment that "they are going to cooperate [with the CIA] to the least extent that they can get away with . . . That doesn't bode well in the search for Bin Laden."

If the CIA's experiences with General Kayani were trying, the agency's problems with his successor, Lt. General Nadeem Taj, who was director-general of ISI from September 2007 to October 2008, were far worse.

By the time General Taj took over the helm of ISI, the joint CIA-ISI intelligence effort against al Qaeda in northern Pakistan was in trouble. Reporting from the CIA station and the U.S. embassy in Islamabad confirmed that al Qaeda had succeeded in regenerating itself in the sanctuaries afforded it in northern Pakistan. Despite the fact that there were fewer than a thousand al Qaeda militants in the FATA, the CIA and the Pakistani military and ISI could not get at them because the terrorists were protected by thousands of Pakistani Taliban fighters who had essentially cleared North and South Waziristan of all Pakistani military forces except for a few isolated garrisons, which the militants kept bottled up.

Beginning in the fall of 2007, several of the joint CIA-ISI intelligence operations in the FATA went horribly wrong. Sensitive intelligence information that the CIA was giving to the ISI on al Qaeda and Taliban activities in the FATA was found to be somehow leaking to the enemy, resulting in a number of CIA clandestine intelligence collection operations being compromised and agents either being killed or disappeared without a trace. Among the casualties were a number of important tribal chiefs and village elders in the FATA, who had been providing the CIA with intelligence on al Qaeda and Pakistani Taliban activities in their regions for some time.

Then in June 2008, the CIA station in Islamabad gave the ISI advance notice that it was going to use its unmanned drones to attack a compound in North Waziristan where a number of high-level Afghan Taliban commanders belonging to a faction known as the Haqqani Network had just been located. What the CIA did not know at the time was that the Haqqani Network and its chief, Jalaluddin Haqqani, had been on the ISI payroll for years. Not only was the ISI secretly bankrolling the Haqqanis, but according to a former CIA official, the Pakistani military was also covertly providing the organization with training, equipment, and logistical support. So not surprisingly, the ISI worked feverishly to delay the drone attack until they could get their clients out of harm's way. According to the CIA officer, the Pakistani Air Force officials at Shamsi Air Base in northwestern Pakistan, where the CIA Predator drones were based, were ordered by Islamabad to delay the takeoff of the drones because of "technical difficulties." While the drones idled in their hangers at Shamsi, the Haqqani officials disappeared from the target locations, with intercepted cell phone calls revealing that they had been warned that they were about to be attacked just before they fled.

A few days later, on June 14, 2008, the CIA thought they had found the hideout of the leader of the Pakistani Taliban, Baitullah Mehsud, and told the Pakistanis they were going to hit the location with a drone strike. According to the CIA official, Mehsud mysteriously disappeared from the house shortly before three Hellfire missiles leveled it.

CIA officials were convinced that the targets of the strikes had been compromised from the inside, with the leaks appearing to come from the very top of the ISI. According to a former senior U.S. intelligence official now associated with a private security contractor, not only were General Taj and some of his deputies leaking sensitive information to the Haqqani Network, as well as elements of the Pakistani Taliban, about ongoing CIA operations in northern Pakistan; sensitive intelligence showed that these same Pakistani intelligence officials also were fully cognizant of the fact that ISI officers in the FATA were providing weapons and logistical support to the Taliban.

The leaks emanating from the top of the ISI forced the U.S. intelligence community to take what some in Washington at the time considered to be extreme measures. A few days after the July 7, 2008, suicide bombing of the Indian embassy in Kabul, which killed forty-one people, CIA director General Michael Hayden gave President Bush a target list of the several dozen al Qaeda and Taliban operatives that the agency had located inside northern Pakistan and wanted to kill. Near the top of the list was the entire senior leadership of the Haqqani Network, which was widely suspected by the CIA of being behind the Indian embassy bombing.

A few mid-level American intelligence officials opposed the new policy, arguing that instead of killing al Qaeda operatives, some effort should be made to try to capture these men if and when the opportunity presented itself. According to two former CIA counterterrorism officials, because no senior or even mid-level al Qaeda official had been captured for several years prior to the initiation of the policy, the CIA's knowledge of al Qaeda's internal organizational structure and management dynamics, as well as the group's plans and intentions, remained very spotty. But their appeals were rejected on purely utilitarian grounds. According to a senior U.S. intelligence official interviewed in 2009, "Capturing al Qaeda officials is a bother. It is so much easier just to kill 'em when you find them."

Without consulting the Pakistani government or military, President Bush approved Hayden's request to use both military commando raids and CIA Predator drone strikes to kill the individuals on the list, which CIA officials refer to privately as either the "Kill List" or the "Murder List." Within hours of President Bush signing the top secret authorization, the CIA operations center at Langley sent a "flash" precedence message giving the go order to the

Predator drones based in Pakistan. In a 2010 interview, Hayden said that "by the time I left office (in January 2009), more than a dozen of those people [on the list] were dead."

But the new round of CIA attacks also produced some particularly horrific collateral damage. For example, shortly before dawn on the morning of September 3, 2008, a twenty-five-man U.S. Special Forces team was landed inside Pakistan by helicopters near the remote border village of Angoor Ada to capture or kill the occupants of what was believed to be an al Qaeda safe house. No one seems to know for sure who the al Qaeda target of the raid was, but whoever it was he seems to have escaped. The local villagers were not so lucky. According to Pakistani officials, at least nineteen civilians were killed in the raid, including women and children.

Five days later, on September 8, 2008, a CIA drone attack on a building in the town of Dande Darpa Khel in northern Pakistan killed twenty-three people, but not its intended targets. The missiles were supposed to kill the leader of the Haqqani Network, Jalaluddin Haqqani, and his son Siraj, who ran the day-to-day operations of the organization. Neither man was at the headquarters complex at the time of the attack. Instead, the missiles killed one of Jalaluddin Haqqani's wives, one of his sisters, his sister-in-law, two nieces, and eight grandchildren.

The one factor that has done the most to poison the U.S. intelligence community's relationship with Pakistan is that for almost a decade the Pakistani military and ISI have not only protected all three major factions of the Afghan Taliban but also secretly provided them with military hardware, training, and financial support. According to an American military intelligence analyst who formerly served on the ISAF intelligence staff in Kabul, "We know that the Pakistanis help the Taliban. We know it. And they know we know it. But we put up with it in the hope that one day the Taliban will bite the hand that feeds it," a reference to the Pakistani government.

Only in the past three years has the U.S. intelligence community somewhat reluctantly come to the conclusion that the Pakistani government's unwillingness to help the United States combat the Taliban was a deliberate act of national policy. It took an extraordinarily long time for the U.S. intelligence community to reach this conclusion.

The first inkling that there was a problem surfaced in 2002, shortly after the Battle of Tora Bora, when, according to senior U.S. intelligence officials, the ISI began to refuse to share any intelligence information about the Afghan

Taliban presence in Pakistan. And when the CIA and the Afghan intelligence service, the NDS, gave the ISI information concerning the whereabouts of senior Taliban officials hiding in Pakistan, the ISI refused to do anything about it. According to a recently retired CIA official, "I held regular meetings in Islamabad with the ISI and gave them the latest intelligence we had on the whereabouts of senior Taliban commanders in his country. And at every meeting they found new ways of politely telling me that their hands were tied . . . No matter what I said, they just would not budge."

Over the next four years (2002 to 2005), the U.S. intelligence community came to believe, based on low-level clandestine agent reporting, that certain "rogue elements" of the ISI were secretly collaborating with the Taliban, but the belief was that this relationship was conducted without the knowledge or consent of President Musharaf. As late as 2005, there were still lingering doubts about the nature and extent of the ISI-Taliban relationship, with a 2005 paper sent to Vice President Dick Cheney reporting that the Taliban "may still enjoy support from the lower echelons of the ISI."

By the end of 2006, all doubts had been cast aside, with a Pentagon report stating unequivocally that "Pakistani Intelligence Service (ISI) elements have an ongoing relationship with the Taliban." The 2006 National Intelligence Estimate on Afghanistan was also quite clear in its judgment. According to a copy of the estimate shown to the author, the report stated that "available evidence strongly suggests that the Pakistani intelligence service maintains an active and ongoing relationship with certain elements of the Taliban."

According to a former DNI official, at some point in 2006 the intelligence community got its first "hard" evidence from what were deemed to be reliable clandestine sources (there were also some incriminating radio intercepts) that the ISI was providing material and financial support to two of the top Afghan Taliban commanders in northern Pakistan: Jalaluddin Haqqani, whose Haqqani Network was based in North Waziristan in the FATA; and Gulbuddin Hekmatyar, whose forces operated from a series of Afghan refugee camps situated around the Pakistani city of Peshawar.

The consensus opinion within the intelligence community at the time was that the principal form of assistance that the Pakistani military and ISI were providing to the Taliban was training, which according to American military intelligence analysts helped to explain the dramatic improvement in the Taliban's fighting skills in 2006. But a restricted-access 2008 Marine Corps intelligence briefing concluded that Pakistani support for the Taliban went far beyond training. According to the briefing papers, the ISI was providing the

Taliban not only with training but also with money and logistical support; while the Pakistani military was providing the Taliban with communications equipment and advanced combat training.

Proof of Pakistani complicity with the Taliban came in July 2008, when the chairman of the Joint Chiefs of Staff, Admiral Mike Mullen, and the deputy director of the CIA, Stephen Kappes, went to Islamabad to try to pressure the Pakistani government to go after the Taliban in their country. The Pakistani reaction was to arrest a single Taliban commander in Quetta named Mullah Rahim, who was picked up because he was leading such a lavish lifestyle that even local newspapermen knew where to find him. But when it came to going after the "big fish" Taliban leaders living out in the open, the Pakistanis followed form and did nothing. And when the Americans complained that the ISI was refusing to go after the top Taliban commanders, the Pakistanis still refused to fire ISI director Nadeem Taj, whom the CIA widely suspected of being "pro-Taliban."

The city of Quetta in northwestern Pakistan, located only fifty miles from the Afghan border, is widely believed to be the headquarters-in-exile and military command center for Mullah Mohammed Omar and his fellow Taliban commanders. Despite ten years of fierce denials from senior Pakistani government officials, it is clear from declassified documents and interviews that the Taliban remain omnipresent in Quetta's sprawling Pashtun slums of Pashtunabad, Satellite Town, Kharotabad, Nawakili, Kachlogh, and Eastern Bypass. The city's Gulshan District, home to tens of thousands of Afghan refugees, remains a hub of Taliban activity, with one major thoroughfare in the neighborhood being dubbed "Taliban Road" by local merchants and taxi drivers. Even lowly reporters have been able to periodically interview senior Taliban officials in Quetta, with the Qasr-e-Gul Hotel downtown being the preferred venue for these assignations.

According to intelligence sources, Quetta serves many other important roles in facilitating the Taliban insurgency inside Afghanistan. It is where senior Taliban field commanders in Afghanistan go once a year for rest and recuperation, as well as to meet with Mullah Omar to plot strategy for the coming year. Money and weapons destined for Taliban fighters in Afghanistan are clandestinely transported to Quetta, then sent across the border via infiltration routes known as "ratlines." In years past, ambulances openly ferried Taliban fighters wounded in Afghanistan from the border crossing at Chaman to a number of hospitals and private clinics in Quetta. The slums in and around Quetta remain an important source of recruits for the Taliban. Taliban officials used to openly recruit volunteers and solicit donations in the local mosques and the eight major religious schools (*madrassas*) in Quetta without any interference from Pakistani police or security officials.

How the Pakistani military and police have over the past decade failed to even accidentally discover the Taliban's substantial presence in Quetta is a mystery, given the fact that some of the Taliban's training and recruitment centers in the city operate literally within steps of Pakistani military facilities and police stations. One building widely reputed by local government officials and journalists to be the Taliban's ex officio headquarters in Quetta is less than a mile from the headquarters compound of the Pakistani Army's XII Corps.

The reason, according to a well-informed Pakistani opposition political leader in Quetta, is that the military, intelligence services, and police have standing orders to look the other way. On those rare occasions when Pakistani security forces do arrest a Taliban official inside Pakistan, the Pakistani military and ISI have historically tried to cover up the event. According to a CIA clandestine service case officer who was stationed in Islamabad from 2007 to 2009, the ISI repeatedly denied him access to several high-ranking Afghan Taliban officials who had been captured by Pakistani security forces. To make matters worse, during his tour the ISI, without explanation, released dozens of Afghan Taliban officials and fighters who had been arrested inside Pakistan.

By late 2008, there was widespread agreement within the U.S. intelligence community that the Pakistani government had secretly given all three major Afghan Taliban factions de facto sanctuary inside northern Pakistan since the U.S. invasion of Afghanistan in the fall of 2001. For example, the Taliban's top spokesman, Dr. Mohammed Hanif, who was arrested in Pakistan on January 15, 2007, told his interrogators that "Mullah Omar is under Pakistani protection." The November 2008 National Intelligence Estimate on Afghanistan, issued by the office of the DNI, concluded that the Pakistanis "permit the Quetta Taliban Shura (the Taliban leadership council) to operate unfettered in Baluchistan province. Inter-Services Intelligence (ISI) provides intelligence and financial support to insurgent groups—especially the Jalaluddin Haqqani network out of Miram Shah, North Waziristan—to conduct attacks in Afghanistan against Afghan government, ISAF, and Indian targets."

The question that gets asked over and over again in Washington is: why has the Pakistani government permitted its military and intelligence service to covertly support the Taliban over the past decade? Opinions vary widely within the intelligence community on this question. According to a 2009 study done for the Marine Corps Intelligence Activity, "The Pakistani military, the Directorate for Inter-Services Intelligence (ISI) in particular, sees the Taliban as a means of pursuing its own strategic interests inside Afghanistan— such as undermining the Karzai government (which can be hostile to Islamabad), putting more conservative Pashtun leaders in power who have connections to Pakistan, and countering India's influence in Afghanistan. Pakistan is also hesitant to move against insurgent groups for fear of a larger backlash."

But there may be another more Machiavellian rationale, which explains why the Pakistanis have secretly thrown their money and support behind the Taliban. According to Dr. Peter Lavoy, a former national intelligence officer for South Asia, "Pakistan believes the Taliban will prevail in the long term."

Pakistan has been a near-perpetual source of angst and frustration for Barack Obama since even before he took office. According to a senior White House official, Pakistan in January 2009 was "a mess and getting worse by the day."

Just after New Year's Day 2009, more than three weeks before Obama was to be inaugurated, intelligence reports and dispatches from the U.S. embassy in Islamabad began arriving in Washington that painted a disturbing picture of what was taking place in northern Pakistan. Without any warning hundreds of Pakistani Taliban fighters had surged out of their mountain strongholds along the Afghan-Pakistani border and captured 80 percent of the picturesque and heavily populated Swat Valley, just ninety miles north of Islamabad, including the district's two largest towns, Mingora and Saidu Sharif. Instead of standing and fighting, the Pakistani Army and police forces in the Swat Valley had abandoned their posts and fled, leaving the residents, according to a cable from the U.S. embassy in Islamabad, "to their fate."

Pakistani government officials claimed that the valley had been lost because they had been forced to withdraw the bulk of their army troops from Swat in order to bolster their forces along the Indian border in the face of "threatening moves" by the Indian Army. American intelligence analysts at DNI headquarters outside Washington were baffled by this claim. Although it was true that the Pakistani military had moved five thousand to seven thousand troops from the FATA to the Indian border in November 2008, no troops had been moved from the Swat Valley. Moreover, all the data they were looking at from their spy satellites and SIGINT sensors showed that the Indian military was doing nothing other than sitting idly in its barracks. The truth came out a few days later when sources inside Pakistan reported that "the decision to pull troops out of Swat was less about needed troops on the border with India as alleged in the press and more about a decision by the GOP [government of Pakistan] to give up on Swat for now."

This information flummoxed U.S. intelligence officials. It defied rational explanation. On the surface, it seemed as if the Pakistani military had deliberately surrendered the Swat Valley to the Taliban without a fight in order to counter a threat from India that did not exist. Both the CIA station and the U.S. embassy in Islamabad concluded that the loss of Swat was a sign of how bad things had become inside Pakistan. Senior U.S. government and intelligence officials concluded that the Pakistani government, wracked by indecision and internal dissension, was falling apart at the seams; and the Pakistani military was paralyzed, refusing to accept that the Taliban were anything more than a nuisance in their backyard, with a leaked February 2009 State Department cable concluding, "The militant takeover of Swat in the Northwest Frontier Province (NWFP) is the most striking example of how far and how fast the government is losing control over its territory."

If American intelligence officers who have served in Pakistan over the past three years are to be believed, their work sometimes bordered on the darker scenes from Francis Ford Coppola's epic film *Apocalypse Now*. "Imagine the worst place you have ever been in your life," a recently retired senior CIA official said over a beer in suburban Virginia, "then multiply it by ten and you got Pakistan."

At the top of the chain of command, the intelligence situation on the ground inside Pakistan at times approached the surreal. The CIA station chief in Islamabad, John D. Bennett, whose cover position was counselor for regional affairs at the U.S. embassy, wrote a lengthy cable to Washington for the new Obama administration describing what he termed the "complicated" state of the U.S.-Pakistani intelligence relationship. The gravamen of the cable was that the state of intelligence cooperation with the Pakistani government, while important in the overall context of the war on terrorism, had not been everything that could have been hoped for. While the CIA's drones continued to relentlessly pound al Qaeda and Taliban strongholds in the FATA, the Islamabad station's principal concern was that the overall collaborative effort between the CIA and the ISI had been rapidly deteriorating since the summer of 2008 with no discernible sign of improvement.

Bennett broke the Pakistani intelligence problem into three equally important and complex parts: (1) how his station was supposed to continue to work with the Pakistani intelligence service, the ISI, knowing full well about its continuing clandestine protection and support of Mullah Omar and the Afghan Taliban; (2) what, if anything, did Washington want him to do regarding the growing menace posed by the Pakistani Taliban; and (3) what new steps, if any, were he and his station to take to combat the residual al Qaeda presence in northern Pakistan other than continuing the practice begun during the Bush administration of hitting the terrorists with missile strikes from the agency's fleet of unmanned drones based in Pakistan.

On the surface, the agency's long-standing problems with the ISI seemed to be improving somewhat. Three months earlier, in October 2008, Pakistani Army Chief of Staff Kayani had finally acceded to Washington's wishes and fired the much-detested director of the ISI, General Nadeem Taj. His replacement, Lt. General Ahmad Shuja Pasha, was handpicked for the post by Kayani in order to, according to a leaked State Department cable, "get control of the ISI."

Although General Pasha was not tainted by the problems of his predecessor, according to interviews with Pakistani intelligence officials, the CIA's Bennett, at their first face-to-face meeting, told the general that the credibility of the organization that he now commanded was low in the eyes of the agency. The tension between the CIA and ISI had grown so bad that it was affecting the conduct of clandestine intelligence gathering and covert action operations against al Qaeda in northern Pakistan. Information exchanges between the two spy agencies on al Qaeda and the Taliban had declined significantly as Washington withheld blocks of information that it had formerly given to the Pakistanis. In one extreme example, the CIA station in Islamabad complained to Washington that the ISI was essentially holding prisoner the CIA case officers who were manning a small number of forward operating bases spread across northern Pakistan rather than letting them perform their duties.

In January 2009, General Pasha flew to Washington for a "Come to Jesus" meeting with outgoing CIA director Michael V. Hayden that was, at times, quite heated. In effect, Pasha was told that his organization was on probation until Langley was convinced that ISI was no longer protecting the Taliban and other terrorist groups. General Pasha tried to convince the incoming Obama administration that it had nothing to fear from putting its trust in the ISI, telling vice-president-elect Joe Biden in January 2009, according to a leaked State Department cable, that "the United States and Pakistan needed to have confidence in each other. Pasha said he was hurt about the inference that he did not have a relationship of trust with CIA."

On January 20, 2009, the "Pakistani mess," as Ambassador Richard Holbrooke described it, became President Barack Obama's problem. The situation that Obama inherited was neatly summarized in a February 4, 2009, cable from U.S. Ambassador to Pakistan Anne W. Patterson: "The [Pakistani] government is losing more and more territory every day to foreign and domestic militant groups; deteriorating law and order in turn is undermining economic recovery. The bureaucracy is settling into third-world mediocrity, as demonstrated by some corruption and a limited capacity to implement or articulate policy."

But to some in the new administration, amid all the gloom, there was reason for hope. The loss of the Swat Valley in January 2009 gave the U.S. government a new degree of leverage to try to force the Pakistani government and the ISI to abandon their support of Mullah Omar and the Afghan Taliban. The Pakistanis desperately needed more American military equipment and money in the aftermath of the Swat defeat. The question was: what price should the White House exact in return for this aid?

In February 2009, General Kayani flew to Washington hat in hand to beg the White House for billions of dollars of additional military aid as well as access to intelligence available to the U.S. intelligence community on the Pakistani Taliban, including live imagery from CIA Predator drones and realtime SIGINT from NSA. The Obama administration decided to give Kayani what he wanted, as well as "forgive and forget" the Pakistani government and ISI's past support for the Taliban.

But there was a steep price tag that came with Washington's forgiveness of Islamabad's past sins. U.S. government officials told Kayani that the Pakistani government had to stop supporting the Afghan Taliban and other terrorist groups based in Pakistan. The Obama administration was not above using less than subtle blackmail to get what it wanted. According to a leaked cable, Washington thought that Kayani would give Washington what it wanted because the general, who had been the director-general of ISI from 2004 to 2007 at the height of the Pakistani government's support for the Taliban, "does not want a reckoning with the past."

Kayani apparently agreed to the conditions stipulated by the White House, but try as it might, the Obama administration just could not change the general's mind about how serious the threat posed by the Pakistani Taliban was, despite the fact that the extremist militiamen now controlled the strategically important Swat Valley. President Asif Ali Zardari and Prime Minister Yousuf Gilani agreed wholeheartedly with the U.S. government that the Taliban were now the chief threat to Pakistan's security, but General Kayani and the rest of the Pakistani high command refused to budge from their age-old mind-set that it was India that remained the main threat to their country's survival. According to a cable from the American embassy in Islamabad, "President Zardari and PM Gilani recognize Pakistan's greatest threat has shifted from India to militancy concentrated on the Pak-Afghan border but is spreading to NWFP [the North-West Frontier Province, whose capital is the city of Peshawar] and beyond. The Army and ISI, however, have not turned that corner."

So instead of pulling troops from the Indian border and fighting, the Pakistani government decided to make a deal with the Taliban in the hope that by giving the militant tribesmen what they wanted, the problem would go away. On February 15, 2009, Taliban representatives signed a cease-fire agreement with the Pakistani government, which, in effect, ceded control of Swat to the Taliban. The Taliban also got a $6 million bribe, as well as permission to immediately implement a harsh form of Muslim religious law called Sharia in the Swat Valley. The "peace treaty" was both cynical and dreadfully short-sighted, and nobody in the U.S. government or intelligence community expected that the Pakistani Taliban would honor it once they realized that they had the Pakistani government and military on the ropes.

When the Taliban did realize just how truly desperate the plight of the Pakistani government and military was, they wasted little time. On February 23, 2009, the top three Pakistani Taliban commanders in the FATA— Baitullah Mehsud, Hafiz Gul Bahadur, and Maulvi Nazir—announced that they had formed an alliance called the Council of the United Mujahideen and merged their respective militias into a single fighting force. The announcement sent shock waves through the Pakistani military and intelligence establishment. One of the three Taliban chiefs, Commander Nazir, was, according to a leaked State Department cable, "the Pakistani government's man," having been on the ISI payroll since 2007. Nazir's defection to the Taliban was not only a huge blow, but more important it showed, according to the cable, that the Pakistani government's "divide and conquer strategy is not working."

Insofar as the al Qaeda presence in northern Pakistan was concerned, there really was not much more that the CIA could do beyond what was already being done. As noted above, the CIA's unmanned drones had taken a dreadful toll on al Qaeda's leadership in 2008, but the drones had not brought the war against al Qaeda any closer to being won. Osama bin Laden and Ayman al-Zawahiri were still alive, and they were still able to direct the operations of the global al Qaeda terrorist franchise from their hiding places in northern Pakistan. According to Dr. Peter Lavoy at DNI headquarters, al Qaeda had been "damaged, [but] not broken."

The decision that President Obama and his newly installed national security team had to make was this: Absent the Pakistani government surrendering its sovereignty and allowing the United States to use American combat troops inside Pakistan, which everyone on Obama's national security team knew would never happen, the CIA's Predator and larger Reaper drones were the only option left through which they could strike al Qaeda inside its sanctuaries in northern Pakistan. The only decision left was whether to continue the drone strikes at the same level as the Bush administration, which was three missile strikes a month, or up the ante and accelerate the number of drone attacks in order to intensify the pressure on al Qaeda.

One of the lead items on the agenda for President Obama's first National Security Council meeting, on Friday morning, January 23, 2009, was to consider whether to approve an urgent proposal submitted by Michael J. Sulick, the head of the CIA's National Clandestine Service (the nomination of the new CIA director, Leon E. Panetta, was not confirmed by the Senate until February 12, 2009), to commence an even more aggressive program of drone missile strikes against al Qaeda hideouts in northern Pakistan.

The entire senior leadership of the U.S. intelligence community, almost to a person, supported the program because the drone strikes seemed to be working. In December 2008, the CIA had concluded that the unmanned drone strikes on al Qaeda targets in northern Pakistan were having the desired effect. According to reports coming in from the U.S. embassy and CIA station in Islamabad, al Qaeda's leadership in Pakistan had been decimated by the drone attacks, reduced to just a few hundred operatives who spent most of their time moving from one hiding place to another in the FATA in order to avoid detection by the CIA's unmanned drones hovering overhead. According to a cable from Ambassador Patterson, "The U.S. has been remarkably successful in disrupting al-Qaida operations in Pakistan's tribal areas. In the past year, 10 of the top 20 al-Qaida operatives, including those responsible for the East Africa embassy bombings in 1998 and tied to Islambad's Marriott bombing [on September 20, 2008, which killed 60 people and wounded 260 more], have been eliminated."

The CIA's new plan was palatable because it was relatively clean and not likely to produce any diplomatic blowback; it enjoyed support at the highest level of the Pakistani government; and it was one of the very few intelligence programs that was wildly popular with the House and Senate intelligence committees, so getting it approved and funded by Congress was not going to be a problem. Without any dissent, the NSC approved the CIA proposal to intensify the number of drone attacks against al Qaeda targets in northern Pakistan.

According to Pakistani military officials, after January 2009 the CIA drones became near-permanent presences in the air over northern Pakistan. During the daytime, two and sometimes three CIA drones armed with Hellfire missiles were continuously in orbit over the FATA looking for targets to hit. A Pakistani Army staff officer who served a tour of duty with the 7th Division at Miram Shah in North Waziristan in 2009 and 2010 told the author in a recent interview that the distinctive and annoying buzzing noise that the drones make could be heard almost continuously during daylight hours from his garrison, if the weather was good. "I hoped God would have pity on those [on the ground] below," he said, "but these infernal machines have no mercy."

In April 2009, to no one's surprise, Baitullah Mehsud, the leader of the Pakistani Taliban, broke the Swat cease-fire agreement that his representatives had signed just two months earlier and resumed hostilities. In a matter of forty-eight hours the Taliban overwhelmed the few remaining Pakistani Army and paramilitary posts in the district and quickly advanced eastward against virtually no resistance into the neighboring Buner District, reaching a point only sixty miles from Islamabad. At the same time, the CIA station in Islamabad and an allied foreign intelligence service reported that Pakistani Taliban militants had been detected moving into the city of Karachi and other cities in the populous Punjabi heartland of Pakistan, where they quickly linked up with other militant groups opposed to the Pakistani government. The office of the director of national intelligence sent to the White House a classified spot report that essentially concluded that the security situation in Pakistan was deteriorating rapidly and that the Pakistani government and military had now lost control of large parts of the northern part of the country.

As the Taliban swept south toward Islamabad, Obama administration officials openly voiced their frustration at the inability or unwillingness of the Pakistani government and military to aggressively confront the Pakistani Taliban militants. The weak and indecisive Zardari government seemed to be mired in political bickering, and the Pakistani Army would not budge from its fixation on India. Testifying before Congress on April 1, 2009, the commander of U.S. Central Command, General David H. Petraeus, issued a less-than-subtle warning to the Pakistani government that the Pakistani Taliban extremists, if not checked, "could literally take down their state."

As the Taliban juggernaut rolled southward, concern spread in Washington about the safety of Pakistan's arsenal of seventy to ninety nuclear weapons. In the minds of some U.S. intelligence officials, a nightmare scenario was beginning to take shape in which Pakistan's nuclear arsenal could fall into the hands of the Taliban unless the military situation in the north of the country was somehow reversed.

One senior American official recalled that in late April 2009, the CIA station in Islamabad reported to Washington that there were no discernible signs that the Pakistani military was taking any steps to beef up security at its nuclear weapons and ballistic missile storage facilities. One of the station's agents inside the Pakistani military reported that there had been no appreciable change in the security measures at the Pakistani Air Force's major nuclear weapons storage sites at Masroor Air Base on the outskirts of the city of Karachi, or at Mushaf Air Base outside the city of Sargodha, 170 kilometers northwest of the city of Lahore. Likewise, there were no signs that the Pakistani Army had increased the alert status of its force of nuclear-armed M-11 ballistic missiles, which were stored in reinforced bunkers at the huge Kirana Hills weapons depot south of Sargodha.

These intelligence reports from Pakistan raised alarm bells in Washington. In early May 2009, CIA director Leon Panetta ordered the CIA station chief in Islamabad to step up surveillance of all Pakistani nuclear weapons storage depots, as well as pump his sources inside the Pakistani military for any information about what they were doing to ensure that Pakistan's nuclear arsenal did not fall into the hands of the Pakistani Taliban or other Muslim extremist groups inside Pakistan. At the same time, U.S. Air Force and Navy planners began contingency planning for air and cruise missile strikes against the Pakistani nuclear weapons storage depots in case these sites were taken over by Muslim extremist groups.

Just as the Taliban juggernaut appeared to be on the verge of rolling unopposed into Islamabad, it suddenly stopped in late May. Realizing how dire the situation was, Pakistani Army Chief of Staff Kayani had ordered an entire army corps sent posthaste from its garrisons along the Indian border to Swat. An attack by 22,000 Pakistani Army troops backed by hundreds of tanks sent the lightly armed Taliban fighters reeling back toward their mountain redoubts. By the end of June the Swat Valley had been retaken largely without a fight, with the Taliban's top commander, Maulana Fazlullah, opting to return to the mountains in order to fight again another day.

The fighting in the FATA during the summer and fall of 2009 between the Pakistani military and the Taliban was remarkable from an intelligence perspective, for a number of reasons. In June 2009, the Pakistani military for the first time allowed U.S. Air Force drones based in Afghanistan to cross the border and fly photo reconnaissance missions over the Pakistani Taliban strongholds in the FATA and the North-West Frontier Province; and the CIA was authorized for the first time to use Predator and Reaper unmanned drones to attack Pakistani Taliban targets not just in the FATA but also in the area to the east around the city of Peshawar.

With the secret and entirely deniable blessing of the Pakistani government and military, the CIA immediately ratcheted up the number of drone attacks in the FATA, conducting fifty-three missile strikes in the FATA in 2009 as compared with only thirty-six the previous year. CIA officials were jubilant when one of their drones on August 5, 2009, killed the leader of the Pakistani Taliban, Baitullah Mehsud, in his house in the village of Zanghara in South Waziristan. But the CIA's jubilation was short-lived.

Not everyone in the U.S. government was as satisfied with the results of the drone strikes as the CIA. Secretary of State Hillary Rodham Clinton told President Obama that the CIA's unmanned drone strikes were *not* the war-winners that many CIA officials said they were. According to Clinton, no matter how many al Qaeda and Pakistani Taliban commanders and fighters the drones killed, the militants would, as they have done for the past decade, just replace the losses within days. In State's view, the only way that al Qaeda would ever be defeated was if the Pakistani military could somehow be coerced or induced into going into the FATA and cleansing the place with, as one of the secretary of state's advisers put it, "fire and sword."

CIA officials thought that the State Department was being overly cautious, with one agency official saying that "State was just doing what they always do—covering their ass." According to the CIA officials, intercepted cell phone calls confirmed that the drone strikes were taking a terrible toll on al Qaeda and the Pakistani Taliban.

There was a serious downside to the missile strikes, however. For their part, Pakistani military officials believed that the drone attacks had proved to be an invaluable recruiting tool for the Pakistani Taliban, with a surreptitiously taken videotape made by Pakistani military intelligence showing hundreds of enraged Waziri tribesmen volunteering to join the Taliban after several particularly bloody CIA drone attacks in North Waziristan in December 2009. According to Wing Commander Irfan Ahmad, a U.S.-educated Pakistani Air Force officer who has been intimately involved in the fight against the Taliban in northern Pakistan since 2004, "It appears that the drone attacks have increased [the] militants' motivation for terrorist activity."

On December 30, 2009, a Jordanian doctor named Humam Khalil Abu-Mulal al-Balawi, who had been recruited by the Jordanian intelligence service while in prison to spy on al Qaeda in Pakistan, detonated a vest containing high explosives inside the heavily guarded CIA compound at Forward Operating Base Chapman outside the city of Khost in southeastern Afghanistan, killing seven CIA officers or contractors and a Jordanian intelligence officer who was Balawi's case officer. The most prominent casualty was the CIA base chief, Jennifer Lynne Matthews, a forty-five-year-old divorced mother of three from Fredericksburg, Maryland, who had served twenty years in the CIA, most of them as an analyst in the CIA's Counterterrorism Center at Langley, Virginia. The Pakistani Taliban immediately took credit for the attack, stating that the Khost attack was in retaliation for the CIA's killing of Baitullah Mehsud in August.

The CIA's retaliation for the Khost suicide bombing proved to be embarrassing. On January 14, 2010, spokesmen for the U.S. and Pakistani governments gleefully announced that a missile fired from a CIA drone had destroyed a compound at Pasalkot in North Waziristan, killing Hakimullah Mehsud, who had succeeded Baitullah Mehsud as head of the Pakistani Taliban. The Taliban's spokesman vehemently denied that Mehsud had been killed, but officials in Washington and Islamabad dismissed his claim as nothing but empty rhetoric. It turns out it wasn't. Four months later, on May 3, the Taliban proved everyone wrong when they released to selected reporters in Islamabad a videotape showing that Hakimullah Mehsud was indeed very much alive and well.

By December 2009, the U.S. intelligence community believed that Pakistan had been saved, but only just barely. Over 11,500 civilians, soldiers, policemen, and terrorists had been killed in 2009, bringing the death toll to more than 25,000 dead since figures started being compiled by the Pakistani government in 2003.

In Washington, the victory over the Taliban was more bitter than sweet. As soon as the Pakistani Taliban militants had been beaten back from the gates of Islamabad, the Pakistani military immediately reneged on its promise to

Washington to break its ties with Mullah Omar's Taliban forces and the other terrorist groups in Pakistan.

According to interviews with U.S. intelligence officials, this was because the Pakistani military and ISI had concluded that the U.S.-led coalition in Afghanistan was going to pull out of the country before the Taliban could be defeated, leaving in Kabul a government hostile to Pakistan and backed by its arch-enemy, India. According to a cable from the U.S. embassy in Islamabad, "Fear that the ISAF mission in Afghanistan will end without the establishment of a non-Taliban, [Pashtun]-led government friendly to Pakistan adds to the Pakistani establishment's determination not to cut its ties irrevocably to the Afghan Taliban."

An angry Secretary of State Hillary Rodham Clinton sent a harshly worded cable to all American embassies in the Persian Gulf in December 2009 that essentially charged Pakistan with continuing to aid and abet terrorist groups within its borders. According to the cable, "Although Pakistani senior officials have publicly disavowed support for these [terrorist] groups, some officials from the Pakistan's Inter-Services Intelligence Directorate (ISI) continue to maintain ties with a wide array of extremist organizations."

Even more difficult to swallow were the end-of-year intelligence assessments, which showed that the Pakistani Taliban had not been defeated in 2009. The Pakistani military had mounted nearly a half-dozen halfhearted offensives against the al Qaeda and Pakistani Taliban fighters in the FATA during the summer and fall of 2009, which while achieving some modest gains failed in their goal to clear the region of militants. When the operations were over, the Pakistani forces returned to their garrisons for the winter and surrendered all of the gains they had made back to the Taliban. But what really angered American diplomats and intelligence officials was that the Pakistani army had refused to go after any of the Taliban factions based in the FATA who were on its payroll, such as the ISI's longtime Taliban client, the Haqqani Network.

In the opinion of the U.S. intelligence community's experts on Pakistan, such as the national intelligence officer for South Asia, Neil H. Joeck, the biggest loser of 2009 was the government of Pakistani president Asif Ali Zardari, whose authority in December 2009 was in free fall in the face of mounting internal opposition to his pro-Washington policies from the Pakistani political elite and the military.

Clandestine intelligence reporting in 2009 and early 2010 revealed that President Zardari had on a number of occasions pressed army chief of staff

General Kayani to intensify his military's efforts against the Taliban in northern Pakistan, only to be rebuffed each time because Kayani still refused to budge from his firmly held belief, which was shared by the entire Pakistani general staff and the ISI, that India remained the principal external threat to Pakistan's national security, not the Taliban.

In a confrontational November 20, 2009, meeting in Islamabad, CIA director Leon Panetta told ISI director General Ahmad Shuja Pasha that his agency had to do more to combat the presence of Taliban and al Qaeda militants in the FATA, and live up to its promise to cease its covert support of all three of the Afghan Taliban factions that continued to operate from their sanctuaries in northern Pakistan. Panetta also told General Pasha that his agency's overt harassment of CIA operatives based in Pakistan had to stop; otherwise, the CIA chief said, "there would be repercussions."

But the Pakistani military and the ISI felt that they were being deliberately manipulated by Washington. Shortly before Christmas 2009, a senior Pakistani military official told a CIA officer in Islamabad that he thought that Washington was deliberately "hyping" the threat from al Qaeda and the Pakistani Taliban in order to get what it wanted from Islamabad. Despite the terrible events of the past year, the general still honestly believed that India was the top threat to Pakistan's national security, not the Pakistani Taliban or al Qaeda. "I could not believe what I was hearing," the CIA official said. "How could this guy be so blind after everything that had just happened?"

As we shall see in chapter 7, this exchange proved to be an ominous portent of things to come.

CHAPTER 5

We Have to Kill Them All

Scenes from the Global War on Terrorism

Too long a sacrifice
Can make a stone of the heart.
—WILLIAM BUTLER YEATS, "EASTER, 1916"

British prime minister Winston Churchill is reputed to have said more than sixty years ago, "We sleep soundly in our beds because rough men stand ready in the night to visit violence on those who would do us harm." Churchill was, of course, referring to the unconventional and often brutal tactics that the badly outnumbered British forces felt compelled to use against the Germans during the darkest days of World War II.

The metaphor may be more than sixty years old, but it remains apt today when describing the decade-long secret war that the U.S. intelligence community and its allies around the world have waged against not only al Qaeda in Pakistan but the dozens of other foreign terrorist groups of every size, shape, and color around the world.

In the days after the 9/11 attacks, the Bush administration made a resolution, which was codified in a top secret directive—National Security Presidential Directive 9, "Combating Terrorism"—that as a matter of the greatest urgency it was necessary to destroy al Qaeda and all of its allies by any means necessary because of the clear and present danger they posed to U.S. national security and, according to a declassified Joint Chiefs of Staff document, "our way of life as a free and open society."

This document was written in stark terms that reduced a very complex global problem down to a simple "us versus them" paradigm in which the overarching doctrine was "we must kill them before they kill us." It was remarkably similar in tenor and tone to a classified directive written almost thirty years earlier in the aftermath of the September 1972 massacre of eleven Israeli athletes and a German policeman at the Munich Olympic Games, wherein the Israeli cabinet ordered the Mossad to wipe out the Palestinian Black September terrorist group because of the danger that it posed to the Israeli state.

Over the past decade, the U.S. intelligence community has waged a secret battle beyond America's borders against a host of foreign terrorist organizations, conducted almost entirely out of view of the American public. The fight has been both remorseless and pitiless, with no quarter asked for or given on either side.

Since entering office in 2009, the Obama administration has continued the policy initiated during the Bush administration of killing al Qaeda leaders and fighters whenever and wherever they are found. The widely held sentiment inside the U.S. intelligence community remains that the only sure way to ensure that there will be no more 9/11s is, as one current senior administration official starkly put it in a 2009 interview, "We have to kill them all, every last one of them."

The U.S. intelligence community's fight against al Qaeda and the hundreds of other foreign terrorist groups around the world is run from the National Counterterrorism Center, which is located in Building LX-1 next to the director of national intelligence's office at Liberty Crossing in northern Virginia.

The chief of the NCTC from June 2008 until his retirement in July 2011, Michael E. Leiter, had an unusual pedigree for the nation's top terrorist hunter. He spent six years flying navy electronic warfare aircraft off the decks of aircraft carriers before graduating from Harvard Law School in 2000 magna cum laude, where he was also the editor of the *Harvard Law Review*. After clerking for Supreme Court Justice Stephen G. Breyer, Leiter spent the next three years (2002–5) as a federal prosecutor in Alexandria, Virginia, before getting his first exposure to the intelligence world when he was chosen to be deputy general counsel of the Robb-Silberman Commission, which examined why the U.S. intelligence community failed so miserably in the run-up to the invasion of Iraq in 2003. That led to a one-year stint as deputy chief of staff for the first director of national intelligence, Ambassador John D. Negroponte, before moving over to take command of NCTC in 2007. When the Obama administration came into office in 2009, Leiter was asked to stay on at his post because of the respect that he had garnered within the intelligence community.

Leiter may have had the respect of his peers in the intelligence community, but the organization he commanded was viewed by many as troubled. The

NCTC was yet another example of the poor compromises that often come out of the U.S. intelligence community's convoluted decision-making process. Its predecessor, the Terrorist Threat Integration Center (TTIC), had been created on May 11, 2003, to be the U.S. intelligence community's one-stop-shopping source for all intelligence information, both raw and evaluated, about domestic and foreign terrorist groups and their activities. The only way such a clearinghouse was going to work cohesively was if it brought together under one single roof the more than one dozen counterterrorism units that then existed within the U.S. intelligence community. But when it came time to consolidate, all sixteen American agencies refused to give up the counterterrorism units that they had lavished so much time and money on since 9/11.

When TTIC was renamed the National Counterterrorism Center in 2005 and placed under the command of the newly created director of national intelligence, it had very few assets to call its own and was almost completely dependent on the charity of the rest of the intelligence community for whatever personnel and resources it got. So today, six years after its creation, NCTC is still trying to evolve and develop its own institutional identity as well as its independence from the rest of the intelligence community.

At the present time, the NCTC staff is rather small by American intelligence community standards, consisting of five hundred full-time military and civilian personnel, only about two hundred of whom are actually NCTC employees. The rest are seconded to NCTC for one- or two-year rotations from sixteen U.S. government agencies, including the CIA, NSA, DIA, and FBI, who continue to operate their own larger and better-funded counterterrorism units.

Because NCTC has no sources of its own, it is completely dependent for its supply of raw data on the U.S. intelligence, military, law enforcement, and homeland security communities. The amount of information pouring into NCTC's operations center every day is mind-boggling—8,000 to 10,000 intelligence reports, each of which has to be read by NCTC's analysts; plus the names of 10,000 individuals, every one of whom has to be cross-checked through NCTC's database of known or suspected terrorists (Terrorist Identities Datamart Environment, or TIDE) to determine if the person has any ties to al Qaeda or other terrorist groups. According to data supplied by the NCTC, as of January 2009 the TIDE database contained the names of more than 564,000 individuals, of whom 5 percent were American citizens. The implications of this figure are staggering. According to NCTC there were in 2009 more than 28,000 American citizens known or suspected to be terrorists, or to have had some association with terrorists!

The problem is that TIDE, according to two intelligence analysts who have served recent tours of duty at NCTC, is far from a perfect system. When TIDE was created in 2004, it was not supposed to be the "Mother of all Counterterrorism Databases" that it is today. The system kept growing and growing as thousands of names were added to it every day. NCTC analysts who have used TIDE say that it is sometimes cranky and unresponsive, and not the easiest system to use. Fixing this relatively simple problem has become increasingly more difficult because the size of the database continues to expand without corresponding software upgrades to handle the greater data load and the ever-increasing number of analysts using the system.

Rather than design a new and more comprehensive database comparable to Google, NCTC's software contractors kept adding on more features and memory on top of the old system, which rather than improve the situation just made the system worse. The system has become so complicated and cumbersome that it isn't unusual for it to come back with a "no records found" response to requests for information on even the most banal subject.

One former NCTC analyst recounted how she typed into the TIDE search engine the name of a well-known African terrorist leader, only to be told that there were no reports in the database matching her description. To put it mildly, the analyst was more than a little angry since she was the lead analyst on this particular terrorist group, and she had personally entered into the system three reports on the subject the week before, which the system for some reason failed to pick up.

Dozens of complaints have been filed in recent years by NCTC analysts about the problems they have experienced trying to use TIDE. A larger and more capable database that was supposed to replace TIDE has been on the drawing board for years, but for unknown reasons the new system has never moved past the design stage. According to a former NCTC terrorism analyst, "We told [NCTC] management that unless a new system was brought online in the near future one of two things was going to happen: TIDE was going to crash or the system would lose a critical piece of information needed to prevent another 9/11." NCTC's management chose not to act on the complaints, however, with the analyst recalling that "we were still waiting for a reply to our complaint when I left a year later."

Senior officials at the NCTC can rightfully point to some major successes in the war on terror since 9/11. The killing of Osama bin Laden on May 1, 2011, tops everyone's list of major accomplishments, but the NCTC's analysts are still waiting to see if his death will lead to the collapse of what is left of al Qaeda in Pakistan. In the meantime, there have been other successes against al Qaeda. Not only has there been a marked decrease in the number of terrorist attacks around the world, but al Qaeda has been unable to mount a successful terrorist attack inside the U.S. for the past decade. Whether this is because of the efforts of the intelligence community or the weakened state of al Qaeda is a matter of fierce debate within the intelligence community today.

There have been occasional attempts, but these plots have all failed miserably, largely because of a combination of technical problems and the ineptitude of the individuals chosen to mount the attacks. Take for example the case of the mentally unstable British-born al Qaeda operative named Richard Reid, who on December 22, 2001, attempted to detonate high explosives packed into his shoes over the Atlantic while on a United Airlines flight from Paris to Miami. The bomb failed to detonate, and Reid was overpowered by the plane's passengers and crew. He is now serving a life sentence in federal prison.

Over the past decade the U.S. intelligence community and its foreign partners have largely succeeded in either destroying or neutralizing the majority of al Qaeda's terrorist networks outside of the organization's stronghold in northern Pakistan. The European intelligence and security services, with some assistance from the U.S. intelligence community, have largely succeeded in stripping bare most of al Qaeda's operational and logistical support networks in Western Europe. European counterterrorism officials believe that today there are only a handful of al Qaeda operatives remaining in Western Europe. Even so, while their numbers are greatly diminished, the remaining al Qaeda operatives in Europe remain potentially lethal.

The Middle East may be the secret success story of the U.S. counterterrorism effort since the Obama administration entered office in 2009. Iran and Syria, the two Middle Eastern countries who are the leading state sponsors of terrorism, have been largely quiescent over the past three years in terms of actively supporting terrorist attacks in the Middle East and elsewhere around the world. Both countries continue to provide sanctuary and financial support to a number of Middle East terrorist groups, but these groups have largely written terrorism out of their playbooks in their efforts to become legitimate political forces in their home countries.

For example, there have been almost no major terrorist attacks on Israel since the Obama administration entered office because the Palestinian terrorist group Hamas is now fully occupied trying to govern the Gaza Strip. There have also been no significant terrorist attacks inside Lebanon over the past three years because the Iranian- and Syrian-backed militant group Hezbollah has largely abandoned terrorism in favor of becoming a legitimate political party in Lebanon. Today, Hezbollah is the single most powerful political force in Lebanese politics, holding eleven of the thirty cabinet posts in the Lebanese government until withdrawing from the Lebanese government in early 2011. It still holds a substantial bloc of delegates in the Lebanese parliament. And thanks to substantial financial subsidies from Iran (estimated at $300 million per annum), it largely governs those parts of southern Lebanon where the country's Shiite population resides independent of the Lebanese government. Behind the scenes, intelligence sources confirm that over the past several years the CIA has succeeded in recruiting a number of agents inside both Hamas and Hezbollah, giving the U.S. intelligence community for the first time relatively reliable information concerning the capabilities and intentions of both these highly secretive organizations.

Iraq is also viewed as a major counterterrorism success within the U.S. intelligence community. Since the Obama administration took power, officials have remained cautiously optimistic about the future of the country. Despite suffering devastating losses during General David Petraeus's "Baghdad Surge" offensive in the summer and fall of 2007, al Qaeda in Iraq (AQI) continues to soldier on, periodically mounting bloody car and suicide bombings in Baghdad and Mosul, which have killed hundreds of Iraqi civilians. But the terrorist networks in Iraq continue to suffer crippling losses, including many of their top leaders over the past three years. The departure of the last U.S. Army combat brigade from Iraq on August 19, 2010, and the shift of former Iraqi Shiite militants like Moqtada al-Sadr, leader of the so-called Mahdi Army militia, toward becoming legitimate political leaders in Iraqi politics have contributed to a further lessening of tensions in the country.

In Indonesia, the CIA and the Australian foreign intelligence service, ASIS, have provided the Indonesian security services and national police with intelligence and technical support that has resulted in the decimation of the al Qaeda affiliate in that country, Jemaah Islamiyah (JI). JI is best known for being behind a series of bloody terrorist attacks in Indonesia, the most notorious of which was the bombing of a nightclub area on the island of Bali that killed 202 people, most of them Australian tourists. According to Indonesian diplomatic officials, since 2002 their country's security services have captured or killed more than six hundred JI operatives and sympathizers, but they admit that JI is still very much alive and kicking in the Muslim slums of Djakarta and other Indonesian cities.

In the Philippines over the past decade, a small force of U.S. Army Green Berets from the 1st Special Forces Group and their supporting intelligence operators, using classic counterinsurgency tactics, have secretly helped the Philippine military capture or kill many of the leaders of Abu Sayyaf, a Muslim terrorist group linked to al Qaeda, who had been terrorizing the populace of the island of Mindanao and the nearby Sulu archipelago since the early 1990s.

But Abu Sayyaf is still very much a going concern. A resilient group of about four hundred fighters is still operating on Basilan and Jolo islands off the coast of Mindanao, occasionally emerging from the jungle to ambush a Philippine army unit or police station. On September 29, 2009, Abu Sayyaf guerrillas killed two American Green Berets and a Philippine marine on the island of Jolo. A great amount of frustration has been voiced by intelligence analysts over the fact that just when American Special Forces advisers thought they had Abu Sayyaf cornered and ready for the kill, senior Philippine military commanders could not be coaxed or cajoled into finishing the job. Instead, as one American Green Beret officer put it, "They [the Philippine military] took a siesta and gave them time to rebuild."

In February 2011, three months before U.S. Navy SEAL commandos killed Osama bin Laden in his hideout in northern Pakistan, senior U.S. intelligence officials told the House and Senate intelligence oversight committees that the U.S. intelligence community still held al Qaeda to be the number one threat to U.S. national security. In fact, well before bin Laden's death in his compound in Abbottabad, al Qaeda had become, in relative terms, a bit player in global terrorism. Al Qaeda's decline has been years in the making. In 2008, former CIA intelligence officer Marc Sageman, now a terrorism analyst with the RAND Corporation, correctly predicted in his book *Leaderless Jihad* that al Qaeda was rapidly declining as a terrorist threat.

The facts back up this contention. According to the latest annual report from the National Counterterrorism Center, al Qaeda accounted for less than 1 percent of the eleven thousand documented terrorist attacks in 2009, indicating the global terrorist threat has evolved dramatically over the past decade to the point where a host of new groups now pose a major threat to U.S. national security and perhaps a greater challenge to the U.S. intelligence community than that formerly posed by al Qaeda. The vast majority of terrorist attacks in 2009 were committed by 240 other terrorist groups around the world, many of whom have lengthier track records of violence and mayhem than al Qaeda. For instance, the worst terrorist incident in all 2009 was not committed by al Qaeda or any other Muslim extremist organization. It occurred on January 17, 2009, near the village of Tora in the Democratic Republic of the Congo, when guerrillas belonging to a group calling itself the Lord's Resistance Army, led by a messianic individual named Joseph Kony who believes that he is the "spokesperson of God," massacred four hundred Congolese villagers in an orgy of violence.

There is even a growing terrorist threat on America's borders to the north and south. In Canada, over a dozen foreign terrorist groups, like the Palestinian group Hamas, Hezbollah from Lebanon, the Egyptian Islamic Jihad, the Armed Islamic Group from Algeria, the Kurdish Workers' Party from Turkey, the Liberation Tigers of Tamil Eelam from Sri Lanka, and the Basque separatist group ETA, operate openly, raising funds, holding rallies, operating Web sites, and publishing newsletters on behalf of their parent organizations. Although none of these groups has shown any sign of trying to mount a terrorist attack inside Canada or the United States, leaked State Department cables reveal that Canadian security forces have on occasion "vigorously harassed" Hezbollah members living in the Toronto area based on what was described as "non-specific intelligence on possible terrorist operations."

Just across the Rio Grande from the United States, an increasingly violent war has been raging for more than a decade between Mexico's government and that country's powerful drug cartels, which has claimed the lives of over 34,000 people in just the last four years. According to a leaked State Department cable, by 2008 the security situation in Mexico had become "a stew of widespread criminality, drug trafficking, [and] corruption."

Although the U.S. government has not designated the Mexican drug cartels as terrorists, the Mexican government has. The cartels have assassinated government officials and policemen, thrown hand grenades into street parties, detonated IEDs outside government buildings, and executed en masse hundreds of innocent civilians.

By the time the Obama administration entered office in 2009, the escalating violence in Mexico was beginning to spill over into the United States. Gun battles between rival Mexican gangs took place in the towns along the U.S.-Mexican border. The Mexican military had requested from Washington intelligence on the drug cartels the previous year, but the Bush White House had delayed granting the request because of concern that the information could end up in the hands of the cartels, who had the Mexican government, military, and police thoroughly penetrated. The sharp escalation in violence across the Rio Grande in early 2009 forced DNI Denny Blair to divert precious intelligence resources, including SIGINT intercept personnel and unmanned drones, to try to help the Mexican military and police combat the cartel gunmen, many of whom were former Mexican military special forces officers trained and equipped for counterinsurgency.

In recent months, the tempo of U.S. intelligence collection activity inside Mexico has been dramatically stepped up. The CIA and DEA stations in Mexico City were augmented in 2010 so as to increase the volume of human intelligence reporting on the Mexican drug cartels, and the army began deploying small SIGINT collection units known as Toric Ice Teams to the Rio Grande. Since February 2011, the U.S. Army has been flying unmanned drones over northern Mexico from Biggs Army Airfield on the grounds of Fort Bliss, located just outside El Paso, Texas. Also on Fort Bliss is the El Paso Intelligence Center, where the Drug Enforcement Administration is currently constructing a sophisticated SIGINT facility to intercept the cell phone calls of drug cartel officials across the border in Mexico.

When asked in 2011 why the U.S. intelligence community was investing so much time and effort in combating the Mexican drug cartels, a senior U.S. government official stated, "We had to. To do nothing would have invited disaster. If the drug violence spread into the United States it would have been a catastrophe."

For the past five years, terrorism has been slowly but inexorably spreading into those parts of the Middle East and North Africa that were peaceful prior to 9/11. A big part of the reason why new terrorist groups, many claiming to be offshoots of al Qaeda, have sprouted up so rapidly across the Muslim world is that thousands of angry young men from virtually every country in the Middle East and North Africa (the colloquial term for these individuals is *jihadis*) went off to Iraq to fight the U.S. military after the fall of Baghdad in April 2003. After getting their fill of action, they returned home, bringing with them lethal new skills in terrorist organization, finance, and bombmaking.

The Israeli foreign intelligence service, the Mossad, detected the first wave of these jihadis returning to their home countries in the Middle East and North Africa from Iraq in late 2004 and warned the U.S. intelligence community that this homecoming meant that trouble was on the way. According to a leaked State Department cable, the head of the Mossad, Meir Dagan, told a visiting U.S. congressional delegation in 2005 that "Israel has evidence that foreign fighters originating from Tajikistan, Uzbekistan, Syria and Yemen have arrived back in their home countries, and he [Dagan] assumes that some had returned to Saudi Arabia as well. Dagan predicted that, as with men who fought in Afghanistan during the 80's and 90's, these returning militants would stay in touch with each other, forming a network based on their common experiences in Iraq . . . He worried however, that these militants' countries of origin—in particular Saudi Arabia, Lebanon, Syria and Sudan—are ill-equipped to control the returning jihadis, who might then pose a threat to stability in the region and, ultimately, to Israel."

Dagan's prediction quickly came to pass. Two years after the Mossad chief spoke to the visiting congressional delegation, the still-classified version of a June 2007 National Intelligence Estimate on terrorism issued by the DNI in Washington revealed that in the four years since the U.S. invasion of Iraq in March 2003, al Qaeda had morphed into something broader based and more insidious as a host of new offshoots suddenly began appearing outside of Pakistan.

In recent years, Africa has quietly become a major hot spot for Muslim terrorist groups. For example, in the last three years a brand-new al Qaeda offshoot calling itself al Qaeda in the Lands of the Islamic Maghreb (AQIM) has appeared in North Africa. Founded in Algeria in 2007 with the expressed purpose of overthrowing the secular Algerian government, AQIM has waged a nasty albeit little publicized terror campaign against the Algerian government, killing hundreds of soldiers, policemen, and civilians with the same kinds of suicide car bombs and IEDs al Qaeda used against U.S. forces in Iraq. In recent years, AQIM has expanded its operations to neighboring Morocco.

To counter AQIM, the CIA and the French foreign intelligence service, the Direction Générale de la Sécurité Extérieure (DGSE), have covertly provided intelligence support to the Algerian and Moroccan governments to try to help them beat back the scourge. The CIA and DGSE have helped the Algerian military's security service, the Département du Renseignement et de la Sécurité (DRS), capture a number of senior AQIM leaders and kill a number of others. But cooperation with the Algerian intelligence service has not been easy; a leaked State Department cable describes the Algerian counterterrorism officials the CIA has to work with as a "prickly, paranoid group."

Next door in Morocco, the CIA and the DGSE have provided similar intelligence information to the Moroccan foreign intelligence service, the General Directorate of Studies and Documentation (Direction Générale des Études et de la Documentation, or DGED) and lavish technical support, including cellular telephone intercept equipment, to the Moroccan internal security service, the Défense et Surveillance du Territoire (DST), helping it capture a number of violent Muslim extremists opposed to the Moroccan regime.

AQIM has rapidly adapted since 2007 and morphed into something potentially more dangerous. It has gained strength and slowly spread its tentacles to the neighboring countries of Niger, Mali, and Mauritania, where in recent years the group has been setting up base camps with impunity because local security forces are so weak and poorly trained that they are incapable of resisting AQIM's encroachment on their territories. This has forced the U.S. intelligence community to expand its efforts to these countries. Green Beret teams from the 10th Special Forces Group began arriving in greater numbers in all three countries in late 2009, and in early 2010 SIGINT teams, including a U.S. Navy EP-3E SIGINT aircraft, were sent to the region on temporary assignment to try to find the AQIM base camps in the desolate northern parts of Mali and Mauritania, signaling that the war in the Sahara was moving to a new and more dangerous phase.

Over the past decade, the tiny and impoverished East African nation of Djibouti, located on the Horn of Africa, has been an important nexus for the U.S. intelligence community's collection efforts against al Qaeda and a host of other Muslim extremist groups who are becoming increasingly active throughout East Africa. The CIA station in Djibouti over the past ten years has run a series of important intelligence collection operations in the neighboring countries of Ethiopia, Eritrea, Sudan, Somalia, and Kenya and across the Red Sea in Yemen.

Four miles south of the U.S. embassy on the outskirts of the city is a former French Foreign Legion base called Camp Lemonnier, which occupies a large tract of land on the south side of the sole major airport in the country, Ambouli International Airport. A number of intelligence collection units are based at Lemonnier, including a U.S. Air Force/CIA Predator drone detachment, a robust HUMINT collection component, and a small SIGINT listening post, which is situated in a separate compound just south of the airfield.

From Camp Lemonnier, the U.S. intelligence community monitors the movement of illegal narcotics between Yemen and Somalia, commerce that finances terrorist groups in both countries. Another target is the notorious Lord's Resistance Army, which has murdered thousands of villagers in Uganda and in Congo but now is based in southern Sudan with the blessing of that government's leaders. In Ethiopia there are two small guerrilla groups operating, the Oromo Liberation Front and the Ogaden National Liberation Front, both of which are based in neighboring Somalia, where they are protected by radical militants. Finally, there are the Janjaweed tribal militias in Darfur Province in western Sudan, who between 2000 and 2007 mercilessly slaughtered anywhere from 200,000 to 400,000 local tribesmen. What currently makes Darfur of such great interest to Washington, according to a senior U.S. intelligence official, is that since at least 2009 the U.S. intelligence community has detected the presence of foreign Muslim fighters claiming allegiance to al Qaeda fighting alongside Janjaweed militia groups against local separatists.

Most of the U.S. intelligence community's attention in the region over the past three years has been focused on the activities of a radical Islamic organization in Somalia called Harakat al Shabaab al-Mujahideen (Mujahideen Youth Movement), usually referred to just as al Shabaab (the Youths), which the United States has long alleged has ties to al Qaeda. A number of American and European counterterrorism analysts interviewed over the past three years find it ironic that al Shabaab probably owes a debt of gratitude to the U.S. government and the CIA for its very existence.

Al Shabaab can trace its origins back to the port city of Kismayo, a longtime Muslim militant stronghold in southern Somalia, where in early 2006 a coalition of moderate and radical Somali militia groups, including al Shabaab, banded together under the banner of an umbrella organization styling itself as the Islamic Courts Union, led by an ambitious and politically astute Libyan-educated man named Sheikh Sharif Ahmed. Ahmed's forces drove northward and captured the Somali capital of Mogadishu in June 2006 from a coalition of local warlords calling themselves by the grandiose title of the Alliance for the Restoration of Peace and Counter-Terrorism, which had been quickly brought together by the CIA and the Ethiopian National Intelligence and Security Service with the help of suitcases filled with brand-new one-hundred-dollar bills.

The fall of Mogadishu set off alarm bells in Washington and the Ethiopian capital of Addis Ababa. Both governments agreed that it was intolerable that Somalia should once again become a haven for radical Muslim extremists and al Qaeda sympathizers, which was what the Islamic Courts Union was believed to be at the time. The CIA station in Addis Ababa was ordered to begin planning a massive covert operation designed to overthrow the Union

of Islamic Courts regime in conjunction with Ethiopia's two intelligence services, the National Intelligence and Security Service (Beherawi Mereja na
Deheninet Agelgelot), headed by a shadowy figure named Getachew Assefa,
and the Military Intelligence Department, headed by Brigadier General Ge-
bredela. Together, the agencies launched an ambitious covert action operation
to provide funding, as well as intelligence and logistical support, to a number
of Somali warlords who were opposed to the Islamic Courts Union. But the
operation backfired, and by late 2006 the Somalia militant militias were on
the verge of taking control of the entire country.

With substantial intelligence and logistical support from the CIA and the
U.S. military, on December 8, 2006, 10,000 Ethiopian troops invaded Soma-
lia. They captured Mogadishu three weeks later after the Islamic Courts
Union fled to strongholds in the south. On January 8, 2007, just days after
the fall of Mogadishu, the U.S. government arranged for Abdullahi Yusuf
Ahmed, the president of what was called the Somali Transitional Federal
Government, to return to Mogadishu from exile in Nairobi. The Somali Transitional Government had been created in Nairobi in November 2004 with the
CIA's financial backing and U.S. government political support, but it had little
support inside Somalia among the four clans who had controlled the country
since the collapse of the last Somali government in 1991. "Ahmed was doomed
from the moment he set foot in Mogadishu," a former State Department official said in a 2009 interview. "No one in Washington seemed to appreciate that
he would instantly be seen by the [Somali] clans as the bagman for the Ethiopians."

The Islamic Courts Union collapsed almost immediately after the invasion
began. Before long, however, Washington recognized that the Ethiopian invasion was not having the desired effect. One of the most radical of the Islamic
Courts' members, al Shabaab, did not disintegrate or disappear. Instead, al
Shabaab announced that it was going to stand and fight from its strongholds
in the southern part of the country. In a matter of months, thousands of militiamen from all of the major Somali clans joined forces with al Shabaab with
the goal of evicting the hated Ethiopians from their country and destroying
President Ahmed's transitional government, which now was widely viewed by
the clans as a puppet of the U.S. and Ethiopian governments. This marked the
beginning of a bloody two-year-long guerrilla war in which al Shabaab spear-
headed the resistance to the Ethiopian occupation.

The Ethiopian invasion also stirred up a hornet's nest of anger within the
Somali diaspora in Africa, the United States, and Western Europe, leading to

an influx into Somalia of a wave of militant foreign fighters who are today the driving force behind the al Shabaab insurgency. According to a leaked 2009 State Department cable, "Many of the foreign fighters currently operating in Somalia, particularly those who entered to fight the Ethiopians from 2006–2008, are ethnic Somalis, recruited from either neighboring countries or diasporas overseas and motivated in the past by a sense of Somali nationalism, jihadist propaganda, and the presence of foreign troops in the country . . . This includes North Americans, including at least 20 young men who were recruited from Minneapolis alone, and recruits from European countries with large Somali diasporas. Fighters have also come from within East Africa, most notably Kenya and Sudan."

During 2007 and 2008, al Shabaab's militia forces racked up one military victory after another against the weak and poorly equipped forces of the Somali Transitional Government. By the end of 2008, almost all of central and southern Somalia was in their hands, including the vitally important city of Baidoa. The CIA and U.S. military tried to help the Somali government by secretly going after the leadership of al Shabaab, killing one of the group's senior commanders, Aden Hashi Ayrow, in an air strike on May 1, 2008.

The U.S. government hoped that Ayrow's death would somehow arrest al Shabaab's progress on the battlefield inside Somalia. Instead, Ayrow was immediately replaced by two veteran and even more militant al Shabaab commanders, Mukhtar Robow and Hassan al-Turki, who intensified their group's attacks on Ethiopian forces deployed in and around the capital of Mogadishu. By late 2008, the situation had deteriorated to the point that Ethiopian government concluded that its troops were rapidly losing control of the countryside outside of Mogadishu and ordered the withdrawal of all its troops from Somalia.

The last Ethiopian troops pulled out of Mogadishu on January 22, 2009, two days after President Obama was inaugurated, leaving only the capital and a tiny pocket of territory surrounding the city in the hands of the Somali Transitional Government, which was now headed by Sheik Sharif Ahmed, who had led the Islamic Courts Union that the CIA and the Ethiopian military had ousted from power two years earlier. With only a tiny number of clan militiamen supporting him, Sheikh Ahmed had to depend on a contingent of almost 2,500 peacekeeping troops from Uganda and Burundi for his personal survival and tenuous control over the capital and surrounding area.

Al Shabaab immediately took advantage of the departure of the Ethiopian forces to consolidate its control of southern and central Somalia and press forward toward Mogadishu, having declared the newly elected Somali government un-Islamic. By the summer of 2009, the Somali Transitional Government was on the verge of collapse. The area around Mogadishu was under relentless attack by al Shabaab militia forces, and the militants even made deep inroads into the few areas in the country that previously were government strongholds, as demonstrated by the June 18, 2009, suicide bombing in the pro-government town of Beledweyne that killed the Somali government's minister of national security, Omar Hashi.

U.S. intelligence analysts in Washington believe that a significant part of the reason for al Shabaab's success on the battlefield was thanks to the substantial supplies of weapons and money that it was getting from a number of Arab states who were determined to counter Ethiopia's influence in Somalia. At the top of the list of countries covertly supporting al Shabaab was tiny Eritrea, Ethiopia's Muslim neighbor to the north, which has secretly provided political and military support for the Somali militant organization for almost a decade. This has brought Eritrea into conflict with the U.S. government. In October 2008, Assistant Secretary of State Jendayi Frazer publicly labeled Eritrea a "state sponsor of terrorism," leading to a near break in relations between the two countries.

Leaked State Department cables show that since 2006, Kenyan-based operatives of the Eritrean intelligence service have been covertly providing al Shabaab with weapons, money, and other forms of logistical support to counter the presence of Ethiopian troops in Somalia. According to intelligence sources, the Eritrean intelligence service has continued to equip and fund al Shabaab even after Ethiopian troops left Somalia in early 2009, with Ethiopian intelligence officials alleging that the Eritrean support of al Shabaab is being directed by the chief of the Eritrean intelligence service, Abraha Kassa.

The State Department repeatedly warned the Eritrean military-led government in early 2009 that its covert support for al Shabaab was perilous and would have diplomatic repercussions if it continued; a leaked February 2009 State Department cable shows that the U.S. ambassador to Eritrea warned government officials that unless the support for al Shabaab ceased, it would "hurt closer ties" with the United States.

At about the same time that the State Department was trying to get the Eritrean government to cease its support of al Shabaab, the U.S. government secretly began flying millions of dollars' worth of weapons and other military equipment into Dire Dawa Airfield in southern Ethiopia bound for the Somali Transitional Government in Mogadishu. The Ethiopian National Intelligence and Security Service then shipped the weapons across the border to the Somali military. The rapid influx of weapons stopped the hemorrhaging, but it was only a temporary respite. While Sheilk Ahmed's transitional government continued to control Mogadishu, al Shabaab and its allies pretty much controlled the rest of the country except for northern Somalia, which had become essentially an independent country with its own government.

Thanks to the covert supplies of weapons and material received from the CIA and the Ethiopian and Kenyan intelligence services, the Somali Transitional Government was able to stabilize the situation on the ground during the fall of 2009 and begin the painful process of rebuilding its military forces. The CIA station in Nairobi, Kenya, quickly became the secret command center for the U.S. government's effort to bolster the Somali Transitional Government. The CIA and U.S. military secretly helped train and equip six thousand newly recruited troops for the transitional government, arranged shipments of much-needed ammunition and fuel for the Somali military forces, and arranged for a select group of Somali officers to be sent to Camp Hurso in Ethiopia to receive advanced training in weapons, tactics, and intelligence gathering.

None of this would have been possible but for the shield provided by some five thousand African peacekeeping troops from Uganda and Burundi who were stationed in Mogadishu protecting Sheikh Ahmed's Somali Transitional Government, although few people knew that the African peacekeepers were secretly being paid for by the U.S. government. The CIA's Nairobi station also coordinated intelligence and logistical support for the African peacekeepers in Mogadishu, including providing near-realtime intelligence in sanitized form about al Shabaab military activities derived from SIGINT intercepts and imagery from Predator unmanned drone flights flown from Camp Lemonnier in Djibouti.

By the spring of 2010, the secret retraining and resupply effort to aid the army of the Somali Transitional Government was complete. In March 2010, the Somali interim government announced its intention to launch a large-scale offensive against the al Shabaab militia forces, which were estimated at about five thousand men. Ugandan peacekeeping troops in Mogadishu knew something big was coming because they suddenly began hearing the near-constant buzz of American unmanned drones flying overhead reconnoitering al Shabaab military positions around the city. But the much-anticipated offensive never materialized, for reasons that remain unclear today.

Today, the security situation in Somalia has largely degenerated into a standoff. Sheikh Ahmed's Somali Transitional Government continues to hold

Mogadishu and the surrounding area, but only because of the almost seven thousand African peacekeepers (up from five thousand troops just the year before) who protect him and the huge bribes paid out to rapacious local Somali warlords in return for their support in keeping al Shabaab at bay.

U.S. intelligence officials interviewed in 2010 admit that there is little that the United States can do directly to affect the trajectory of the war in Somalia. On September 14, 2009, attack helicopters flying from a U.S. Navy assault landing ship off the coast of Somalia blew up a car with Hellfire missiles carrying Saleh Ali Saleh Nabhan, the leader of al Qaeda in East Africa, who was wanted by the U.S. government in connection with the 1998 East Africa embassy bombings and the 2002 bombing of an Israeli-owned resort in Kenya. The decision was made in Washington to kill Nabhan as a matter of practical expediency. The *New York Times* quoted an American defense official as saying, "We may have been able to capture the guy but the decision was made to kill him."

But Nabhan's death changed nothing. According to U.S. intelligence officials, the al Shabaab militants are still lurking just outside the Mogadishu city gates. Over the past two years al Shabaab has increased the size of its militia to over five thousand men who are better armed in most respects than the Somali government troops they face. It is actively recruiting more foreign militants over the Internet to come to Somalia and join their jihad. Al Shabaab also provides safe havens in the western part of the country for two Ethiopian terrorist organizations, the Oromo Liberation Front and the Ogaden National Liberation Front.

On July 11, 2010, the final day of the World Cup soccer tournament being held in South Africa, al Shabaab militants executed two simultaneous bombings in the Ugandan capital of Kampala, killing seventy-four men who were watching the final soccer match between Spain and the Netherlands on huge outdoor televisions. The Kampala bombings were the militia's first attack outside of Somalia, with an al Shabaab spokesman confirming that the bombings were in retaliation for the presence of several thousand Ugandan troops in Somalia who were protecting the transitional government in Mogadishu.

The next day, one of the National Counterterrorism Center analysts responsible for covering Somalia wrote a brief memo entitled "Is al-Shabaab the Next al Qai'da?" The analyst's conclusion was that given the fact that the Pakistani Taliban, through Faisal Shahzad, had tried to detonate a car bomb in Times Square just two months earlier, he wondered if the bombing signaled that yet another local terrorist organization had crossed the Rubicon and "gone global."

*   *   *

Rarely visited by Westerners, and virtually unknown to Americans save for the most avid readers of *National Geographic* magazine, Yemen is a country steeped in history and legend. Located on the southwestern tip of the Arabian Peninsula, Yemen can rightfully claim to be one of the cradles of civilization because it lay astride the ancient incense and spice trade routes that ran up and down the Red Sea. Walking through the downtown of Yemen's capital, Sana'a, is to be transported back to the time of the *Arabian Nights*. A small piece of Yemen's former glory can be seen in the medieval Old City of Sana'a, which is dominated by an ornate 2,500-year-old fortified citadel. As they have for centuries, every Yemeni male proudly owns a rifle (there are 65 million guns in a nation of only 18 million people) and wears an ornate curved dagger called a *jambiya*.

As picturesque as it may be, Yemen today is one of the poorest and least developed nations on the planet. Although the Yemeni government is dedicated to trying to modernize the nation, the deeply religious and tradition-bound Yemeni tribesmen have stubbornly resisted the central government's efforts to bring the country into the twenty-first century, becoming a bastion of support for al Qaeda. Yemen is not only the ancestral home of Osama bin Laden's family, but it has produced more al Qaeda fighters per capita than any other country in the world. At one point in time, bin Laden's personal body-guard was made up entirely of Yemenis because of their loyalty. As of 2009, of all the al Qaeda fighters being held at the U.S. military-run confinement facility at Guantánamo Bay, Cuba, the ninety-nine Yemenis made up by far the larg-est single group.

In April 2002, seven months after the 9/11 terrorist attacks, a company of 150 U.S. Army Green Berets arrived in Sana'a to begin the process of training Yemeni security forces to hunt down the al Qaeda terrorists hiding in Yemen. According to a former official at the CIA's Counterterrorism Center, at the time there were at least twenty top al Qaeda officials and over one hundred fighters hiding in northern Yemen. The top two al Qaeda fugitives in Yemen that the U.S. intelligence community wanted, dead or alive, at the time were Mohammed Hamdi al-Ahdal and Ali Qaed Senyan al-Harthi, both of whom were suspected of being involved in planning the October 12, 2000, suicide bombing of the destroyer USS *Cole*, which killed seventeen American sailors. But the Yemeni military training program never got off the ground because in late 2002 the last of the Green Beret teams were withdrawn from Yemen as part of the military buildup for the invasion of Iraq in March 2003.

It took six years before the U.S. intelligence community once again began to pay attention to Yemen. In early 2008, reporting reached Washington from the small CIA station in the U.S. embassy in Sana'a indicating that al Qaeda, long dormant in the region, was beginning to make a comeback in Yemen. In March 2008, al Qaeda operatives launched a mortar attack on the U.S. embassy in Sana'a. The mortar shells missed the embassy and landed instead in the playground of a nearby girls' school. Six months later, on September 17, 2008, a team of al Qaeda militants dressed in Yemeni police uniforms attacked the main gate of the U.S. embassy in Sana'a. After a twenty-minute gun battle with Yemeni police, the attack was beaten back and six of the attackers were killed, but so were six Yemeni policemen and seven civilian bystanders.

A few days before President Obama was inaugurated in January 2009, the leaders of the Saudi and Yemeni branches of al Qaeda announced on a Web site that they had just merged their two organizations into a single entity, which they named al Qaeda in the Arabian Peninsula (AQAP). In an instant, Yemen went from a forgotten backwater in the global war on terror to the front of the line. The National Counterterrorism Center in Washington elevated Yemen to the top of the U.S. intelligence community's terrorism watch list.

Washington's newfound concern about events taking place in Yemen was enunciated in a private discussion that Obama's newly appointed deputy national security adviser John O. Brennan had with King Abdullah of Saudi Arabia in Riyadh on March 15, 2009, during which Brennan told the monarch that "the U.S. feared Yemen could become another Waziristan," referring to the al Qaeda and Taliban stronghold in Pakistan.

But heightened interest in Washington did not translate into effective action in Yemen itself, as has been too often the case in the war on terrorism. In order to go after al Qaeda in Yemen, the first problem that the U.S. government had to overcome was the country's colorful and fast-talking sixty-eight-year-old president, Ali Abdullah Saleh, who according to a former CIA station chief "runs his country like [TV game show host] Bob Barker."

The glib Saleh, at least on the surface, has professed to be eager to cooperate with the U.S. government in the war on terror, telling one delegation after another of visiting American officials of his profound desire to eliminate the scourge that is al Qaeda. But dozens of leaked cables from the U.S. embassy in Sana'a show that Saleh's enthusiasm for the war on terror is directly commensurate with how much money he could shamelessly extract from Washington and other countries by playing the "al Qaeda card."

Senior Obama administration officials have privately admitted that they have real concerns that Saleh and his top aides are really in it for the money and do not take the threat posed by al Qaeda very seriously. This was made abundantly clear in a May 2009 meeting outside the city of Taiz, where Saleh initially told the deputy director of the CIA, Stephen Kappes, that there were three insurgencies in Yemen, one by rebel Shiite Houthi tribesmen in the northern part of the country, a secessionist tribal movement in the southern part of the country, and a third in the form of al Qaeda in the Arabian Peninsula, all of which in his opinion were "on the same level." He then realized who he was talking to and quickly changed his tack. According to a leaked State Department cable, he "corrected himself to prioritize AQAP as the most severe threat." The U.S. ambassador to Yemen, Stephen Seche, realizing that what Saleh was doing was essentially telling the U.S. government what it wanted to hear, cabled Washington that "Saleh's decision to reverse himself and characterize AQAP as the most serious threat facing Yemen was almost certainly taken with his USG interlocutors in mind."

According to 2009 and 2010 interviews with a number of Yemeni government and security officials, from their perspective the lowest priority is for the Yemeni Army to hunt down the two hundred or so al Qaeda fighters who operate freely in seven desolate southern provinces where the Yemeni government has virtually no presence. According to Yemeni security sources, Shabwah Province in the south has become the de facto capital of al Qaeda in the Arabian Peninsula. U.S. and European intelligence sources generally agree that the fugitive American-born extremist cleric Anwar al-Awlaki is probably hiding somewhere in Shabwah, where he is protected by heavily armed tribesmen from his family's Awliq clan.

The same Yemeni officials believe that the White House has greatly exaggerated the threat that al Qaeda poses to the Yemeni government in order to get what Washington wants from Sana'a. In a 2010 interview, a senior Yemeni national security official close to President Saleh said, "You Americans say that al Qaeda is under every rock here. But there are only a couple hundred of them down in the south [of Yemen] . . . We do not think they pose much of a threat to us. And we have other problems here which are far more serious."

The Yemeni official was probably correct when he said that the two other insurgencies are a far more dire threat to the Yemeni government than al Qaeda. Since 2004, the Yemeni Army has been trying to subdue a rebellion by a group of Shiite tribesmen called the Houthis in the northern part of the country. Despite facing the Yemeni Army's best units, the Houthis have not only held their own but have captured large parts of Sa'ada and Amran provinces along the border with Saudi Arabia. In the southern part of the country, for the past several years the Yemeni Army has been unsuccessfully trying to put down a rebellion by secessionist tribesmen, who now control huge chunks of territory in the mountains north of the port city of Aden. According to a U.S. Army Special Forces officer who has been a frequent visitor to Yemen over the past three years, "Most of the southern part of Yemen is presently outside the control of Sana'a."

Reversing the situation and helping the Yemenis restore a semblance of order in the country may very well be impossible. The Yemeni government and military bureaucracy is corrupt, inefficient, and ineffective, in part because President Saleh has stacked the entire government bureaucracy, the military high command, and the top posts of all the intelligence and security services with members of his extended family or political cronies. For example, Saleh's half brother commands all Yemeni forces in the northern part of the country; and his eldest son, Ahmed Ali Abdullah Saleh, who is widely seen as being groomed to succeed his father as president, commands both the Yemeni Republican Guard and the special forces.

Virtually all Yemeni division, brigade, and battalion commanders were chosen for their posts based on their political loyalty to the Saleh regime rather than their military command expertise. Corruption runs rampant throughout the top echelons of the Yemeni military. According to a senior U.S. Army Special Forces officer who served two rotations in Yemen, "You could never find the [Yemeni Army] commanders at their desks because they were absentee landlords, spending most of their time on outside business interests rather than leading their troops."

So it should not come as a great surprise that the Yemeni military is, in the words of a former U.S. Army military adviser, "a duck that cannot quack." A 2010 survey by the Pentagon found that the Yemeni Army had virtually no fighting capability whatsoever. Only a few of the Yemeni Army's thirty combat brigades were sufficiently trained and equipped to conduct independent operations, and these units never left Sana'a because their primary mission was to guard the Saleh regime. The survey found that Yemeni troops, 80 percent of whom are illiterate, were poorly trained, infrequently paid, suffering from low morale, and equipped with fifty-plus-year-old Russian military equipment that should have been consigned to a museum decades ago. Only a handful of the Yemeni Air Force's Russian-made MiG fighters and helicopters were found to be airworthy. The chewing of the narcotic leaf qat (or khat) by the military's enlisted men was so widespread that all daily operations and training activities had to be completed by noon, after which most of the troops were comatose in a drug-induced stupor.

All of the weaknesses of the Yemeni Army have been on display in recent years in the war against the rebellious Houthi tribesmen in northern Yemen. In August 2009, the Houthis captured a Yemeni Army company and stole all its heavy weaponry before releasing the soldiers. Later that month, the rebels routed the Yemeni Army's 82nd Infantry Brigade, capturing huge quantities of heavy weaponry, including tanks and armored personnel carriers. In December 2009, Houthi tribesmen surrounded the Yemeni Army's 107th Infantry Brigade for two weeks. Cut off and out of food, the brigade commander was forced to sign a humiliating agreement with the rebels, whereby his troops were allowed to withdraw in return for surrendering all of their tanks, armored vehicles, and heavy weapons.

Frustrated by the string of defeats that his forces had suffered, President Saleh tried repeatedly to get the U.S. government to provide military equipment for his forces fighting the Houthis, telling John O. Brennan in September 2009, "The Houthis are your enemies too." But the Obama administration has consistently refused, with the U.S. embassy repeatedly telling Saleh that it was al Qaeda in the Arabian Peninsula who was the main enemy, not the Houthis.

With no assistance coming from Washington and desperate to stem the tide of losses in the north, in September 2009 Saleh's elite Counter-Terrorism Unit (CTU), which had been trained and equipped at great expense by U.S. and British special forces specifically to combat al Qaeda since 2003, was deployed instead to Sa'ada Province to combat the Houthis. The decision infuriated American government and intelligence officials, who had for months begged Saleh to send the CTU to the south to find and kill the al Qaeda fighters that U.S. intelligence had tentatively located in the region. When the U.S. ambassador to Yemen, Stephen Seche, and the CIA station chief in Sana'a registered a formal complaint on December 9, 2009, about this flagrant misuse of the Yemeni military's sole counterterrorism asset, Colonel Akram al-Qassmi, the deputy commander of Yemen's small counterterrorism agency, the National Security Bureau, told them that "the war against the Houthis is not a distraction from the CT [counterterrorism] fight. It is the CT fight."

The CIA station in Sana'a has had a tense and sometimes acrimonious relationship with its Yemeni counterparts since 9/11. While the CIA has had

generally good relations with the National Security Bureau, headed by a pol-
ished former diplomat named Ali Muhammad al-Anisi, the same cannot be
said of its relations with Yemen's more powerful internal security service, the
Political Security Bureau, which is headed by an aged Saleh loyalist named
Ghalib Mutahi Qamish. Over and over again since 9/11, the Political Security
Bureau has withheld information from the CIA and even denied CIA and FBI
investigators access to captured al Qaeda operatives and documents. In the
minds of many CIA and State Department officials, the obstructive behavior
of Qamish's organization has become the principal obstacle to success against
al Qaeda in Yemen, with a leaked cable from the U.S. embassy in Sana'a com-
plaining that "there continue to be frequent and troubling lapses in the [Ye-
meni government's counterterrorism] performance, including the release of
extremists and failure to share information."

But it has to be said that the U.S. government's interest in Yemen has been
anything but consistent, fluctuating wildly based on the crisis du jour. For
much of the Obama administration's first year in office, the NCTC ranked
Yemen far below Afghanistan and Pakistan as a priority in the war on terrorism. But on November 5, 2009, U.S. Army psychiatrist Major Nidal Malik
Hasan went on a shooting spree at Fort Hood, Texas, killing thirteen American soldiers and wounding dozens more. An investigation revealed that in
the months leading up to the shooting rampage, Major Hasan had exchanged
about twenty e-mails with the American-born radical cleric Anwar al-Awlaki,
who as noted above was still in hiding in the portion of southern Yemen that
the Sana'a government did not control.

Retaliation from Washington for the Fort Hood shootings was swift. On
December 17, 2009, a U.S. Navy warship off the coast of Yemen fired a cruise
missile at what was believed to be an al Qaeda training camp in Abyan Province just north of the port city of Aden, killing forty-one people. Seven days
later, on December 24, another cruise missile struck what was believed by
U.S. intelligence sources to be the headquarters of al Qaeda in the Arabian
Peninsula deep inside remote Shabwah Province in southern Yemen. The
principal targets of the attack were Nasser al-Wuhayshi, the leader of AQAP,
and his deputy, Said Ali al-Shihri. But postattack intelligence reports showed
that neither man was at the site when the missiles hit. According to Yemeni
newspaper reports, the only casualties of the attack were five al Qaeda fighters.

The following day, December 25, 2009, a Nigerian native named Umar
Farouk Abdulmutallab, who had been trained as a suicide bomber at an al
Qaeda training camp in southern Yemen, attempted to detonate a bomb on a

Northwest Airlines plane over Detroit. Once again, Yemen jumped to the top of the U.S. intelligence community's terrorism watch list. Within seventy-two hours of the bombing attempt, more than two dozen CIA and military clandestine intelligence officers, SIGINT collectors, and intelligence analysts were put on planes to beef up the CIA station in Sana'a. NSA and its SIGINT partners in Great Britain and Australia immediately began intercepting all international telephone calls going into or coming out of Yemen. The Saleh government gave the CIA permission to conduct daily Predator drone missions over the southern part of the country from Camp Lemonnier in Djibouti, and the U.S. Navy was allowed to begin flying manned reconnaissance missions over southern Yemen from warships stationed offshore. There was also a dramatic influx of Green Berets from the 5th Special Forces Group to intensify the training of Yemeni counterterrorist units at a special training camp in Dhamar Province south of Sana'a.

Even so, it is America's foreign intelligence partners in the region who are currently doing most of the heavy lifting in Yemen. A contingent of veteran Jordanian intelligence officers arrived in Sana'a in December 2009 to reinforce the somnolent Yemeni intelligence and security services. The Saudi Arabian foreign intelligence service, the General Intelligence Directorate, has also been quietly supplying intelligence, including cell phone intercepts, about al Qaeda activities in Yemen, in the hope that the escalating violence can be prevented from spreading into the restive tribal areas of southern Saudi Arabia.

Yet actionable intelligence on al Qaeda activities in southern Yemen is still extremely difficult to come by. For more than two years, al Qaeda has been systematically assassinating Yemeni intelligence officers stationed in their strongholds in southern Yemen, and the CIA believes that al Qaeda has bought off many of those intelligence officials still remaining. Intelligence collected over Yemen by CIA unmanned drones flying from Djibouti has only led to two air strikes by U.S. warplanes since the beginning of 2010, neither of which appears to have accomplished much.

The simple truth is that we cannot get into the al Qaeda sanctuaries to kill or capture the terrorists. President Saleh will not allow any CIA or U.S. military intelligence personnel to work outside the city limits of Sana'a for fear that their presence in the countryside would further antagonize the already rebellious tribesmen in the country's south, where al Qaeda operates. He has also placed very strict limits on American aerial reconnaissance missions, requiring that all imagery collected by CIA unmanned drones over Yemen go to an operations center that had been set up with CIA and U.S. military assistance

in the headquarters building of the Yemeni Ministry of Defense for this purpose. The one concession that Saleh was willing to make was to allow U.S.
warplanes to strike al Qaeda targets inside Yemen if and when actionable intelligence became available. He even told the commander of U.S. Central
Command, General David Petraeus, at a private meeting in Sana'a in January
2010, "We'll continue saying the bombs are ours, not yours."

In effect, by imposing these onerous conditions Saleh has tied the hands
of the U.S. intelligence community. Unless these restrictions are lifted, there
is not much of a substantive nature that the U.S. government can do in the
near future to take the war to the al Qaeda forces in southern Yemen except
watch and wait for the next shoe to drop.

The Obama administration decided early in 2009 to revamp and reorient the
U.S. intelligence community's stalled efforts to interdict the flow of money
from rich Arab businessmen in the Persian Gulf to al Qaeda and the Taliban.
In August 2009, President Obama's special representative for Afghanistan
and Pakistan, Ambassador Richard C. Holbrooke, created a special interagency group called the Illicit Finance Task Force to restart the effort to disrupt
or, if possible, shut down the clandestine financial and logistical support networks located throughout the Persian Gulf States that were keeping al Qaeda,
the Taliban, and a host of other terrorist groups alive and kicking.

In order to track terrorist finances, it is absolutely essential that you get the
countries where the terrorists are raising their money and doing their banking to cooperate. In the case of America's allies in the Persian Gulf, where al
Qaeda and the Taliban traditionally raise most of their money, this cooperation has been hard to come by.

Some of the Gulf States have gone the extra mile to help the U.S. intelligence community block the flow of money originating in or transiting through
their countries to terrorist groups. For instance, according to a leaked 2009
State Department cable, the United Arab Emirates (UAE) has been extraordinarily helpful to the U.S. government in "countering financial support for
al-Qa'ida, and more recently, in constricting Iran's ability to use UAE financial institutions to support its nuclear program." In 2009 Crown Prince
Sheikh Mohammed bin Zayed ordered the UAE's two security services to
"disrupt any Taliban-related financial activity that can be identified in the
UAE." True to their word, for the past three years the Emiratis have diligently
sought to block the flow of money from banks in Dubai to the Taliban in

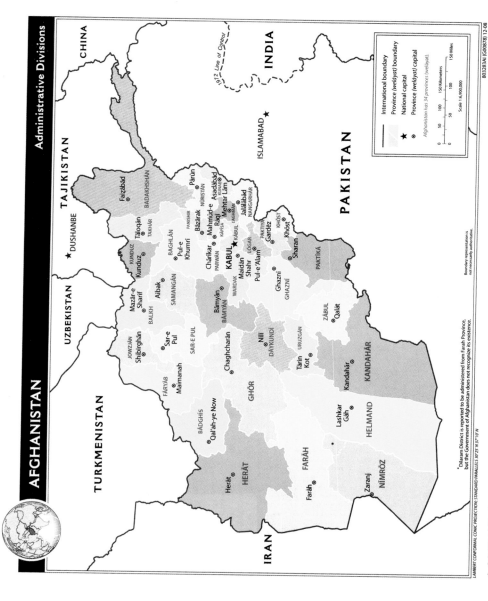

A 2008 U.S. Army map of Afghanistan's political divisions.

The view from a gun position at Firebase Phoenix, overlooking the Korengal Valley, on July 10, 2007. Courtesy of Department of the Army.

Corporal Scott Harvey, a cryptologic linguist with Operational Command Element 2, 2nd Radio Battalion, Task Force Belleau Wood, uses a radio scanner to listen to Taliban radio activity in Helmand Province, Afghanistan, May 2011. Courtesy of United States Marine Corps.

Air force ordnance personnel load a Hellfire missile on an MQ-9 Reaper unmanned drone in April 2010. Courtesy of United States Air Force.

U.S. Marine Corps Lance Corporal Samuel Kautz, with Alpha Company, 1st Battalion, 7th Marine Regiment, launches an RQ-11B Raven unmanned drone at Combat Outpost Viking, Iraq, June 2, 2009. Photo by Corporal Robert S. Morgan, courtesy of United States Marine Corps.

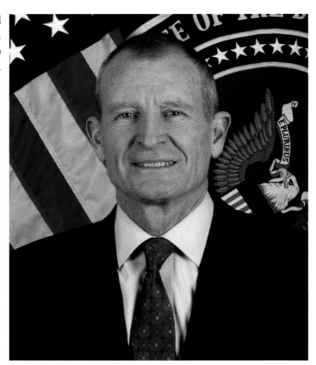

Former director of national intelligence Dennis Blair. Courtesy of the Office of the Director of National Intelligence.

Sergeant Marcel Ruales, with the U.S. Army's 636th Military Intelligence Battalion, and assigned to the human intelligence collection team, Forward Operating Base Ghazni, Afghanistan, shakes hands with children in the Afghan village of Warghez on September 17, 2009. Photo by Master Sergeant Sarah R. Webb, courtesy of United States Air Force.

Secretary of Defense Leon Panetta, director of the CIA from 2009 to 2011, and White House chief of staff under President Bill Clinton from 1994 to 1997. Photo by Monica King, courtesy of Department of Defense.

U.S. Army RC-12X Guardrail SIGINT aircraft flying an operational intelligence collection mission over Afghanistan. Courtesy of United States Army.

U.S. Air Force personnel with the 380th Expeditionary Aircraft Maintenance Squadron conduct preflight services on an RQ-4 Global Hawk unmanned drone at Al Dhafra Air Base in the United Arab Emirates, February 12, 2010. Photo by Master Sergeant Scott T. Sturkol, courtesy of United States Air Force.

President Barack Obama and senior staff attend a briefing in the White House Situation Room. Courtesy of the White House.

National Security Agency director Lieutenant General Keith B. Alexander being briefed on SIGINT operations in Afghanistan by Rear Admiral Paul Becker, director of intelligence of the International Security Assistance Force (ISAF) Joint Command, in July 2010. Note that the map on the wall has been censored. Courtesy of ISAF Media Relations Office.

Stills from a Taliban propaganda video aired on the Al-Emara network showing insurgents en route to an attack on a United States Army outpost in Nuristan Province in 2009, as well as an arsenal of RPGs. The title card reads "Foreign Press Center of the Islamic Emirate of Afghanistan."

The tracking device that college student Yasir Afifi found mounted to the undercarriage of his car in October 2010, later reclaimed by FBI agents. Photo courtesy of Flickr user floorsixtyfour, used under a Creative Commons license.

A U.S. Air Force MQ-1B Predator unmanned drone taxis down the runway on October 13, 2008, at Ali Air Base, Iraq. Photo by Senior Airman Christopher Griffin, courtesy of United States Air Force.

Afghanistan. In return, leaked State Department cables show that the U.S. has provided the UAE authorities with intelligence information about Taliban front companies in the UAE, as well as details of the travel from Pakistan to Dubai by senior Taliban finance officials to raise or move funds. But the UAE has been the exception rather than the rule. Convincing the leaders of other Persian Gulf States to do more to shut down al Qaeda's and the Taliban's financial lifelines running from their countries to terrorist groups in Afghanistan and Pakistan has proven extraordinarily difficult, a surprising development from countries that are actively cooperating with the U.S. intelligence community in the war on terrorism.

For example, the Kuwaiti government has refused to shut down a charitable organization called the Revival of Islamic Heritage Society, which the U.S. intelligence community has determined is a major source of money for al Qaeda and a host of other terrorist organizations. Kuwait has even blocked attempts by the U.S. government to list the charity as a terrorist financier with the United Nations Security Council. The government of Qatar has also stubbornly refused to cooperate with the U.S. intelligence community in its efforts to interdict the flow of money to terrorist groups; a December 2009 State Department cable charges that "Qatar's overall level of CT [counterterrorism] cooperation with the U.S. is considered the worst in the region."

Ironically, perhaps the most recalcitrant of the Arab states has been America's top ally in the region, Saudi Arabia, with a leaked December 2009 State Department cable revealing that "donors in Saudi Arabia constitute the most significant source of funding to Sunni terrorist groups worldwide." Despite years of effort by the U.S. government, according to a State Department cable, "it has been an ongoing challenge to persuade Saudi officials to treat terrorist financing emanating from Saudi Arabia as a strategic priority."

So where are we today? In Pakistan, the toll of al Qaeda fighters and other terrorists killed over the past three years has been massive, although no one in the U.S. intelligence community seems to know, much less care, how many enemy combatants have died because to them the body count is an irrelevant measure of success.

Some have tried to keep a tally of the death toll, at least for posterity's sake. A young intelligence analyst at the National Counterterrorism Center, whose responsibilities included maintaining an up-to-date organization chart of al Qaeda's top leadership in Pakistan, in frustration stopped keeping her posterboard-sized chart of who was who in al Qaeda up to date in late 2009 because the CIA's six Predator and Reaper unmanned drones based in Pakistan were killing the terrorist leaders faster than she could keep up.

Outside of Pakistan, the White House has quietly approved an expanded series of classified counterterrorism operations against al Qaeda affiliates in North Africa, Yemen, and Somalia, including commando raids, cruise missile attacks, and clandestine air strikes. The number of individuals on the CIA's "Kill List" has grown exponentially since the list was first conceived in the summer of 2008, growing from just a couple of dozen al Qaeda militants hiding in northern Pakistan to over two thousand today, including its first American, the radical cleric Anwar al-Awlaki, still believed to be in hiding somewhere in southern Yemen.

On the negative side of the ledger, none of the al Qaeda terrorists that are currently in U.S. custody have yet been brought to trial to answer for their crimes. Secret legal opinions prepared by Justice Department lawyers since Obama was inaugurated indicate that successfully prosecuting many of these individuals in American civilian courts may be next to impossible. Key parts of the government's legal case against these prisoners are based on evidence obtained by torturing three of the top al Qaeda leaders currently in U.S. custody—Abu Zubaydah, 'Abd Al-Rahim Al-Nashiri, and Khalid Sheikh Mohammed. Justice Department officials are convinced that all of these individuals are guilty but fear that they may never be able to try them because federal prosecutors have not been able to obtain corroborative evidence independent of what the CIA obtained from torture. Without evidence untainted by torture, prosecution of these defendants is problematic, at best, and obtaining convictions in a federal court is even less certain. The only remaining option is to try these individuals before military tribunals at Guantánamo, where the rules of evidence are not as strict as in civilian courts. If the U.S. government takes this route, it will almost certainly generate vast amounts of controversy around the world, especially if the government tries to use evidence obtained from torture.

The military-run Guantánamo Bay detention facility in Cuba remains open despite the president's executive order signed during his first week in office ordering its closure. Three years later, the fate of the detainees there remains in limbo. Since 2009, about 200 of the 245 Guantánamo detainees that Obama inherited from the Bush administration have been transferred to prisons in their home countries, leaving forty-eight prisoners that the Justice Department has decided to continue to hold indefinitely without trial although according them the status of prisoners of war. A senior Justice Department official admitted in a 2010 interview that this state of affairs is not popular and almost certainly will result in a legal challenge from civil liberties groups, who will challenge the constitutionality of the government holding anyone prisoner for the rest of his life without due process of law. According to the Justice Department official, "It's the only option open to us . . . If we can't try them, then we have to keep them behind bars."

Counterterrorism officials in the United States and Europe tend to be a rather dour bunch, who generally believe that things will get worse before they get better. One of the nightmare scenarios that keeps these men and women awake at night is the gnawing fear that they may never be able to win the war on terrorism, no matter how hard they try.

They are worried that the global battlefield may be expanding faster than the ability of the U.S. intelligence community and its allies to contain it. For example, the al Qaeda affiliate in North Africa, although small in size, is rapidly expanding to countries outside of its base in Algeria. There are signs that new terrorist groups not affiliated in any way with al Qaeda are beginning to take root in a number of East African countries, like the Lord's Resistance Army in Uganda, Congo, and Sudan. Al Shabaab is continuing to grow in size and power in Somalia, and there is very little realistically that the U.S. government can do about it other than try to prevent the group from expanding into neighboring Kenya, Uganda, and Ethiopia. In Yemen, the options of the U.S. government are constrained by strict limitations imposed by a host government that does not believe that al Qaeda is really a significant threat to national security. The efforts of the U.S. government to choke off the flow of money to terrorist groups like al Qaeda have met with fierce resistance from many governments in the Persian Gulf, almost all of whom are close allies with American troops stationed on their soil for their protection.

In Pakistan, despite killing Osama bin Laden and hundreds of his fellow terrorists over the past three years, the U.S. intelligence community still has not been able to destroy the last battered vestiges of al Qaeda because it cannot uproot them from their sanctuaries in the FATA. Nor does the Pakistani military appear to have the capacity, or the willingness, to do the job. As long as al Qaeda continues to survive and some of its top leaders, like Osama bin Laden's longtime deputy and al Qaeda's new leader Ayman al-Zawahiri, remain at large, everything that has been accomplished to date could potentially come undone, especially if the Pakistani government ceases cooperating with the CIA in the fight against al Qaeda.

While many Americans rejoiced at the news of Osama bin Laden's death, many in the intelligence community believe that his death will probably not be the end of al Qaeda, or terrorism in general. In the fall of 2006, a team of U.S. government officials and consultants sat down at the Pentagon to consider what the U.S. strategy should be in order to win what was then popularly called "the Long War." The panel concluded that even if al Qaeda was crushed and Osama bin Laden was captured or killed, that would not be the end of the struggle: A war on terrorism would almost certainly continue for at least another generation or even longer, because as long as even a small number of angry Muslim men hate America, extremism and the terrorism that it breeds will continue to exist well after al Qaeda is dead and gone.

If there is a single overarching lesson to be taken away from America's decade-long war on terrorism, it may very well be that no matter how hard we try, for every terrorist group that we neutralize or every jihadi fighter we kill, more will take their place. In reality, Osama bin Laden's death, while an emotional milestone for the American public, does not change the dynamics of the war on terrorism in any meaningful way. This idea is just now beginning to sink in at the White House and elsewhere around Washington, with one senior Obama administration counterterrorism official lamenting, "Killing him [Osama bin Laden] will probably change nothing."

CHAPTER 6

Men of Zeal

Homeland Security and Domestic Terrorism

*The greatest dangers to liberty lurk in insidious
encroachment by men of zeal, well-meaning
but without understanding.*
—U.S. SUPREME COURT JUSTICE
LOUIS D. BRANDEIS (1928)

On most days, the Situation Room in the basement of the West Wing of the White House hums with activity. On weekdays there is almost always a meeting taking place in the Sit Room's famous conference room. President Obama comes down to the Sit Room several times a week to chair National Security Council meetings with all of his senior national security advisers, as well as to chair the weekly meetings of his homeland security and Afghanistan-Pakistan policy teams.

Unlike how it is portrayed in popular television shows like *The West Wing*, the Sit Room's windowless conference room is cramped and somewhat claustrophobic. The room's wooden conference table can seat only a dozen or so people, and not particularly comfortably. Complaints about the cold in the Sit Room are legion because the system is set to keep the room at near-arctic temperatures.

It used to be much worse, before the advent of laptop computers and powerful air-conditioning systems. President Richard Nixon's national security adviser, Henry Kissinger, hated the Sit Room's conference room, describing it in less than glowing terms as a "tiny, uncomfortable, low-ceilinged, windowless room."

During the weekly National Security Council principals' meetings, the president sits at the head of the conference table with an ever-present can of Diet

Coke in front of him. Vice President Joe Biden sits on his right, usually reading through a pile of unread policy papers while sipping on a bottle of water. Until he was fired in October 2010, Obama's national security adviser, retired General James L. Jones, or Secretary of State Hillary Rodham Clinton, sat on the president's left. Against either wall of the conference room are rows of leather chairs that can seat up to twenty junior staffers and note takers. On most occasions, the large video screens at the far end of the conference room display the visages of foreign government officials or senior American military commanders thousands of miles away who have been patched in so that they can participate in the conference via secure video teleconferencing technology.

But the Sit Room is much more than just a snazzy high-tech conference room. Since it was created back in the summer of 1961 in what used to be the White House bowling alley, the Sit Room's principal function has been to be the president's eyes and ears on the world, a combination of watch center and intelligence fusion facility, whose mission is to provide the president with up-to-the-minute intelligence and alerts of significant events taking place around the globe, as well as with secure communications allowing him and his senior staff to talk securely to cabinet secretaries, military commanders, and the nation's top intelligence officials anywhere around the world, twenty-four hours a day.*

The Sit Room has its own staff of thirty senior intelligence officers and military personnel seconded by the CIA and other branches of the U.S. intelligence community, who work in a cramped watch office in rotating eight-hour shifts scanning the more than one thousand classified messages and intelligence reports, plus over a thousand wire service reports, that come into the Sit Room every day, looking for anything that might rise to the level that requires informing the president immediately. Even at night, the Sit Room staff is responsible for keeping the president and all of his senior national security staff informed if a crisis situation happens anywhere around the world. Because of who they work for, these men and women are cleared for access to virtually every type of classified information generated by the U.S. government. A former Sit Room watch officer recalled that when he returned to his regular job at the National Security Agency, he had to spend the better

---

* Its wartime counterpart, the President's Emergency Operations Center, located in the basement of the East Wing of the White House, is the ultramodern nuclear war bunker that houses many of the same command and communications systems found in the Sit Room.

part of an hour signing a stack of forms taking away the dozens of special security clearances that he had formerly held.

Intelligence reporting on terrorist incidents at home and abroad comes into the Sit Room every day of the week. Both the FBI and the Department of Homeland Security operations centers have standing orders to inform the White House Sit Room immediately of any significant domestic terrorist incidents or arrests. There were ten instances in 2009 when the yellow-colored secure phones in the Sit Room rang, with the FBI watch officer on the other end reporting a major arrest of a terrorist suspect inside the United States.

During the first ten months of 2009, the FBI successfully broke up plots by groups of homegrown terrorists who were planning attacks in Boston, Massachusetts; Dallas, Texas; Newburgh, New York; Raleigh, North Carolina; and Springfield, Illinois. All had been duly reported to the White House. Only two of the plots involved individuals with ties to foreign terrorist groups. One, Najibullah Zazi, was arrested in September 2009 on charges of going to Pakistan to get explosives training from al Qaeda with the intent of planting bombs on New York City subways. The second, David C. Headley, was arrested in Chicago in October 2009 and charged with scouting the locations for the November 2008 attack by Pakistan-based Lashkar-e-Taiba terrorists in Mumbai, India. All in all, according to one of the counterterrorism analysts at the NCTC, it had been a "pretty hum-drum year."

Then, as described in the previous chapter, on November 5, 2009, a Muslim U.S. Army psychiatrist named Major Nidal Malik Hasan went on a shooting spree at Fort Hood, Texas, killing thirteen American soldiers and wounding thirty-two more. Two months later, on Christmas Day 2009, a twenty-three-year-old Nigerian national named Umar Farouk Abdulmutallab failed to bring down his Northwest Airlines flight from Amsterdam while it was on final approach to Detroit International Airport. Disaster was averted only because the crude explosive device sewn into his underwear failed to detonate, earning him for all eternity the nickname of "the Tighty Whities Bomber."

The Hasan and Abdulmutallab incidents proved to be huge embarrassments for the U.S. intelligence community because they showed that the terrorists had adapted their tactics and found new chinks in the armor of America's homeland security defenses. For years before the incidents, a number of NCTC analysts had tried to get their superiors to pay greater heed to the growing terror threats to the homeland, but failed. The leadership of the U.S. intelligence community and the White House were focused on al Qaeda in Pakistan and the growing threat posed by al Qaeda in Yemen and, according to the analysts, did not take the domestic terrorism problem very seriously, placing the problem way down on their counterterrorism priority lists.

Both incidents also confirmed that there were still serious systemic problems in the U.S. intelligence community's counterterrorism effort. In both cases the U.S. intelligence community possessed information that, if properly analyzed and correlated, would have allowed the United States to prevent the attack from happening. But the intelligence analysts overlooked key pieces of intelligence, and for the information they did have, they failed to "connect the dots."

In the case of Major Hasan, three postmortem reviews found that the intelligence community "collectively had sufficient information to have detected Hasan's radicalization to violent Islamic extremism but failed to understand and to act on it." Months before the shooting rampage, Major Hasan had exchanged more than a dozen e-mails with the American-born radical cleric Anwar al-Awlaki, who was then hiding in southern Yemen. The e-mails were intercepted by NSA and examined by FBI counterterrorism analysts, who concluded that there was nothing in them which warranted further action. This should not have been the end of the matter, though. At the very least someone at the FBI should have told Hasan's army superiors that the major was communicating with an individual on the U.S. intelligence community's terrorism watch list. As a congressional investigation later revealed, the FBI committed the unpardonable sin of failing "to inform Hasan's military chain of command and Army security officials of the fact that he was communicating with a suspected violent Islamist extremist."

Insofar as Umar Farouk Abdulmutallab was concerned, three separate internal reviews of the incident found that exactly the same glaring mistakes were made as in the case of Major Hasan. Four months before Abdulmutallab had been allowed to board Northwest Airlines Flight 253 in Amsterdam, NSA had intercepted al Qaeda cell phone calls in Yemen indicating that an unidentified Nigerian was being trained for a terrorist attack. In and of itself, this was not enough to cause anyone to do anything. But the National Counterterrorism Center in Washington failed to link the intercepts with information obtained from Adulmutallab's father, who on November 20, 2009, told officials at the U.S. embassy in Abuja, Nigeria, that he had received text messages revealing that his son was in Yemen and "had become a fervent radical." For reasons nobody seems to be able to explain, nobody at NCTC connected the dots between these two disparate pieces of information.

President Obama was understandably furious. Even before he was inaugurated, he had been assured in briefings by President Bush's DNI, Admiral

Mike McConnell, that the most serious systemic deficiencies identified by the 9/11 Commission in its 2004 report had been fixed. He had received the same assurances from his own DNI, Denny Blair. Seeking to assuage the president's anger, Blair told Obama that he should not rush to a premature judgment before all the facts were in.

The Abdulmutallab affair marked the beginning of the end of Blair's tenure as DNI. President Obama, rightly or wrongly, blamed Blair for Abdulmutallab being allowed to get onto the Northwest airliner, not the analysts at the National Counterterrorism Center for failing to connect the dots. It did not help that Blair's enemies inside the intelligence community joined in the barrage of criticism aimed at him. John O. Brennan, the president's counterterrorism adviser, and Blair's nemesis within the intelligence community, CIA director Leon Panetta, both blamed Blair for the Christmas Day intelligence failure.

According to one of Blair's former deputies, the criticism from Panetta was particularly hard for Blair to bear. He and Panetta had known each other for years, and Blair thought that he would not have any problems working with the easygoing Californian when he was named DNI in January 2009.

But relations between the two men quickly soured as the hard-nosed Panetta furiously resisted all attempts by Blair to assert his office's authority over the CIA. Underestimating Panetta's bureaucratic infighting skills was to prove to be Blair's undoing. For instance, on May 19, 2009, Blair sent out a memo announcing that his office would hereafter appoint all CIA chiefs of station, not Langley. Within hours of Blair's memo going out, Panetta sent out his own message to his staff telling them, in essence, to ignore Blair's memo. Blair refused to back down and demanded that the White House confirm his statutory authority over the CIA. The fighting between the two escalated to the point that in the fall of 2009 the White House felt that it had to intervene and settle the dispute once and for all. In early December, Obama's national security adviser, General James L. Jones, issued an order that came down firmly on the side of the CIA, finding that Panetta alone had the authority not only to appoint the agency's station chiefs but also to direct the CIA's covert action operations in Afghanistan and Pakistan, including the CIA's Predator drone strikes in northern Pakistan.

The Abdulmutallab affair was the final straw. On May 20, 2010, President Obama fired Denny Blair after only sixteen months on the job as DNI. Blair had learned earlier in the day what the president intended to do and had tried repeatedly to make an appointment to see him. Blair knew that his time was up when Obama, who was at the time hosting a state visit by President Felipe

Calderón of Mexico, did not answer his phone calls. When the two men finally spoke later that day, the president told Blair that he intended to replace him as DNI. Blair told the president that he would have his letter of resignation by the end of business. Word quickly leaked to the White House press corps that Blair was on his way out.

In retrospect, Blair was a tragic figure. Unlike his predecessors, he had tried to assert the authority of his office over the rest of the U.S. intelligence community, and lost his job for his troubles. He had not committed any egregious mistakes that warranted his dismissal, although he clearly failed to establish anything approaching an intimate relationship with his top client, President Obama. In his short time in office he could point to some significant successes. For instance, he had largely fixed the relationships with America's foreign intelligence partners that had been damaged during the Bush administration. Full intelligence-sharing relations were restored with New Zealand in August 2009; they had been broken off in 1985 after New Zealand refused to allow U.S. Navy warships armed with nuclear weapons to dock in its ports. Also in 2009, Canada, France, and Germany once again became full-fledged partners of the U.S. intelligence community, ending nearly seven years spent without access to high-level American intelligence because their governments had refused to back the U.S. invasion of Iraq in 2003. The only problem area was the U.S. intelligence community's relationship with the Mossad and the other Israeli intelligence services, which continued to slowly deteriorate because of differences between the two countries over whether Iran intended to build a nuclear weapon. Blair had also increased the number of intelligence resources in Afghanistan, ramped up the number of unmanned drone attacks on al Qaeda in northern Pakistan, and responded quickly to the growing narco-violence in Mexico, to name a few of his successes. Those mistakes that had been made on his watch, such as failure to "connect the dots" in the cases of Major Nidal Malik Hasan and Umar Farouk Abdulmutallab, were not in any way directly attributable to his actions.

Reflecting on these events a year later, one of Blair's former deputies said, "It just proved that the laws of physics were wrong. Shit does roll uphill."

On Saturday, May 1, 2010, at 9:30 P.M., the senior duty officer in the White House Situation Room called the National Security Council duty officer upstairs in the West Wing to tell him that three hours earlier the New York Police Department had found a 1993 Nissan Pathfinder parked at the crowded intersection of 45th Street and Broadway in the heart of Times Square containing a large homemade car bomb made from gasoline, propane, fireworks, and 250 pounds of the fertilizer ammonium nitrate, which was the same explosive used by Timothy McVeigh when he blew up the Alfred P. Murrah Federal Building in Oklahoma City on April 19, 1995, killing 168 people.

According to the first reports from the New York Police Department, the bomb had failed to detonate but had started a fire inside the vehicle. Two street vendors, Duane Jackson and Lance Orton, noticed a plume of smoke coming from the backseat of the vehicle and alerted a nearby mounted police officer. The bomb squad was called in, and the device was disarmed without any difficulty.

The Sit Room senior watch officer immediately called John O. Brennan, the president's special assistant for homeland security and counterterrorism, and briefed him over the secure telephone on what was known so far. It took a little more than an hour for Brennan to drive to the White House and read through the rapidly accumulating stack of reporting from the FBI, the Department of Homeland Security, and the New York Police Department's command center in downtown Manhattan. At 10:44 P.M., Brennan spoke briefly on the phone with David Cohen, the deputy commissioner for intelligence of the NYPD, to get the latest update, then called President Obama in the White House residence to give him a brief rundown on what was known at that point. It was the beginning of a long and arduous three days.

It took the FBI less than forty-eight hours to trace the ownership of the Nissan Pathfinder to a thirty-year-old naturalized American citizen from Pakistan named Faisal Shahzad, who was living in suburban Connecticut in the town of Shelton. Shahzad was immediately put under surveillance by the FBI and his name placed on the "Do Not Fly" watch list maintained by the Transportation Security Agency (TSA).

On Monday, May 3, Shahzad slipped his surveillance and drove to New York City on the first leg of a trip to get himself out of the country. Somehow, he managed to buy a ticket on the Emirates Airlines midnight flight to Dubai with a connection to Pakistan at the ticket counter at John F. Kennedy International Airport and board the aircraft without triggering any alert. But just as the plane was due to depart, the names of all the passengers on the flight were checked again against the TSA "Do Not Fly" watch list, and this time Shahzad's name triggered alarm bells. U.S. Customs and Border Protection agents raced to the gate and boarded the Emirates Air airliner and arrested Shahzad without a struggle. Twenty minutes later Shahzad was booked and formally charged with being the culprit behind the abortive Times Square bombing.

A memorandum on the case sent to President Obama and his homeland security policy team noted with concern that Shahzad had not had any problem getting his hands on either a handgun or the explosives for his bomb, highlighting the fact that ten years after 9/11 there are still virtually no controls in place to ensure that people like Shahzad can't get hold of these materials. In 1953, there were an estimated 10 million handguns in the United States. Today, there are an estimated 65–66 million guns in private hands in the United States, with 2.5 million new handguns being sold every year.

Shahzad had no problem buying 250 pounds of the fertilizer ammonium nitrate for his crude but potentially deadly bomb. If Shahzad's car bomb had detonated, the carnage would have been unimaginable. The only reason that dozens if not hundreds of people were not killed on the crowded sidewalks of Times Square that Saturday evening was Shahzad's crass ineptitude as a bomb maker.

Shahzad was a blank page as far as the U.S. intelligence community and state and law enforcement agencies were concerned. No one in the U.S. intelligence community or law enforcement had ever heard of Faisal Shahzad before May 1, 2010. According to a senior White House counterterrorism official, "Shahzad wasn't on our radar screen . . . NSA was not intercepting his phone calls or monitoring his e-mails. The CIA didn't know he was in Pakistan training to be a suicide bomber. Treasury did not take any note of the money being wired to him from Pakistan. And the FBI, state and local law enforcement had no file on him because he had never done anything wrong . . . He was the perfect terrorist recruit."

The FBI only learned later from Shahzad that he had returned to his native Pakistan in October 2009 for what he told friends was a family visit that lasted five months. In December 2009, he slipped away for five days to undergo an intensive course in explosives at a Pakistani Taliban training facility outside the town of Miram Shah in North Waziristan. After his training was completed, he went back to his family home to spend the holidays with his father and the rest of his family. Two months later Shahzad flew back to the United States, not telling anyone in his family that he was now a full-fledged terrorist. On February 25, 2010, a week after he had returned from Pakistan, Shahzad received $5,000 in cash that had been wired to him by a Pakistani Taliban operative in Pakistan. Six weeks later, on April 10, Shahzad got another $7,000 in cash that had been wired to him from Pakistan. Neither of these cash transfers was detected by the U.S. intelligence community because the amounts were so small.

Coming only four months after Abdulmutallab's abortive attempt to detonate a bomb on a Northwest Airlines plane over Detroit, Shahzad's admission that he was working for the Pakistani Taliban came as a major shock for the U.S. intelligence community. In early April 2009, four months before he was killed in Pakistan by a Hellfire missile fired by a CIA unmanned drone, the leader of the Pakistani Taliban, Baitullah Mehsud, had issued a warning that his group was planning to strike targets in Washington, D.C., itself. Mehsud's threat was dismissed at the time by senior U.S. intelligence officials, with one official telling the Senate intelligence committee behind closed doors in executive session that the threat was "blather." When Shahzad admitted that he was a Pakistani Taliban operative, the officials at the National Counterterrorism Center who had dismissed Mehsud's claims a year earlier were not forthcoming with an apology for having dismissed the threat so casually. Such is the way government bureaucracies work, where accountability for mistakes is often a fungible concept.

After his arrest, Shahzad made no effort to defend himself and cooperated fully with his FBI interrogators, telling them that he had nothing to hide. Shahzad admitted that his attempt at terrorism was a simple act of revenge, born of raw hatred that was not meant to right a wrong or to achieve anything tangible other than killing as many people as he could. He admitted that the bombing was planned specifically to generate as much carnage as possible. When asked later about whether he had any moral doubts about the killing of innocent civilians, such as women and children, Shahzad told his interrogators that not only was it justified, it was necessary.

At his arraignment in U.S. District Court in New York City, Shahzad freely admitted that he was the Times Square bomber, telling the presiding judge that he did what he did because he was convinced that his adopted country was trying to destroy Islam. When it came time to face judgment, Shahzad pleaded guilty to all the charges against him, and on October 5, 2010, he was sentenced to life in prison without the possibility of parole. His parting words to the court were a warning, stating that he would not be the last man to try to exact some measure of revenge for what he thought the United States was doing in the Muslim world.

Seen in retrospect, Faisal Shahzad was simply giving voice to what an entire generation of Muslims, not just the young and disenfranchised, now take as gospel. Tens of millions of Muslims, regardless of their age, social status, educational level, tribal affiliation, or country of origin, honestly believe that America is trying to destroy their religion. By failing to mount any form of an effective, sustained public diplomacy program to counter this perception, the U.S. government conceded defeat without even bothering to fight for the hearts and minds of the Muslim world. In short, the United States has now replaced Israel as the symbol of all that is evil throughout the Muslim world, giving al Qaeda, the Taliban, and every other like-minded terrorist group a virtually limitless supply of recruits and financial backers for the foreseeable future.

Even many of America's allies in the Arab world implicitly believe that there is something insidious about the U.S. government's policies in the region. One Pakistani intelligence official interviewed in 2009 made no secret of his view that "America will not be satisfied until we are all dead." A government minister in Yemen felt the same way, stating, "You [the United States] did not invade France or Germany when they disagreed with you," referring to the failure of these two countries to support the U.S.-led invasion of Iraq in 2003. "You do not bomb Tel Aviv when the Israelis kill innocent Palestinians . . . So why are we different?"

Most alarmingly, this view of the U.S. role in the Arab world is beginning to permeate the thinking of young Arab Americans here at home. This sentiment reared its ugly head at a 2009 book signing in Washington, D.C., when an American-born student of Egyptian extraction attending Georgetown University asked me a question one frequently hears across the length and breadth of the Arab world, "Why does America hate Islam?"

Since 9/11, U.S. intelligence and law enforcement officials have returned over and over again to one particularly troublesome question: Do the more than 3 million Muslims living in the United States (some estimates of the number of Muslim Americans run as high as 6 million people) constitute a potential terrorist fifth column in our midst? In the corridors of power in Washington, it is a vitally important and at the same time an enormously politically sensitive issue because it has to some degree driven the U.S. intelligence community's and our nation's law enforcement efforts to protect America from terrorist attacks over the past decade.

No government official in Washington that I have spoken to over the past several years honestly believes that the 3 million Muslim Americans constitute a fifth column. The vast majority of Muslim Americans have eagerly embraced America's democratic and multicultural traditions while at the same time proudly preserving their religious and cultural heritage. As a demographic group, they tend to be better educated than most, professionally or business oriented, economically successful, and very politically astute. Like many of their fellow Americans, Muslim Americans have tended to vote in presidential elections with their pocketbooks, hence their conservative voting habits. With a few notable exceptions, such as Senator Robert F. Kennedy's killer Sirhan Sirhan, Muslim Americans have historically rejected political violence and extremist religious views.

Until relatively recently, very few American Muslims have been involved in terrorist plots. A 2010 study done by the RAND Corporation found that between 9/11 and the end of 2009, only 125 Muslim Americans, many of whom were career criminals who had converted to Islam in prison, had been implicated in forty-six separate cases of plotting to commit terrorist acts in the United States. According to the study's author, Brian Michael Jenkins, the fact that a little more than one hundred Muslim Americans have been involved in terrorist plots indicated "an American Muslim population that remains hostile to jihadist ideology and its exhortations to violence."

However, things have been slowly but inexorably changing since 9/11. Muslim American political and community leaders sadly remember what happened during the state of siege that pervaded America after the 9/11 terrorist attacks, when the FBI and state and local law enforcement agencies furiously scoured the country looking for al Qaeda sleeper cells widely believed at the time to be hiding within the large Arab American populations in New York City, Detroit, Miami, and Los Angeles.

For all the time and effort, the FBI found only a few al Qaeda operatives in the United States. There was a thirty-two-year-old Muslim convert with a long criminal record named José Padilla, who was arrested by the FBI at Chicago O'Hare International Airport as he was returning from an al Qaeda terrorism training camp in Pakistan. Four months later, in September 2002, the FBI arrested six Americans of Yemeni descent living in Lackawanna, New York, who had received terrorist training at an al Qaeda training camp in Afghanistan before 9/11.

Thousands of ordinary Muslim illegal immigrants and political refugees living in the United States were caught up in the FBI and law enforcement dragnet, arrested, and held incommunicado in prison for months, often in solitary confinement. Their legal right of habeas corpus was declared null and void. They were detained without bond or access to legal counsel. Their right to a speedy court hearing and adjudication of their cases was suspended. Their families were not told what had become of them. They just disappeared from work or off the streets without notice.

Almost 70 percent of these unfortunates were eventually deported en masse in one of the more shameful and underreported episodes in American history, leaving behind wives and children, many of whom had been born in the United States, who suddenly had to make do without their husbands. For example, one third of the Pakistani and Bangladeshi natives living in the Brooklyn neighborhood known as "Little Pakistan" were arrested and deported in the months after 9/11. By the end of 2002, an estimated 45,000 residents of Little Pakistan had been deported or left voluntarily for countries like Canada, which had a more tolerant attitude toward immigrants from South Asia. Not one of them was ever proven to have any affiliation with al Qaeda or any other terrorist group. Their only crime was that they all had overstayed their visas and were working illegally in this country.

A former FBI special agent who specialized in counterterrorism work, who is now an attorney in private practice in New York City, said of this episode, "I lie awake at night thinking about the hundreds of guys I got tossed out of this country. I honestly don't know if I did the right thing . . . At the time I did. I thought I was protecting America. Now I'm not so sure."

Many Muslim Americans still ruminate on this episode. An official with a Muslim American political advocacy organization in Washington who wishes to remain anonymous said, "We were sleepwalking before 9/11. The way we were treated after 9/11 led some of my brothers to think that they would always be treated as second-class citizens in their own country, feared and watched. We had become 'the usual suspects.' "

What few Americans realize is that the discovery of so few al Qaeda sleeper cells in the U.S. after 9/11 led to a split within the U.S. intelligence community that still has not resolved itself. The intelligence analysts in Washington concluded that the discovery of no sleeper cells meant that the nearly 3 million Muslim Americans had rejected al Qaeda's extremist political and religious views. With few modifications, this has remained the consensus opinion of the intelligence community ever since.*

---

* A July 2007 National Intelligence Estimate on terrorism found that "the arrest and prosecution by U.S. law enforcement of a small number of violent Islamic extremists inside the United States—who are becoming more connected ideologically, virtually, and/or in a physical sense to the global extremist movement—points to the possibility that others may become sufficiently radicalized that they will view the violence here as legitimate. We assess that this internal Muslim terrorist threat is not likely to be as severe as it is in Europe, however."

But officials with America's lead agency responsible for investigating domestic terrorist acts and threats, the FBI, disagreed with this view and concluded that the internal threat was potentially more dire than what the intelligence professionals believed, taking the position that America's Muslim population represented a huge potential recruiting base for al Qaeda and other Muslim terrorist organizations that needed close scrutiny.

So since early 2002, the FBI, with the concurrence of the Department of Justice, has been engaged in a large-scale effort to monitor those Muslim American groups or individuals the bureau believes might be inclined to give aid or comfort to al Qaeda or other foreign terrorist groups.

To get a sense of how extensive the FBI's counterterrorism efforts are, consider that an estimated 10,000 FBI special agents, intelligence analysts and reporters, and technical surveillance operators are doing nothing else but working on active counterterrorism investigations, accounting for almost 40 percent of the bureau's annual budget.

Virtually every one of the FBI's fifty-six field offices and fifty resident offices across the United States has been involved in these counterterrorism operations to one degree or another. Every FBI office has its own Joint Terrorism Task Force, which coordinates all bureau counterterrorism operations in its jurisdiction. Even the FBI's tiny field office in Helena, Montana, population 29,000, has its own terrorism task force despite the fact that virtually no Muslims live in the state and there has not been a serious terrorism-related incident in the state in almost forty years, with the exception of Theodore "Ted" Kaczynski, the so-called Unabomber, who killed three people and wounded twenty-three others with mail bombs sent between 1978 and 1995 from his cabin outside Lincoln.

The FBI has also brought to bear a vast array of technical surveillance assets to covertly monitor those groups or individuals the bureau suspected of having some involvement with terrorism. The FBI's Operational Technology Division at Quantico, Virginia, intercepts targets' telephone calls, e-mails, and text messages; the National Security Agency monitors their international e-mails and phone calls.

Twenty-five miles southwest of downtown Washington, D.C., is the city of Manassas, Virginia, best known for being the site of the first and second Battles of Bull Run during the Civil War. Three miles south of the city is the Manassas Regional Airport, where on the north end of the field the FBI secretly operates a hangar complex. The sign outside identifies the occupant as a company which according to FAA data is the owner of record of ten Huey helicopters. Research at the Delaware Corporations Division revealed that the company is, in fact, an FBI front company, incorporated in Delaware in September 2000 for the purpose of providing operational cover for the FBI's surveillance flight operations at the Manassas Regional Airport.

According to flight data provided in 2010 by two amateur ham radio operators who live in the Washington metropolitan area, Manassas is the principal staging point for all FBI aerial surveillance missions over the Washington, D.C., metropolitan area. Since 2009, the ham radio operators have noted ten different FBI Cessna surveillance aircraft flying operational surveillance missions over Washington from Manassas. FBI helicopter surveillance flights over D.C. are flown from Davison Army Airfield at Fort Belvoir, Virginia. The flight-tracking logs of the amateur radio monitors show that twenty-four hours a day, seven days a week, weather permitting, FBI aircraft and helicopters equipped with the latest electro-optical, infrared, and video imaging cameras, and some of the most modern electronic surveillance equipment available, are in the air over Washington, D.C., and its surrounding suburbs.

No one seems to know for sure what the FBI is looking for on the streets and rooftops of the nation's capital every day of the week. Congressional sources confirm that these aircraft are being paid for with money appropriated by Congress specifically for counterterrorism purposes, but no official interviewed knew of any domestic terrorist threat lurking among the townhouses and upscale apartment buildings of downtown Washington that warranted this kind of 24/7 surveillance coverage by the bureau. As is so often the case, nobody on Capitol Hill seems to have performed any oversight of these surveillance activities, much less asked whether there were indeed al Qaeda terrorists walking the sidewalks of Connecticut Avenue or sitting on park benches in downtown Washington that could only be monitored by the FBI from the air.

All across America, over the past decade the FBI joint terrorism task forces have quietly been keeping close tabs on a number of Muslim political and religious organizations looking for the slightest sign of trouble. Since 9/11, the FBI has narrowed its domestic terrorism watch lists down to a relatively small number of individuals who remain under full-time surveillance to this day. According to two former FBI intelligence analysts, as of early 2009 the FBI had active case files open on several hundred individuals in the United States, including almost two dozen imams and Muslim American community leaders, all of whom were under near fulltime surveillance by the bureau.

The FBI's domestic surveillance efforts were quietly stepped up after Faisal Shahzad's failed attempt to detonate a bomb in Times Square on May 1, 2010. The abortive Times Square bombing led a number of senior FBI officials to conclude that the next terrorist threat was not al Qaeda but rather Muslim Americans like Shahzad, who were already living here in America, working normal nine-to-five jobs, biding their time, waiting for someone or something to trigger them into action. New names were added to the FBI's domestic terrorism watch lists, and investigative efforts were intensified on those individuals already suspected of ties to terrorism.

The number of these watch lists and the names on them has continued to increase in recent years. Today, nobody seems to know for certain how many of these watch lists actually exist, whose names are on them, or, more important, how these names got put on the lists in the first place. In short, there is no way of knowing who is being monitored or why.

Take for example the case of Yasir Afifi, a twenty-year-old marketing major at a community college in San Jose, California, who in October 2010 discovered while getting an oil change at a local garage that someone had hidden a GPS tracking device behind the rear exhaust of his car. One of Afifi's friends posted photographs of the device on the Web site Reddit. Two days later armed FBI agents wearing full body armor turned up at his apartment in San Jose and demanded the device back.

From the evidence available, it would appear that Afifi had done nothing wrong. Rather, the whole matter seems to be a case of guilt by association. In a lawsuit filed on March 2, 2011, by the Council on American-Islamic Relations, Afifi's lawyers alleged that he was placed under surveillance by the FBI because he traveled frequently to the Middle East and made numerous phone calls to Egypt, where two of his brothers and other family members still lived. In other words, he may have been put on an FBI watch list for no other reason than that his travel and telephone calls to Egypt led someone at the bureau to conclude that he fit the profile of a potential terrorist. Not surprisingly, the FBI refused to comment on the case.

Once someone ends up on one of the FBI's terrorism or counterintelligence watch lists, it is nearly impossible to get the person's name removed. According to a former FBI intelligence official, "Getting on a watch list is easy. All it takes is a single report, and a file is instantly opened and your name goes on one of these lists. But getting off the list is impossible. It's like proving a negative . . . There is no way that the bureau can prove that the individual is not a bad guy!"

A personal example will suffice to explain the nature of the problem. Shortly after 9/11, I gave a speech at a historical conference. After the speech was over, a man came over and asked a few pointed questions about the book I was writing at the time about the history of the National Security Agency, then gave me his business card before disappearing just as quickly as he had come. The business card identified him as a researcher with a conservative think tank, the American Enterprise Institute (AEI), giving both a telephone and fax number for him at AEI's Washington, D.C., headquarters. Only later did I learn from a fellow intelligence historian that he was, in fact, a counterintelligence officer with the National Security Agency. And his office was not at AEI in Washington, but rather at NSA's headquarters at Fort George G. Meade, Maryland, forty miles north of Washington, D.C.

At the time, it did not bother me that someone from NSA's Counterintelligence Division was checking up on what I was saying about the agency or the status of my book. I may have even found the encounter somewhat humorous, and the use of AEI as an operational cover by an NSA counterintelligence operative a bit over the top. But over time, I have often found myself wondering if the encounter was not as innocent as it sounds; if somehow I had ended up on somebody's computerized watch list. And if so, why?

Since 9/11, most of the FBI's counterterrorism surveillance efforts have centered on those major urban areas with large Muslim populations, such as New York City, Los Angeles, Detroit, Chicago, Miami, Dallas, Houston, and northern Virginia. The huge Joint Terrorism Task Force in the FBI's New York field office in downtown Manhattan has been quietly keeping tabs on a number of mosques, Muslim American political and community activist groups, and charitable organizations in New York City to ensure that they are not being used as recruiting grounds or logistical support centers for terrorists. The bureau's Detroit field office has been quietly monitoring a small number of community and religious leaders in the huge 600,000-person Muslim community in Dearborn, Michigan.

The FBI's Minneapolis–St. Paul field office has since 2007 been closely monitoring the large community of Somalis living in the area after it was discovered that twenty young Somali Americans had secretly gone to Somalia to fight with the al Qaeda–affiliated terrorist group al Shabaab. According to a senior Minnesota law enforcement official, the Abubakar as-Saddique Mosque in Minneapolis has been under surveillance by the FBI since 2009 because some of its members facilitated the travel of the Somali American teenagers to Somalia.

The bureau's Washington field office is still keeping close tabs on the activities of a number of Muslim national political activist organizations and charities based in the nation's capital. One long-standing target has been the Council on American-Islamic Relations (CAIR), the leading Muslim American political activist organization, because of allegations that it has been a front organization for the Palestinian terrorist organization Hamas.

One senior official with a D.C.-based Muslim American charitable organization recalled that in the months after 9/11, a black panel van with Virginia license plates was permanently parked near his suburban Washington home, even on holidays. None of his neighbors ever saw anyone get in or out of the vehicle, and the van's windows were tinted so that no one could see inside. When he woke up in the morning, he often found that overnight the van had changed its parking place but was still located within shouting distance of his home.

The FBI has tacitly admitted that its agents are currently conducting surveillance inside a number of mosques in the United States. However, according to an FBI spokesman, these surveillance operations only target specific individuals who are members of the mosque congregation, not the mosques as a whole. A play on words perhaps, but an important distinction since the FBI's senior leadership knows that this issue is politically explosive, as evidenced by the huge political battle taking place in New York City over plans to build a mosque near Ground Zero in Lower Manhattan.

When it comes to trying to find al Qaeda adherents hiding among the congregations at the more than 1,200 mosques in the United States, the FBI has focused its surveillance efforts on a relatively small number of mosques whose imams were known to have advocated at one time or another a more militant or extremist interpretation of the Koran than their more mainstream counterparts.

One of the radical imams that the FBI closely monitored in the months after 9/11 was Anwar al-Awlaki, then the thirty-one-year-old imam of the Dar al-Hijrah Mosque in Falls Church, Virginia, which two of the 9/11 hijackers briefly attended before the terrorist attacks.

Born in Las Cruces, New Mexico, in April 1971, al-Awlaki has a bachelor's degree in civil engineering from Colorado State University and a graduate degree in educational leadership from San Diego State University. According to law enforcement officials, al-Awlaki became radicalized after graduating from San Diego State. While preaching at the Masjid Ar-Ribat al-Islami Mosque in San Diego, California, from 1996 to 2000, he quickly attracted the attention of the FBI for his fiery sermons that came perilously close to calling for jihad.

After being repeatedly interrogated by the FBI about his alleged involvement with the 9/11 hijackers, al-Awlaki was allowed to leave the United States in late 2002. He moved to England, then two years later returned to his family's native Yemen, where he has since become a leading ideological force behind al Qaeda in the Arabian Peninsula, earning him the dubious distinction of being the first American placed on the CIA's terrorist "kill on sight" list, by President Obama in April 2010. Since then, according to a senior U.S. intelligence official, five other U.S. citizens have joined al-Awlaki on the CIA's list of individuals authorized to be killed if they are located.

Al-Awlaki may have left the United States nine years ago, but the leaders of Dar al-Hijrah mosque are still trying to repair the damage to their institution's reputation. The FBI and the 9/11 Commission found no evidence that the mosque's leaders had any role in the 9/11 terrorist attacks, but suspicion lingers on. Days after Osama bin Laden's death in Pakistan in May 2011, Dar al-Hijrah held an open house to try to build a greater sense of trust between the mosque and the local community. According to two Muslim American political leaders in Washington, congregants at Dar al-Hijrah are certain that the FBI still has agents planted among them to make sure the mosque is not being used as a recruiting ground by al Qaeda adherents.

In conversations with senior U.S. intelligence officials over the past three years, two questions came up repeatedly about the future of the American domestic counterterrorism effort. First, can the U.S. intelligence and law enforcement communities detect another terrorist plot by a "lone wolf" homegrown terrorist with no ties to al Qaeda or any other foreign terrorist group? If a number of American intelligence officials are to be believed, probably not. The second question that many lower-level counterterrorism analysts are currently asking: Is the intelligence community adapting as fast as the terrorist threat is? The answer, again, is probably no.

The biggest problem that the FBI and U.S. law enforcement are facing right now, according to intelligence officials, is that they do not understand the emerging homegrown terrorist threat. For foreign terrorist groups like al Qaeda, the U.S. intelligence community has a reasonably good understanding of the group's hierarchy, command structure, and membership list; the same cannot be said for homegrown domestic terrorists, who tend to operate alone or in extremely small cells that by their very nature are extremely difficult for the FBI or law enforcement agencies to penetrate. And as the case of Faisal Shahzad proved, existing FBI profiles of potential terrorists may be inadequate for the task at hand.

According to FBI officials who have read his case file, there was absolutely nothing in Shahzad's background or his behavior that would have attracted the attention of American counterterrorism or law enforcement officials before May 1, 2010. On the surface Shahzad was a relatively well-off family man who had never uttered an anti-American word in his life and had no discernible ties to any foreign terrorist organization. The youngest of four children, Shahzad came from a well-to-do and highly respected Pakistani family. His father, Bahar ul-Haq, was a retired air vice marshal in the Pakistani Air Force who at the time of the May Day bombing attempt was a deputy director of the Pakistani Civil Aviation Authority, Pakistan's equivalent of our Federal Aviation Administration. Shahzad had moved to the United States in January 1999, received a bachelor's and a master's degree in business administration from the University of Bridgeport in Connecticut, then worked as a financial analyst for a number of companies in the Stamford, Connecticut, area. He was married, had two vivacious children, and owned a home in a nice bedroom community in suburban Connecticut. In April 2009, he had been granted his U.S. citizenship after living in this country for ten years. Most important, he had never had any run-ins with the law except for a few speeding and parking tickets. Only after his arrest did FBI officials learn that Shahzad's personal life was not as rosy as it seemed.

Is Faisal Shahzad the model for the next generation of domestic terrorists that we will have to contend with in the future? Opinions vary widely depending on who you talk to, but virtually all of the former or current-serving officials interviewed over the past three years are concerned that the FBI and U.S. law enforcement may not be equipped to deal with this new kind of "lone wolf" terrorist. According to an e-mail received from a retired senior FBI counterterrorism official:

> The odds are the next attack will be by an American who [we] will never have heard of . . . He will probably have no criminal record or history of mental illness. He will probably be a family man . . . have

a Facebook or MySpace page. Maybe takes his kids to weekend soccer games or ballet lessons . . . All his friends and neighbors will say
that he seemed perfectly normal and did nothing out of the ordinary.

You get a clear sense of the conundrum currently facing the FBI and U.S. law
enforcement when you look at the 2010 edition of the U.S. intelligence community's guide to "Identifying Homegrown Violent Extremists Before They
Strike," prepared jointly by the National Counterterrorism Center, the Department of Homeland Security, and the FBI. The "indicators" of what America's
spies and police should be looking for contained in the document are ridicu-
lously vague, offering little, if any, concrete guidance to federal, state, and local
law enforcement officials about what they should be looking for.

For example, the document asks federal, state, and local intelligence and
law enforcement officials to forward to Washington any information received
from their sources about Americans who have "new or increased interest in
critical infrastructure locations and landmarks, including obtaining aerial
views of these locations."

This particular item produced gales of laughter at a recent gathering of intelligence analysts at a private home in the Washington suburbs, with a number of the attendees wondering if parents, teachers, and supervisors at work
should call the FBI anytime someone they know or work with shows an interest in Web sites concerning the White House, the Empire State Building, or
the Hoover Dam. One analyst questioned how anyone could be legally reported to the FBI for merely going to Google Maps and pulling up a publicly
available map or aerial photograph of the Washington Monument.

In short, we do not know where to begin in what promises to be a never-
ending quest to find the next homegrown terrorist. The intelligence community's current fixation on al Qaeda obscures the fact that one does not have to
be a Muslim to be a terrorist, or even have a political or social agenda. All it
takes to become a terrorist is a sense of rage, alienation, and resentment so
profound that violence becomes in the mind of the individual the sole viable
means of striking back. It also helps if the individual does not care if they live
or die in order to accomplish their goal. Once that line is crossed, the next
step to becoming a bona fide terrorist is simply a matter of gaining access to
guns and/or explosives, finding a target, and doing the dirty deed.

Take for example what happened on Saturday morning, January 8, 2011,
when a troubled twenty-two-year-old American named Jared Lee Loughner
joined the list of angry and alienated individuals who chose to commit mass

murder. Loughner surged into a crowd attending a political meeting outside a Safeway supermarket near Tucson, Arizona, killing six people, including U.S. district court judge John M. Roll, and wounding nineteen others, including Congresswoman Gabrielle Giffords (D-AZ), who was the target of the attack. Giffords was immensely unpopular with many conservatives in her district because of her criticism of Arizona's tough new immigration laws, as well as her vote in 2010 in favor of President Obama's national health care law.

No one yet knows if Loughner's murderous attack was prompted by disagreements with Congresswoman Gifford's liberal political positions, or if he was just trying to get his fifteen minutes of fame by killing a popular political personality as so many other mentally disturbed assassins have done before. On May 28, 2011, a judge in Arizona declared Loughner to be mentally incompetent to stand trial for the shooting spree. A mental health evaluation found that he was not only delusional, but was also schizophrenic and suffered from a severe paranoia disorder. The judge ordered that Loughner be held indefinitely in a Missouri prison hospital until he was determined to be sane enough to stand trial.

But it may not matter. Whatever the reason or reasons for his murderous rampage, Jared Loughner perhaps personifies the problem that American law enforcement now faces. On the surface Loughner was a perfectly normal individual with no prior criminal record, other than being suspended from attending the local community college for disruptive behavior. He was not a political activist, he was not a member of any extremist political or religious group, and he had never made any threatening statements against the U.S. government or any political figures. He was a blank slate as far as federal, state, and local law enforcement agencies were concerned. In effect, Jared Loughner represents the new kind of enemy that the U.S. law enforcement's vast network of agents, informers, and technical surveillance gear is worthless against.

Intelligence officials at the FBI and the Department of Homeland Security are fully aware of the long-term threat posed by this new generation of "lone wolf" domestic terrorists. They just don't know what to do about it except to periodically send out bulletins reminding all federal, state, and local law enforcement agencies to report immediately any suspicious activity that they may come across. But there is a clear sense of frustration among some law enforcement officials that they do not have the tools needed to do their job.

For example, a number of state and local police chiefs across America have for years lobbied for restrictions on who can purchase the chemical fertilizer ammonium nitrate, which Timothy McVeigh used to construct his car bomb that killed 168 people in Oklahoma City in 1995, and which is now the Taliban's explosive of choice for their IEDs in Afghanistan. Some foreign governments have moved decisively on this issue. Both the Afghan and Pakistani governments have banned the sale of ammonium nitrate to civilians. For reasons defying easy explanation, however, the U.S. government has not yet imposed any restrictions whatsoever on the sale of the chemical, even after Faisal Shahzad built a massive car bomb with this material in May 2010.

The problem for the lack of action is that the U.S. government's bureaucracy is moving forward at a snail's pace on this issue. In 2008, Congress granted the Department of Homeland Security the authority to regulate the sale and transfer of ammonium nitrate to individuals in the United States. Three years later DHS still has not acted on the mandate given to it by Congress. No rules have yet been issued stipulating who can purchase the chemical because these guidelines are still working their way through the creaky DHS bureaucracy. Is it any wonder that American law enforcement officials are becoming increasingly frustrated that a decade after 9/11 they still do not have the means at their disposal to detect and prevent a domestic terrorist attack before it happens?

Another question that government intelligence analysts are asking with greater frequency is: Are the U.S. intelligence community and American law enforcement doing anything to try to prevent Americans from becoming terrorists? Again, the answer from intelligence insiders is a resounding no.

Despite the recent spate of Americans being arrested for plotting terrorist attacks, the U.S. government is still paying virtually no attention to the question of why ordinary Americans are deciding in increasing numbers to throw their lives away and become terrorists, a process government officials call radicalization.

Over the past decade, America's European allies have invested hundreds of millions of dollars trying to get to the bottom of the radicalization problem. The British government, for example, is spending more than $200 million a year studying Muslim extremism and radicalization at home and abroad. Overseas, the British Foreign Office has funded studies of what is driving Muslim extremism in Pakistan, while at home the British government has gotten moderate British Muslim community and religious leaders to make public service announcements on television and radio and in the newspapers trying to convince their fellow Muslims that the violent extremist ideology espoused by al Qaeda and other like-minded groups violates the basic tenets of Islam and is morally wrong from any perspective.

On this side of the Atlantic, action on the problem has been notably absent. Virtually no substantive effort has been made to study the problem in depth, much less do anything about it. The Bush administration put almost no money into studying radicalization because senior U.S. government officials did not believe it was worthwhile. The Obama administration has made exactly the same mistake as the previous administration, making no effort to even look into why Faisal Shahzad and other seemingly ordinary Americans became terrorists, because, according to President Obama's counterterrorism and homeland security adviser, John O. Brennan, it "risks reinforcing the idea that the United States is somehow at war with Islam itself." So today, we have a situation where the Obama Justice Department is willing to continue the practice of spying on Muslim religious institutions in the United States looking for terrorists in their midst, but not to put any effort into finding out why a small but growing number of Muslim Americans have become involved in terrorist activities.

Some senior U.S. government officials, who did not wish to be identified because their views conflict with current White House policy, believe that this rationale for not doing anything is comparable to ignoring the problem in the hope that it will magically go away. According to a source on Capitol Hill, "We have not paid heed to the lessons that the Europeans learned a decade ago about just how difficult it is to detect and neutralize domestic terrorists . . . We will never win the war on terror unless we admit we have a problem and take steps to try to understand the causes of terrorism."

A Washington, D.C.–based nonpartisan think tank, the Bipartisan Policy Center, agreed with this sentiment, stating in a 2010 report written by two noted terrorism experts, that it is "fundamentally troubling . . . that there remains no federal government agency or department specifically charged with identifying radicalization and interdicting the recruitment of U.S. citizens or residents for terrorism."

Taking its cue from the White House, the U.S. intelligence community has also paid very little attention to the subject. The U.S. intelligence community just does not think that the subject is important enough to warrant serious study or require any action. Today, there is only one intelligence analyst at NCTC who specializes in radicalization, and although her work has received generally high praise from America's foreign partners, she has been virtually ignored by her colleagues here at home.

The U.S. intelligence community has not even tried to seriously block al Qaeda's use of the Internet to spread its message of violence and hatred. Only in the past year or so have U.S. intelligence officials publicly admitted that the Internet is a major driver of terrorist activities. According to FBI director Robert S. Mueller III, "The Internet has expanded as a platform for spreading extremist propaganda, a tool for online recruiting, and a medium for social networking with like-minded violent extremists, all of which may be contributing to the pronounced state of radicalization inside the United States." Director Mueller's views are entirely accurate, but according to current-serving bureau officials, the FBI, like the rest of the U.S. intelligence community, is currently devoting far too few resources to monitoring militant chatter on the Internet.

While the U.S. intelligence community has dawdled in responding to the homegrown terrorist threat, choosing to devote the vast majority of its resources to al Qaeda, America's European intelligence partners have not. For instance, the British intelligence services recognized years ago the inherent danger posed by homegrown terrorists and the fact that their own vast intelligence and law enforcement network may be useless against this new type of threat. According to a May 2008 secret assessment by the British foreign intelligence service, MI6, the "internal threat in the UK is growing more dangerous because extremists are conducting non-lethal training without ever leaving the country and, should they turn operational, HMG [Her Majesty's Government] intelligence resources, eavesdropping and surveillance assets would be hard pressed to find them on any 'radar screen.'"

Washington's allies in Europe are frankly baffled by the near-total lack of interest on the part of their American counterparts as to why Muslim Americans are showing an increased willingness to commit terrorist attacks. A senior European security official attributed the lack of interest within the U.S. government in the whole question of radicalization to the almost complete absence of evidence of any homegrown jihadi terror networks among America's nearly 3 million Muslim citizens found immediately after the 9/11 terrorist attacks: "When you guys found no [al Qaeda] sleeper cells after 9/11, all interest in the subject disappeared." The official added, "But things are different now . . . Many things have changed in the last ten years."

An important part of the reason why the U.S. government was not paying much attention to why a growing number of Muslim Americans were choosing to become terrorists was that the junior member of the U.S. intelligence community responsible for protecting the United States from terrorist attack—the Department of Homeland Security—was not paying nearly as much attention to the subject as it deserved.

Whether it is merited or not, no branch of the U.S. government seems to attract more derision from American government and intelligence officials than the Department of Homeland Security. Created by an act of Congress a little more than a year after the 9/11 attacks, in November 2002, conceptually DHS was supposed to be the U.S. government's all-powerful guiding brain and central nervous system responsible for bringing under one roof all of the various U.S. government agencies performing domestic intelligence, counterterrorism, and security missions, plus coordinating the efforts of the nation's 17,000 state and local law enforcement agencies, who collectively were responsible for protecting the United States from attack.

The agency that was eventually created was a shadow of what its creators envisioned. Bombarded by telephone calls from senior FBI officials and the bureau's powerful friends in Washington, all of whom demanded that the bureau's independence not be abridged, Congress decided to exempt the FBI from DHS control, which in essence neutered DHS before it was even born. Without control over the FBI, DHS was condemned in perpetuity to be nothing more than a poor cousin of the older and more politically connected bureau.

Although DHS has a congressional mandate to protect the U.S. homeland, the FBI remains, as it was before 9/11, the lead agency of the intelligence community responsible for protecting the United States from terrorist attack. In the years since 9/11, the FBI has used its considerable political clout in the White House and on Capitol Hill to strengthen its control over the homeland security mission at the expense of DHS. Not surprisingly, the current relationship between DHS and the FBI can best be characterized as tense and hypercompetitive. While intelligence analysts from the two agencies work closely together on domestic counterterrorism issues, the higher up the chain of command of both agencies you go, the less cordial the relations become. According to two congressional sources, in closed-door hearings FBI officials have never missed an opportunity to denigrate the Department of Homeland Security as part of their never-ending campaign to further strengthen the bureau's stranglehold on domestic security and counterterrorism functions in the United States.

It is an open secret in Washington that if a reporter wants a negative comment about DHS, there is no shortage of current or retired FBI officials who will happily oblige—albeit on a "not for attribution" basis. For instance, when asked for his assessment of DHS, a recently retired FBI official quipped over a beer at a downtown Washington, D.C., eatery that the "the place is literally falling apart. That's why we call it the Department of Homeland Insecurity."

During the Bush administration, DHS was so badly managed that even the staunchest of the White House's supporters on Capitol Hill despaired. Senator Jay Rockefeller (D-WV), a former chairman of the Senate intelligence committee, was so despondent about DHS and its inability to perform its domestic intelligence analysis mission that he told the 9/11 Commission that DHS was a "disaster" that was incapable of conducting its statutory domestic intelligence mission because of its "inability to stand up any kind of intelligence function."

The department's senior management was renowned for being intensely political, in large part because a large number of Bush administration political appointees were given senior management positions in the agency, none of whom were particularly well qualified for their jobs.

According to two former senior intelligence officials, DHS frittered away its resources during the Bush administration on a host of wasteful and unnecessary programs that did little to protect America from attack. For example, Vice President Dick Cheney was so concerned for his personal safety that he had the U.S. Secret Service, on orders from DHS, maintain continuous helicopter surveillance over his residence at the Naval Observatory in northwest Washington, D.C., at a cost to the taxpayers of tens of millions of dollars each year. Dozens of complaints from local residents about the noise made by these helicopters were studiously ignored by the Secret Service.

Cheney also had the Secret Service order the Internet giant Google to digitally "fuzz" the satellite images of his residence that were available on the company's Google Maps Web site, despite the fact that these same satellite images were widely available elsewhere on the Internet. No one seems to have told the Secret Service that anyone, including foreigners, could purchase these aerial photographs online for a nominal charge from the U.S. Geological Survey. Only after the Obama administration was inaugurated was the practice of "fuzzing" the satellite images of the vice president's residence halted.

Interviews with over a dozen former and current DHS intelligence officials and analysts have confirmed that the agency's intelligence organization has always been somewhat dysfunctional. The DHS's intelligence branch, known as the Office of Intelligence and Analysis, had a troubled track record during the Bush administration. One former DHS official referred to it as "the gang that could not shoot straight."

Two U.S. intelligence officials independently recalled an incident in 2006, when the Department of Homeland Security's classified daily intelligence summary carried an item that mistakenly identified the Saudi national oil company Aramco as a terrorist organization known to be linked to al Qaeda. How this item appeared in the department's daily intelligence summary without being caught in the editorial process before publication is still a source of considerable embarrassment within DHS, as evidenced by the number of robust "no comment" responses I received from government intelligence officials when I asked about the incident.

The department's intelligence organization has been beset from the beginning by weak leadership at the top and by a cadre of less than stellar middle-level managers, some of whom were castoffs from other intelligence agencies. Its young and relatively inexperienced intelligence analysts were often found to be poorly trained and got very little support from the rest of the intelligence community. DHS has been unable to effectively control the six subordinate intelligence units under its command, such as the intelligence activities of the Transportation Security Agency, Customs Service, and Border Patrol. No wonder that the rest of the U.S. intelligence community has tended to view the DHS intelligence organization like an illegitimate stepchild.

Since taking over as head of DHS intelligence in February 2010, Caryn Wagner has slowly been trying to right the ship. A number of notable improvements have been made in the way the DHS intelligence organization performs its mission, but the problems she faces are considerable. Plagued by a combination of poor management, constantly changing missions, heavy personnel turnover, and the continuing challenge of attracting and retaining talented people, morale among DHS's intelligence workforce has remained at or near rock bottom, and the DHS intelligence organization routinely comes in near the bottom of the surveys of government employees conducted annually by both the Office of Personnel Management and the director of national intelligence.

Nowhere have the problems been more apparent than with the centerpiece of the DHS intelligence organization, the network of seventy-two state- and local-run intelligence fusion centers, which are supposed to be the frontline soldiers in the war against terrorism in the United States. Each of the fifty states has its own intelligence fusion center. Twenty-two of America's largest cities also have their own, which essentially duplicate what the state fusion centers are doing.

For example, there are four intelligence fusion centers in California, all of which are to some degree duplicating each other's work. So why does California have four fusion centers? The answer is bureaucratic power politics. The Los Angeles and San Francisco mayor's offices and police departments demanded their own fusion centers because they said they needed one. It did not hurt that millions of dollars of federal and state money came with the centers, which the L.A. and San Francisco police departments desperately needed to make up for budget shortfalls. No one in Washington or in the state capital in Sacramento apparently bothered to ask if the redundancy was necessary.

California, according to a former DHS intelligence official, is just another example of the fact that "there are too many vested interests now perpetuating an entire layer of inefficient, ineffective resources." The official asked a trenchant question, "Why did Idaho need a whole FC [fusion center] devoted to terrorism issues? Montana? New Mexico? They all jumped on the bandwagon in a race to get federal and state homeland security dollars. But terrorism only keeps them busy for about fifteen minutes a day."

DHS is nominally responsible for helping fund the centers. Since 2004, it has pumped over $425 million into them. But because the fusion centers are controlled by the states or municipalities where they are located, DHS has had very little say in how the money it gave them was spent—or misspent, as has often been the case. A number of senior DNI and DHS intelligence officials admit that the money that has been spent on the fusion centers is but a fraction of what is needed to allow these units to perform their mission. DHS's budget is limited, and the states and cities are so strapped because of the current financial crisis that they are being forced to make cutbacks in funding for the fusion centers in order to keep police stations open and cops on the beat. Two California state law enforcement officials admitted in recent interviews that their state's depressed financial status means that they are going to have to cut back on spending on their fusion centers unless DHS can somehow make up the difference.

As originally envisioned, DHS was supposed to feed the fusion centers with high-level intelligence information derived from national sources about terrorist threats to their communities. But state and local intelligence officials interviewed for this book acknowledge that the quality of the intelligence information they received from DHS was usually not germane to their localities. A Las Vegas police official admitted at a recent national conference of state and local law enforcement officers that the daily intelligence bulletins that he got from DHS in Washington rarely had any items that were pertinent to his department's concerns. "I get better intel from the casino security chiefs than from Washington," he said.

Intelligence officials in Washington admit that some of the fusion centers have proven to be better run and to produce better intelligence than others. The well-funded New York State Intelligence Center in Albany generally gets high marks for the above-average quality of its work. A number of senior intelligence officials in Washington heaped considerable praise on the reporting and analysis produced by the New York Police Department Intelligence Division, headed by David Cohen, the head of the CIA's clandestine service from 1995 to 1997. Studies produced over the past several years by the NYPD on how European countries are combating Muslim radicalization and how the Israeli police and security services handle counterterrorism were rated as being particularly insightful by DNI officials in Washington.

But since the first fusion center was opened in 2006, DHS has failed to regulate them. A number of senior intelligence officials admit that the quality of the intelligence reporting emanating from the fusion centers leaves much to be desired. At times it has been of such poor quality that it has proven to be embarrassing for intelligence officials in Washington. A senior DNI intelligence official recalled an incident in 2009, when one of his aides brought him a secret intelligence report produced by one of the Texas intelligence fusion centers that was lifted almost word for word from an ultraconservative Web site that openly advocated harsh measures to stem the flow of illegal immigrants into the United States. The incident was particularly mortifying for the official because his boss had earlier that day testified before the House intelligence oversight committee about the dramatic improvements that had been made in the quality of the analysis coming out of the U.S. intelligence community.

The crux of the problem is that these state and local intelligence fusion centers are not subject to the same rigorous fact-checking and editorial quality-control standards that are the norm in the U.S. intelligence community. According to a senior DHS official, the biggest problem that he has experienced is that these centers are run by cops who have little if any prior intelligence experience. "They don't know it; they don't understand it; and they don't want to do it," the official stated in a recent interview. According to the DHS official, many of the state and local law enforcement officials who are in charge of the fusion centers have ruthlessly taken the money they get gratis from DHS and then, without informing Washington, have converted their centers from counterterrorism analysis to criminal investigation in clear violation of the intent behind the creation of the fusion centers.

The result is that much of what passes for intelligence coming out of the fusion centers has nothing to do with counterterrorism whatsoever. For example, the August 6, 2010, daily intelligence report issued by the Central Florida Intelligence Exchange, a state-run fusion center in Orlando, reported on its front page that Dondi, an Asian elephant, had died suddenly at the Southwick Zoo outside Boston, Massachusetts, at the ripe old age of thirty-six. The center reported Dondi's passing because during the winter months she performed at an establishment known as Flea World in Sanford, Florida, and the fusion center was using the report to alert state and local police that animal rights activists might stage protests at Flea World to mark her death in captivity.

CHAPTER 7

Distant Battlefields

Mission Creep and the U.S. Intelligence Community

All the business of war, and indeed the business of life, is to endeavor to find out what you don't know by what you do; that's what I called "guessing what was on the other side of the hill."

—ARTHUR WELLESLEY, 1ST DUKE
OF WELLINGTON

On June 5, 2010, just two weeks after Denny Blair had vacated the DNI's office at Liberty Crossing, President Obama appeared in the White House Rose Garden with his new pick to head the nation's intelligence community, retired U.S. Air Force Lt. General James R. Clapper Jr. Clapper and the president had met for the first time only a month earlier in a May 6 private meeting in the Oval Office, where Obama asked the general if he would take over as DNI. Clapper said yes, subject to the president letting him run his organization in his way.

Genial and easygoing, the sixty-nine-year-old Clapper had spent his entire forty-five-year career in intelligence, beginning as an air force lieutenant flying airborne signals intelligence collection missions over Laos and South Vietnam during the Vietnam War in the 1960s. Renowned for his sense of humor, Clapper hated bureaucracy and was not afraid to mix it up with his superiors. While head of the National Geospatial-Intelligence Agency, Clapper clashed repeatedly with Secretary of Defense Donald Rumsfeld for advocating that his agency and the rest of the Pentagon's intelligence organizations be placed under the command of the newly created office of the director of national intelligence. Rumsfeld, a fierce opponent of the creation of the DNI's office, and intelligence reform in general, rejected Clapper's proposal and forced him out of his post as head of NGA in June 2006.

Clapper did not have to wait long to get back into the game. In November 2006, President Bush forced Rumsfeld out of office and replaced him as secretary of defense with Robert M. Gates. Among Secretary Gates's first decisions was to completely overhaul the Pentagon's massive intelligence establishment, which was headed at the time by Stephen A. Cambone, whose reputation within the intelligence community left much to be desired. Cambone resigned in January 2007, and within days Gates nominated Clapper to replace Cambone as undersecretary of defense for intelligence.

With the exception of a few members of Congress who wanted a career civilian official at the helm of the intelligence community, President Obama's decision to nominate Clapper to be the new DNI was met with approval by the Washington establishment because of his long experience in the intelligence world. A now retired senior intelligence official who served under Clapper during the Bush administration said of him, "Jim's a really great guy. Funny, sharp-witted, completely apolitical, and smart as hell . . . He knows the intelligence business better than just about anybody I know."

But there were those within the intelligence community, many of whom were angry about Denny Blair's firing, who were not happy with Clapper's nomination, largely because they viewed him as too committed to keeping the Pentagon's intelligence resources divorced from the control of the office of the DNI. One of Denny Blair's former aides warned, "Don't overestimate him [Clapper]. He seems warm and cuddly. But he's not the expert that everyone makes him out to be."

Clapper inherited the same predicament as his predecessor sixteen months earlier, only he had more resources to play with. The U.S. intelligence community was slightly larger (210,000 people), and its annual budget had risen to $80.1 billion, equal to the combined amount spent by the U.S. Departments of Transportation and Education. Other government departments were having their budgets slashed, but not the intelligence community, which continued to get pretty much what it wanted. A May 2011 report to the president revealed that in addition to the money spent on intelligence, the U.S. government was spending $10.1 billion trying to keep its classified information a secret, which included the hefty sums currently being spent to upgrade the security of a variety of computer systems holding classified information in the aftermath of the massive leak of classified Pentagon and State Department documents to WikiLeaks in 2010.

But the intelligence community was still failing to get its sometimes contrarian views taken seriously within the Obama administration. For instance, the White House and the Pentagon were still locked in a contest of wills with the intelligence community about how the wars in Afghanistan and neighboring Pakistan were going. The intelligence community's view in the summer of 2010 was that they were not going well. The intelligence analysts at Liberty Crossing took the position that the military situations in both countries were largely locked in a stalemate, which was not what the White House or the Pentagon wanted to hear. Having promised to begin withdrawing U.S. combat troops from Afghanistan in July 2011, the Obama administration urgently needed some proof to demonstrate that progress was being made on these fronts. According to intelligence insiders, the White House and the Pentagon began following the Bush administration's penchant of ignoring or suppressing any information from the intelligence community that reflected negatively on how the wars in Afghanistan and Pakistan were progressing, while at the same time spinning a message that dramatic progress was being made on the battlefield.

Today, the disconnect between what the White House and Pentagon are publicly saying and the stark reality on the battlefields in Afghanistan and Pakistan has once again become as apparent as it was during the Bush administration. Take for example the classified report submitted to President Obama on December 16, 2010, which concluded that the White House's strategy in Afghanistan and Pakistan was "showing progress." In Afghanistan, the report asserted, General David H. Petraeus, who arrived in Kabul in June 2010 to replace General Stanley A. McChrystal as commander of U.S. and NATO forces in Afghanistan, had managed to right the ship, and the Taliban's momentum had been "arrested in much of the country and reversed in some key areas." In neighboring Pakistan, the report boldly announced, "significant progress [had been made] in disrupting and dismantling the Pakistan-based leadership and cadre of al-Qaeda over the past year." Curiously, it said nothing about whether the Pakistani military and intelligence service had made any effort to go after Mullah Omar's Afghan Taliban forces hiding in the northern part of their country or had made any progress attacking the militant Pakistani Taliban strongholds in the FATA.

At almost the same time President Obama's status report was released, two highly classified National Intelligence Estimates on Afghanistan and

Pakistan, which were prepared by the national intelligence officer for South Asia, Dr. Neil H. Joeck, were sent to Washington policymakers, contradicting much of what was contained in the unclassified version of the president's progress report. The intelligence estimate on Afghanistan painted a particularly bleak picture of the situation. According to the estimate, the "positive trends" that the White House was claiming were based solely on relatively minuscule improvements in the security status of five districts in Kandahar and Helmand provinces. The gains that had been made were extremely tenuous, leaving both provinces still very much up for grabs. In other key provinces, like Paktika in eastern Afghanistan, the report showed that the Taliban were still prevailing, with some districts in the province being 80–90 percent controlled by the insurgents. These were hardly impressive indicators of success. According to a Canadian intelligence officer interviewed after he returned from a tour of duty in Afghanistan in the spring of 2011, the Taliban used the winter months to reinfiltrate hundreds of fighters into the districts cleared during the fall.

Left unsaid in the estimate was that it is now widely accepted inside the U.S. intelligence community that, barring a complete collapse of the Taliban from within, it is probably not possible to defeat them militarily, no matter how many more American troops are sent to Afghanistan. Not only were the Taliban continuing to gain strength and expand the scope and intensity of their operations, but their underground "shadow governments" were now probably dug in too deep to be uprooted, especially in the rural areas of southern and eastern Afghanistan.

If one accepts this basic premise, as many (but not all) intelligence officials do, then direct negotiations with Mullah Omar's Taliban are an unpalatable but necessary step if the war in Afghanistan is to be resolved. Secret peace negotiations with the Taliban are currently taking place outside of Afghanistan with Mullah Omar's representatives. The United States is directly involved in the talks, as well as a number of NATO governments and Hamid Karzai's Afghan regime. But the outcome of these talks is very much up in the air. With President Obama facing what promises to be a stiff reelection fight in 2012, there is only a very narrow window of opportunity to ink a deal with the Taliban, because no one seeking the Oval Office wants to be seen as negotiating with terrorists.

Pakistan remains an even more complex and perhaps intractable problem. According to Ambassador Richard Holbrooke, President Obama's special adviser on Afghanistan and Pakistan, "Pakistan may be a knot that we may never be able to untangle." The intelligence community's view was that the security situation in Pakistan, while significantly better than it was in 2009, was nowhere near as good as President Obama's progress report made it out to be.

According to the December 2010 National Intelligence Estimate, Pakistan remained a safe haven for virtually every major terrorist or insurgent group on the U.S. intelligence community's "Most Wanted" list. Osama bin Laden may be dead, killed in Abbottabad in northern Pakistan on May 1, 2011, but his deputy, Ayman al-Zawahiri, and the rest of al Qaeda's leadership are still hiding in northern Pakistan. In the aftermath of the killing of bin Laden, questions are now being asked in the United States and Pakistan about whether the terrorist leader was protected by the ISI or elements of the Pakistani security forces. Mullah Mohammed Omar and the rest of the Afghan Taliban's leadership continue to operate freely inside Pakistan with the apparent blessing of the Pakistani government. Tens of thousands of heavily armed extremist fighters belonging to the Pakistani Taliban still control huge segments of the lawless tribal areas of northern Pakistan. Pakistan is also the home for over a dozen other homegrown terrorist groups, which the Pakistani government refuses to go after, despite intense pressure from the U.S. government, because almost all of them were created decades ago by the Pakistani intelligence service to serve as covert proxy foot soldiers in Pakistan's never-ending war against neighboring India over the disputed province of Kashmir.

Even with incessant pushing and prodding by Washington over the past three years, and the presence of 140,000 heavily armed Pakistani troops and paramilitary forces in the region, the Pakistani military seems unwilling to make a concerted effort to clear the Federally Administered Tribal Areas of the Pakistani Taliban and their Afghan Taliban and al Qaeda allies. The attacks that the Pakistani military made into the FATA in 2010 achieved very limited short-term gains, which the Pakistanis then promptly surrendered to the Taliban after their troops returned to their barracks. The frustration of the Obama White House with the Pakistani military was all too apparent in an earlier report sent to Congress in September 2010, which stated that "unless these challenges are overcome, the Government of Pakistan risks allowing the insurgency the opportunity to reestablish influence over a population that remains skeptical of its staying power."

So the unmanned drone remains the only reliable weapon available to the U.S. intelligence community to go after al Qaeda targets inside Pakistan. In 2010, the CIA carried out 112 drone attacks on al Qaeda and Taliban targets in northern Pakistan, double the number of attacks in the previous year, according to figures published by the authoritative Web site *The Long War Journal*. These drone attacks proved to be far more lethal than in previous years, thanks to a new generation of technical intelligence sensors, such as automated cell phone intercept and unattended ground sensor systems, which have vastly shortened the interval between the time that an al Qaeda target was located in northern Pakistan and the time that a drone could put a missile on the target in the FATA. These new sources have also allowed the CIA to dramatically lessen its dependence on the Pakistani intelligence service, whose agent sources have become viewed at Langley as increasingly unreliable.

While the number of al Qaeda and Taliban fighters killed inside Pakistan jumped significantly in 2010, a small but vocal group of mid-level intelligence officials at DNI headquarters has argued that classified statistics showed that the vast majority of the militants being killed were low-level fighters, not high-level commanders. This argument is supported by a tally compiled by Reuters, which showed that the CIA drone strikes had killed about five hundred al Qaeda and Pakistani Taliban militants during the two-year period from May 2008 to May 2010. Of the five hundred dead, only fourteen were rated by the intelligence community as senior "high-value" al Qaeda or Taliban officials, and another twenty-five were rated as being mid-level al Qaeda militants.

Events that have taken place in Pakistan since the issuance of President Obama's December 2010 progress report reveal just how dangerous the situation had become. On December 16, 2010, the same day that the report was issued in Washington, the secret war in Pakistan claimed its most important victim. It wasn't a senior al Qaeda commander hit by a missile in the FATA. Nor was it a Taliban commander grabbed by a U.S. Special Forces "capture-kill" team.

The victim was Jonathan D. Bank, the CIA station chief in Islamabad. A veteran of several high-profile assignments in the Middle East and elsewhere around the world, Bank had replaced John Bennett as head of the Islamabad station in the summer of 2009.

The weapon that suddenly ended his tenure in Islamabad was not a bullet, a missile, or a bomb. It was a lawsuit filed in the city of Peshawar on December 10, 2010, by a Pakistani journalist named Karim Khan, which alleged that Bank and his boss, CIA director Leon Panetta, were responsible for the deaths of Khan's brother and son, who were killed in a CIA drone strike at Mir Ali in North Waziristan a year earlier, in December 2009.

On December 16, 2010, CIA headquarters sent a flash "Eyes Only" message to Bank advising him that his cover had been blown and ordering him to leave the country immediately. Station security personnel hustled Bank to the airport in a convoy of black armored SUVs, where he was put on a plane bound for the United States along with a security escort.

Bank's hasty departure was big news in India and Pakistan, where newspapers splashed his name and Khan's allegations all over the front pages. Back in Washington, CIA officials were furious. Unidentified CIA officials told the *New York Times* and the *Washington Post* that they "strongly suspected" that Bank's name had been leaked by ISI officials in retaliation for the filing of a lawsuit in federal court in Brooklyn, New York, in November 2010, which alleged that the current director of the ISI, General Ahmad Shuja Pasha, was partly responsible for the November 26, 2008, terrorist attack in Mumbai, India, by the Pakistan-based terrorist group Lashkar-e-Taiba that killed 173 people. ISI officials vehemently denied this charge.

In the months that followed, the CIA-ISI intelligence relationship rapidly went from bad to worse. On January 27, 2011, Raymond A. Davis, a thirty-six-year-old CIA contract security officer stationed in the U.S. consulate in Lahore, Pakistan, was arrested by Pakistani police after he killed two Pakistanis he claimed had tried to rob him in broad daylight at a busy intersection. The case caused an immediate sensation in the Pakistani press and quickly became a diplomatic incident when the Pakistani government refused to honor Davis's diplomatic status, holding him in prison pending trial for murder.

Pakistani security officials further inflamed the situation by leaking details of the matter to the local press, including the fact that Davis, a former Special Forces soldier, was working for the CIA. Davis spent several weeks in prison, then was released and quietly flown out of Pakistan after the CIA made what was described a large "blood money" payment to the families of the two slain men.

When the Pakistani government initially would not release Davis, the CIA suspended all intelligence-sharing activities with the Pakistani government and the ISI. In retaliation, the Pakistanis halted all joint intelligence collection programs with the CIA and the rest of the U.S. intelligence community, including a number of joint human intelligence collection projects in the FATA, and banned the CIA from using Pakistani airfields for unmanned drone flights over northern Pakistan. A number of CIA case officers and contractors were also ordered to leave the country immediately.

The killing of Osama bin Laden on May 1, 2011, in Abbottabad only further inflamed the already deeply troubled relations between the CIA and the ISI. On Saturday, May 7, 2011, a private Pakistani television network and a right-wing newspaper published the name of the new CIA station chief in Islamabad a day after the chief of ISI and the CIA station chief had held an angry meeting in Islamabad over the killing of bin Laden. Although the name given in the broadcast and the newspaper article was incorrect (the name given in the Pakistani press was Mark Carlton), CIA officials immediately claimed that the name had been leaked to the press by the ISI in retaliation for the embarrassment caused by the killing of Osama bin Laden on Pakistani soil. The Pakistanis then arrested five of the Pakistani military officers and police officials who had helped the CIA monitor bin Laden's home in Abbottabad, and ordered the immediate closure of three intelligence fusion centers that U.S. special forces were secretly running in Peshawar and Quetta.

At the time that this manuscript went to press in mid-2011, U.S.-Pakistani intelligence relations had reached their lowest levels since 9/11. Officials in Washington confirmed that intelligence cooperation between the two countries had come to almost a complete stop. When asked to comment about the state of his agency's relations with Pakistan, a senior CIA official put it bluntly: "They couldn't be much worse than they are right now."

A typical New Year's Day in Washington, D.C., is a surreal experience. The streets are almost completely empty of cars, and the sidewalks empty of people. In a town of serial workaholics, January 1 is one of the very few days of the year when the city's population of politicians, government workers, and lobbyists are not at the office working a typical ten- to twelve-hour day. It may be one of the very few days of the year when you can actually be assured of reaching people at home because they are all parked in front of their television sets watching a never-ending series of college football games.

New Year's Day 2011 was no different. But breaking with tradition, I abandoned my television set and attended a party at a private home in the Washington suburbs because I was promised that a number of senior intelligence officials would be present. The talk among the multitude of diplomats and spies in attendance centered on a polite debate as to whether the wars in Afghanistan and Pakistan were going as well as President Obama said they were. But in one knot of partygoers the conversation focused on a topic that at the time I did not think was particularly important—the Middle East.

Almost everyone participating in the conversation was of the opinion that the Middle East and North Africa had become a backwater on the global stage, upstaged by the more pressing events taking place in Afghanistan and Pakistan. There was a dissenting voice, though. One State Department official, apparently a veteran Middle East hand, was not so sure. "Things have been too quiet over there for too long. I think something's going to blow," he intoned with great seriousness. Judging by the derisive comments his assessment received, he was clearly a minority of one.

It is easy to see why no one thought that the Middle East or North Africa warranted much serious concern at the time. The region had been remarkably quiet during President Obama's first two years in office. The Israeli and Syrian militaries had not fired a shot at one another in almost five years, and the number of terrorist attacks inside Israel since Obama became president could be counted on one hand. The rest of the region seemed, at least on the surface, relatively peaceful.

That changed rapidly in the days immediately after New Year's as waves of popular unrest exploded across the region. On January 14, 2011, massive nationwide protests forced Tunisian president Zine El Abidine Ben Ali, a longtime U.S. ally, to resign and flee the country. Less than a month later, on February 11, Egyptian president Hosni Mubarak was forced to step down from his post after eighteen days of public demonstrations on the streets of Egypt's cities.

The U.S. intelligence community had been reporting for years that popular unrest with the Ben Ali and Mubarak regimes was building, but according to a senior U.S. intelligence official, nobody at DNI headquarters at Liberty Crossing foresaw that mass street demonstrations would lead to the collapse of both the Tunisian and Egyptian regimes. The thinking among the intelligence analysts at the time was that the massive police and security services of both countries were more than capable of suppressing any public unrest. The analysts were wrong.

It is small comfort, but all of our foreign intelligence allies, many of whom have better connections in the region than the United States, also did not see the unrest coming. According to a senior CIA official, the Mossad incorrectly predicted that Hosni Mubarak would be able to ride out the mass demonstrations in downtown Cairo without any difficulty. And the French foreign intelligence service, which had agents operating at all levels of the Tunisian government, had no inkling that the Ben Ali regime was so structurally weak that it would collapse of its own volition.

The collapse of the Mubarak regime in Egypt will almost certainly have serious long-term consequences for the U.S. intelligence community's efforts in the Middle East, especially in the realm of counterterrorism. Leaked State Department cables show that for twenty years the U.S. intelligence community enjoyed excellent relations with all four of Egypt's intelligence and security services. Particularly important was the CIA's intimate relationship with the Egyptian General Intelligence and Security Service (Al-Mukhabarat al-'Ammah), headed by Major General Omar Suleiman, which worked closely with Langley combating terrorism in the countries around Egypt, spying on the terrorist group Hamas in the Gaza Strip, as well as acting as a middleman during the on-again, off-again Arab-Israeli peace negotiations. The FBI worked closely with the Egyptian State Security Service (Jihaz Amn al Daoula), headed by Hassan Abdul Rahman, which was the principal agency for combating terrorism and militant extremism inside Egypt, as well as crushing political dissent. On foreign intelligence matters, the CIA and the DIA (Defense Intelligence Agency) depended on the Egyptian Military Intelligence Service (Mukhabarat el-Khabeya), which monitored all external threats to Egypt, including Israel, Sudan, and Libya.

In the weeks that followed the collapse of the Tunisian and Egyptian regimes, mass street demonstrations, some of them violent, erupted in Bahrain, Jordan, and Yemen, all American allies. This marked the beginning of what has since become known as the "Arab Spring." The Obama administration was particularly concerned about the potential collapse of the government of Bahrain, which in addition to being a key ally in the war on terrorism is the headquarters of the U.S. Navy's Fifth Fleet and homeport for all American warships operating in the Persian Gulf. A small detachment of U.S. Navy SIGINT aircraft, which fly daily intelligence collection missions off the coast of Iran, operates from the airbase outside the Bahraini capital of Manama. The Bahraini military and police were ordered to break up the protests by force. In the ensuing street battles, hundreds of protesters were killed or wounded.

Another country engulfed in violence following the fall of the Tunisian and Egyptian governments was Libya, whose leader, Colonel Muammar Qaddafi, has for more than forty years been America's principal antagonist in North Africa. In February 2011, street protests erupted throughout Libya, quickly leading to a full-scale armed revolt across the country. The fighting spread to the capital of Tripoli by February 20. Opponents of Qaddafi took control of the city of Benghazi and by early March had evicted pro-government forces from all of eastern Libya. By March 2011, Libya was embroiled in a full-scale civil war. Qaddafi's forces controlled most of western Libya, while the rebels, who controlled the eastern part of the country, were led by a group based in Benghazi styling itself as the Transitional National Council, headed by former Libyan minister of justice Mustafa Abdul Jalil.

By mid-March 2011, the U.S. intelligence community was fully involved in the fighting inside Libya. CIA paramilitary personnel were operating on the ground in eastern Libya. Administration officials claimed that they were there only to "assess the situation." In fact, they were helping direct air strikes against Qaddafi's forces and helping British and French intelligence personnel funnel arms shipments to the Libyan rebels, as well as trying to determine if any of the Libyan rebels were allied with al Qaeda or other Muslim militant organizations.

As time went by, more American intelligence-gathering resources were deployed to Sigonella Air Base on the island of Sicily, from where U.S. and NATO operations against Libya were being run. The CIA reportedly established a headquarters on the base to direct all of the agency's operations inside Libya. U.S. Air Force RC-135 SIGINT aircraft based at Souda Bay on the Greek island of Crete were being used to monitor Libyan air force and air defense communications. On March 21, 2011, President Obama authorized the use of Predator unmanned drones to identify the locations of pro-Qaddafi forces so that they could be hit with air strikes by U.S. and NATO forces. The end, when it came, was anticlimactic. In mid-August 2011, Qaddafi's forces collapsed and the Libyan rebels rolled into Tripoli virtually unopposed on August 22, 2011, all without the help of the U.S. military or intelligence community.

There is one country in the Middle East where the CIA has been actively trying to foment civil unrest for years. The country is Syria, another longtime nemesis of the United States because of its opposition to a peaceful settle of the Arab-Israeli conflict and its support of foreign terrorist groups, both dating back decades.

After 9/11, intelligence sources confirm, the Bush administration authorized a series of covert action operations designed to promote internal and external opposition to the Syrian regime. The CIA and the British foreign intelligence service, MI6, began actively providing covert financial support to a number of London-based opposition groups seeking to overthrow the regime of Syrian strongman Bashar al-Assad. Some of the leaders of these groups had fled to London after the Syrian military brutally crushed a popular uprising in the city of Hama in 1982.

Although not explicitly stated, the purpose of these covert operations was to unseat Assad, who has ruled Syria since his father, Hafez al-Assad, died in

2000. If the U.S. government had hoped that the younger Assad would moderate his father's hard-line anti-Israeli policies and support for terrorism, these hopes were quickly dashed. Assad has continued to thumb his nose at the United States since Obama became president in 2009. Assad has strengthened his country's long-standing alliance with Iran, and Syria remains firmly opposed to any attempt to peacefully resolve existing Arab-Israeli disputes, such as the Palestinian problem in the West Bank and the Gaza Strip.

According to U.S. intelligence officials, Syria remains one of the top state sponsors of terrorism in the world. Together with Iran, Syria is a major backer of the militant Shiite group Hezbollah in Lebanon and of Hamas in the Gaza Strip, giving Damascus an extraordinary degree of influence over Lebanese politics and the Arab-Israeli peace process.

Classified intelligence reports reviewed by the author reveal that the two top Syrian intelligence services, Syrian Military Intelligence and the General Intelligence Directorate, continue to covertly permit Iraqi insurgents and foreign fighters belonging to al Qaeda in Iraq to freely operate from its soil. Syria's not-so-secret involvement in the war in Iraq between 2003 and 2008 was considerable. According to a study done for the Marine Corps Intelligence Activity by the Center for Naval Analyses, "Inside Syria, [Iraqi] insurgent leaders could take refuge, financiers could organize money flows into Al Anbar [Province], foreign fighters could transit en route to Al Anbar, and insurgent cadres could even establish a few training camps. The Syrian government seemed to turn a blind eye to much of this activity, although they never allowed insurgents to truly mass inside their territory."

Attempts to modify Syria's behavior through the imposition of harsh economic sanctions have not worked. Intelligence reports show that Iran has provided Damascus with substantial economic subsidies to keep the Syrian economy afloat, and Russia has covertly provided the Syrian military with modern weapons and technological assistance in violation of U.S.-backed economic sanctions.

It is not known at present if the CIA has attempted to take advantage of the civil unrest that has wracked Syria since the collapse of the Ben Ali and Mubarak regimes in Tunisia and Egypt in early 2011. The Syrian military and security forces have been aggressive in the efforts to suppress the popular uprising, using tanks and elite commando units to quell anti-government demonstrations. Thousands have died in the fighting, which is still continuing as this book heads to press. According to a British security source, since the unrest began, a number of the London-based groups supported by the CIA and MI6 have been actively involved in beaming news and video podcasts into Syria over the Internet using social media vehicles such as Facebook and Twitter.

Iraq, the U.S. intelligence community's top priority for much of the past decade, has not been affected by the popular unrest sweeping the rest of the Middle East, but the country remains in a state of flux. Despite the fact that the Iraqi insurgency was soundly defeated in 2007, the U.S. intelligence community continues to hold that without a comprehensive and binding resolution to the outstanding political differences between the country's Shiite majority and the minority Sunnis and Kurds, all of the progress that had been achieved on the battlefield could easily collapse overnight. Even General David H. Petraeus, the architect of the 2007 victory over the Iraqi insurgents, remains concerned, telling a group of analysts in Washington in June 2009 that the security situation in the country was, in his opinion, still "fragile and reversible."

Al Qaeda in Iraq is still very much alive and carrying out terrorist attacks, but it is much smaller and far less capable than it was in its heyday prior to the 2007 Baghdad surge. It is probably purely coincidental, but the number of deadly suicide bombings in Iraq has been steadily rising since Obama's inauguration in 2009. Moreover, Sunni insurgent groups have begun resurrecting themselves in Al Anbar Province, recruiting Sunni officers in the Iraqi Army and the tribal "Awakening Council" militias created and funded by the United States in 2007.

In another ominous portent of things yet to come, the U.S. government's relations with Nuri al-Maliki's Iraqi government have been slowly slipping because the Baghdad regime has been quietly moving away from the United States toward closer ties with Iran. Iran's ability to influence the policies of the Iraqi government is a source of heated debate within the U.S. government and intelligence community, although nobody disputes the fact that the Iranian intelligence services are striving to ensure that the policies of al-Malaki are to Tehran's liking.

There is, however, widespread agreement within the intelligence community that Iran's attempts to influence Iraqi politics are not directed by its diplomats, but rather by the operatives of the Iranian foreign intelligence organization, the Quds Force. According to a leaked 2009 State Department cable, "Since at least 2003, Brigadier General Qasem Soleimani, the commander of the Islamic Revolutionary Guards Corps–Qods Force (IRGC-QF), has been the point man directing the formulation and implementation of the

[Iranian government's] Iraq policy . . . Through his IRGC-QF officers and Iraqi proxies in Iraq, notably Iranian Ambassador and IRGC-QF associate Hassan Kazemi-Qomi, Soleimani employs the full range of diplomatic, security, intelligence, and economic tools to influence Iraqi allies and detractors in order to shape a more pro-Iran regime in Baghdad and the provinces."

Because of the concern that al-Maliki's Iraqi government might move toward rapprochement with Iran, the CIA station in Baghdad has devoted significant resources to closely following the inner workings of the al-Maliki government and its policies toward Iran. According to a senior U.S. intelligence official, we have al-Maliki's government "wired from top to bottom." It goes without saying that the CIA station is also paying close attention to the activities of Iran's spies in Iraq.

Washington's concerns about the future political course of the Iraqi government are shared by some senior Iraqi security officials, who fear that Prime Minister al-Maliki's government is inept, corrupt, and incapable of fairly addressing the Sunni minority's concerns in a country where Shiites constitute the vast majority of the population. According to an Iraqi security official interviewed in 2010, "Malaki is weak and too dependent on the Shiite parties like [hard-line Iraqi Shiite politician Moqtada al-] Sadr. . . . He will move us towards Tehran. God help us. I know he will."

Seeking a glimpse of an intelligence battlefield of the future, one need look no further than the tiny Persian Gulf mini-state of Dubai, which is one of the seven principalities that comprise the United Arab Emirates. Only about 17 percent of Dubai's 2.2 million inhabitants are Emiratis. The rest come from India, Pakistan, the Philippines, and over two dozen other nations; among them are several thousand American expatriates, all of whom have flocked to Dubai because of the emirate's massive wealth.

From an intelligence standpoint, Dubai is critically important because it has become a global financial powerhouse, replacing Beirut as the banking center and tax shelter of choice for the rich and powerful of the Middle East. If there is a major business transaction taking place anywhere in the Middle East or Near East, whether a sale on the world petroleum market or a major construction project, chances are very good that a bank or investment house in Dubai is financing the deal.

Over the past decade, Dubai and the other principalities comprising the United Arab Emirates have become the principal source of financing for Mullah Omar's Taliban guerrillas and all of the Afghan drug kingpins. According to a leaked September 2009 State Department cable, "It comes as no surprise that Taliban financing originates in and transits the UAE to Afghanistan and third countries. Afghan drug proceeds, including laundered funds, both transit the UAE and are invested here. Cash couriers are believed to carry the majority of illicit funds to and from Afghanistan." The cable went on to note that the U.S. Drug Enforcement Administration believed that "over $2 billion in drug proceeds has transited through the UAE over the last three years."

Dubai's position as the leading banking center in the Middle East has made it a mecca for spies from around the world. According to senior U.S. intelligence sources, Dubai is today the principal listening post for monitoring what is taking place across the Persian Gulf inside America's arch-nemesis in the region, the Islamic Republic of Iran, led by an aging conservative religious autocracy that derives its strength from feeding its people with the notion that they are beset on all sides by enemies. The Iranian government's aggressive, some would say confrontational, attitude toward the United States over the past thirty years, its sponsorship of international terrorist groups, its work on building a nuclear weapon, and its development of long-range ballistic missiles capable of hitting Israel and perhaps even the United States have kept the country near the top of the list of the U.S. intelligence community's most important targets for almost three decades.

The CIA has had no station inside Iran since Washington broke diplomatic relations with the regime after Iranian militants stormed the U.S. embassy in Tehran on November 4, 1979, and took sixty-six embassy staff members hostage, including the entire CIA station headed by Thomas L. Ahern Jr. This has forced the agency to improvise. In the 1980s and 1990s, the CIA's "Iran station" was situated inside the I. G. Farben Building in downtown Frankfurt, Germany, from where the agency directed its global efforts to recruit and run agent networks inside Iran. But try as it might, the agency's efforts to penetrate Iran during this time period were marked by one failure after another, with the single greatest loss occurring in April 1989, when Iranian security forces rolled up virtually the entire CIA network of agents inside Iran.

For the last two decades, the agency's "Iran station" has been hidden away inside the U.S. consulate in Dubai because of its close proximity to Iran, which is only one hundred miles to the north across the Strait of Hormuz. The Iranian presence in Dubai is massive. Not only does Iran maintain a sizable embassy in Dubai, complete with a large complement of intelligence officers, but according to a leaked State Department cable, banks in Dubai currently

hold about $12 billion of Iranian government money, which the Tehran re-
gime secretly uses to finance terrorist groups, its overseas weapons purchases, and its clandestine acquisition of nuclear technology.

By monitoring the flow of money in and out of Iranian government bank
accounts in Dubai, the U.S. intelligence community has determined that despite strict United Nations economic sanctions, a number of major European
oil companies have continued to covertly purchase large amounts of Iranian
oil and natural gas on the international petroleum market, knowing full well
that the Iranian government uses the proceeds from these sales to finance its
nuclear weapons and ballistic missile programs. According to an American
intelligence official, as long as Iran can continue to freely sell its oil and natural gas on overseas markets, "traditional diplomacy and economic sanctions
are unlikely to ever work."

As valuable as Dubai may be to the CIA as a base from which to spy on
Iran, it does not come close to compensating for the agency's lack of a presence on the ground in Tehran. In theory, the CIA should not have to be con-
tent with watching Iran from the relative comfort of the skyscrapers of Dubai.
Compared to North Korea, where a siege mentality and acute paranoia are the
norm, Iran is far more open. Thousands of Americans visit Iran every year,
many of whom are Iranian expatriates who have settled in the sunny climes
of Southern California and are now American citizens. They just can't do any
business there, which would violate the economic sanctions that are currently
in place to curb Tehran's nuclear ambitions.

There is also an enormous reservoir of residual friendship toward the
United States among young Iranians born since the 1979 seizure of the U.S.
embassy in Tehran, who now comprise 50 percent of Iran's population. Thanks
to modern technology, like satellite television, cell phones, and the Internet,
Iran's under-thirty set are well versed in Western culture and, unlike their
parents, generally well disposed toward improved relations with the West,
including the United States. Walk down any street in downtown Tehran and
you will find yourself surrounded by teenagers and twenty-something college
students who want to talk about America and their desire for better relations
with the West.

An American television film crew filming a documentary about Iran in
2009 was taken aback by the eagerness of young Iranians to criticize their
government on camera, even with a team of glum Iranian plainclothes secret
police standing just off to the side. One young Iranian man even went so far
as to walk past the plainclothesmen flaunting a copy of *Newsweek* that the

Americans had given him, which contained an article highly critical of Iranian president Mahmoud Ahmadinejad. In another time, their earnest candor would have gotten the youths arrested and perhaps even a stiff prison sentence for, as one of the wittier of the students put it, "revealing state secrets." This time, the Iranian plainclothes security men observing the affair, perhaps having teenagers of their own at home, decided that the prudent thing to do was nothing and hope that it would not end up on the nightly news.

In this more permissive environment, America's clandestine intelligence collectors should thrive. But because there is no CIA station inside the country, it is very difficult for the agency to recruit agents or gather firsthand intelligence information. Unable to operate from inside Iran, the CIA has been forced to try to recruit and run agent networks inside Iran from outside the country, which as any intelligence professional will tell you is an extremely difficult proposition, especially given the effectiveness of the Iranian security services in rooting out spies.

The CIA's Baghdad and Kabul stations have been infiltrating Iranian-born agents into Iran since 2003 with marginal success. The agency has been forced to largely depend to some degree on the intelligence services of a number of friendly European and Middle Eastern governments with embassies in Tehran to provide it with much of what it knows about what is going on inside Iran.

The CIA is not the only branch of the U.S. intelligence community actively spying inside Iran. The National Reconnaissance Office's fleet of spy satellites keeps very close tabs on Iran's uranium enrichment facilities at Natanz and Qom and on the Iranian missile test ranges at Semnan, Shahrud, and Garmsar. American spy satellites are currently maintaining a constant vigil on a new missile launch facility fast approaching completion with the help of North Korean technicians at Semnan east of Tehran. According to Michael Elleman of the International Institute for Strategic Studies in London, who is the author of a new study of the Iranian missile program, this new facility will be used to launch a spy satellite into space on top of a large new booster rocket called the Simorgh, which many analysts believe is the prototype of an Iranian intercontinental ballistic missile. According to Elleman, "The launch, if it occurs as scheduled, will set off a fire-storm, especially by proponents of missile defense" in the United States who want to build a massive new defense system designed to shoot down these missiles before they can strike the United States.

The National Security Agency also devotes a significant amount of its

SIGINT intercept resources to listening to Iranian military and internal security communications networks every day of the week. For example, NSA and its British counterpart, the Government Communications Headquarters (GCHQ), keep a sizable number of Farsi linguists at the huge NSA listening post at Menwith Hill in northern England listening around the clock to Iranian communications. U.S. Navy and Air Force reconnaissance aircraft based in the Persian Gulf States of Bahrain and Qatar, and Air Force U-2 spy planes and Global Hawk high altitude reconnaissance drones based at Al Dhafra Air Base in the United Arab Emirates, fly daily SIGINT and imagery collection missions along Iran's borders with Iraq and Afghanistan and along Iran's Persian Gulf coastline. Without live sources on the ground inside Iran, however, these technical intelligence sources are limited in terms of what they can tell us about what the Iranian regime is up to.

The need to know what the Iranian government's intentions are has never been greater, as the U.S. intelligence community has become increasingly concerned about the direction that Iran is headed. Since the U.S. invasion of Iraq in March 2003, Iran has rapidly become a regional political and military power whose influence is seen to be on the rise. According to three Middle Eastern intelligence officials interviewed in 2009 and 2010, Iran, as a matter of national policy, is exporting instability throughout the Middle East, the Near East, and South Asia through coercive tactics, such as its continuing lavish support of terrorist groups like Hezbollah in Lebanon and Hamas in the Gaza Strip. According to Lt. General Ronald L. Burgess Jr., the director of the DIA, "Iran uses terrorism to pressure or intimidate other countries and more broadly to serve as a strategic deterrent."

Iran is also continuing to provide clandestine support to a number of extremist Shiite groups in Iraq. The U.S. intelligence community has a substantial volume of reliable intelligence showing that not only are the Iranian Ministry of Intelligence and Security (MOIS) and Iran's covert intelligence organization, the Quds Force of the Islamic Revolutionary Guard Corps, running massive intelligence-gathering operations inside Iraq, but, according to leaked State Department cables, Iran is also providing weapons and money to extremist Shiite political and militia groups in Iraq opposed to the continuing U.S. military presence in that country.

There is some circumstantial evidence that Iran has covertly become involved in the war in Afghanistan. In September 2007, British forces in Afghanistan captured a shipment of Iranian-made advanced IEDs destined for Taliban fighters in Helmand Province. The British intelligence community's

evaluation of the matter, according to a leaked State Department cable, was
that it demonstrated that Iranian intelligence operators belonging to the Quds
Force were now engaged in the same sort of mischief in Afghanistan that they
had exported to Iraq for years. But the British report left open the question of
whether the Iranian government knew what the Quds Force operatives were
up to, quoting a senior British official as saying that the Quds Force "may have
attempted to conceal its activities from other branches of the Iranian government."

The best that the U.S. intelligence community could conclude at the time,
according to a DNI briefing, was that it was "likely" that the Iranian intelligence services were supporting the Taliban because they were the "enemy of
my enemy," that is to say, the United States. Now the U.S. intelligence community believes that the Iranians were just being prudent, supporting both
sides in the conflict to ensure that they have a seat at the table regardless of
who wins the war in Afghanistan. As a matter of policy, Iran has consistently
opposed the Taliban, whom Tehran clearly views as an equal threat to its security as the American military presence in Afghanistan, if not a greater one.
According to a little-noticed presentation to Congress made by DNI Denny
Blair in February 2009, "Iran has opposed Afghan reconciliation talks with
the Taliban as risking an increase in the group's influence and legitimacy . . .
Iran distrusts the Taliban and opposes its return to power but uses the provi-
sion of lethal aid [to the Taliban] as a way to pressure Western forces, gather
intelligence, and build ties that could protect Iran's interests if the Taliban
regain control of the country."

The Iranian government has gone out of its way to maintain friendly relations with Afghan president Hamid Karzai and his closest advisers. According to U.S. intelligence sources, CIA surveillance of the activities of senior
Iranian diplomats and intelligence officers in Kabul has revealed not only
that the Iranian ambassador in Kabul, Feda Hussein Maliki, is a frequent
visitor to Karzai's presidential palace but also that the ambassador has for
years been giving Karzai's chief of staff, Mohammad Daudzai, a plastic bag
filled with cash once a month. The sums involved have never been specified,
but according to the *New York Times*, the payments over the years have totaled
in the millions of dollars.

Senior U.S. intelligence officials believe that Tehran's motive in making
these large cash payments to Karzai is to drive a wedge between Washington
and the Afghan government. According to these officials, Tehran has also
been making comparable payments to two other members of Karzai's kitchen

cabinet, Information and Culture Minister Abdul Karim Khoram, and Education Minister Farooq Wardak, who are infamous in Kabul diplomatic circles for their attempts to use their positions of influence to push Karzai away from his alliance with the United States. According to a leaked State Department cable, these three men "provide [Karzai] misleading advice and conspire to isolate Karzai from more pragmatic (and pro-Western) advisors in a purposeful effort to antagonize Western countries, especially the United States."

But it has been Iran's extremely controversial nuclear weapons development program that has dominated the U.S. intelligence community's interest in Iran since it began working on the project back in 1985. The CIA's "Iran station" in Dubai has covertly tried to disrupt Tehran's nuclear program for more than a decade by tracking Iranian clandestine purchases of nuclear-related technology from countries such as the People's Republic of China and North Korea using money held in Iranian government bank accounts in Dubai. Thanks to cooperation from the UAE intelligence services, the U.S. intelligence community has been able to interdict some of these clandestine nuclear shipments, but American officials admit that most of these shipments have managed to get through despite their best efforts.

Information provided by an Iranian dissident group in 2002 led to the discovery of a secret underground uranium enrichment plant at Natanz, located halfway between the cities of Isfahan and Kashan in central Iran. According to U.S. intelligence sources, the discovery of Natanz led the CIA in 2004 and 2005 to use its Predator unmanned drones to conduct secret reconnaissance overflight missions over the facility and the deployment sites for Iran's long-range ballistic missile units. Some of these drone missions were conducted from Balad Air Base in Iraq; others were launched from Karshi-Khanabad Air Base in Uzbekistan. The Iranians formally protested these overflights, but the U.S. government refused to confirm or deny that it was behind these secret flights.

Five years later in 2007, intelligence information provided by the NSA revealed that a team of Iranian engineers, led by a shadowy figure named Mohsen Fakhrizadeh, had been diligently working on designs for a nuclear weapon to be carried by one of Iran's new generation of long-range ballistic missiles, but that this work had been ordered halted in 2003 shortly after the U.S. invasion of Iraq. This new information formed the basis for a controversial November 2007 National Intelligence Estimate on the Iranian nuclear program, which concluded, "We judge with high confidence that in fall 2003, Tehran halted its nuclear weapons program."

But two years later, according to senior American intelligence sources, the intelligence community had to reverse many of its 2007 findings after an Iranian nuclear physicist named Shahram Amiri defected in May 2009 while making the pilgrimage to Mecca in Saudi Arabia. Sources confirm that Amiri's defection was entirely voluntary, facilitated by the cooperation the CIA received from the Saudi General Intelligence Directorate.

The information Amiri brought with him was deemed so important that the CIA offered him a $5 million cash reward. The CIA leaked his name to the press in March 2010, describing his defection as "an intelligence coup." But in July 2010, Amiri returned to Iran without the $5 million in cash that the CIA had given him, claiming that he had been kidnapped by CIA officers in Saudi Arabia. The CIA formally denied the allegation, claiming that Amiri had been a willing defector whose information had significantly enhanced the U.S. intelligence community's knowledge of the Iranian nuclear program.

In the U.S. intelligence community, the Amiri re-defection was a huge embarrassment, the latest in a string of high-level defectors dating back to the 1970s who later chose to return home. In the eyes of some intelligence officials, Amiri's re-defection was a stark reminder of the peril innate in placing one's faith in human agents with all their foibles.

Despite doubts about Amiri's reliability, the U.S. intelligence community stuck by the information he provided. Based in part on the information provided by Amiri, as well as information provided by the Mossad, on September 27, 2009, President Obama and the leaders of Great Britain and France publicly accused Iran of building a secret underground uranium enrichment facility one hundred miles south of Tehran on the grounds of an Islamic Revolutionary Guard Corps base at Fordow, located outside the holy city of Qom. At the time of the announcement, the Qom site was far from complete, but the analysts believed that at the rate construction was going it would be ready by 2010.

The discovery of the secret uranium enrichment facility outside Qom dramatically changed how the U.S. intelligence community assessed the Iranian nuclear program. What it boiled down to was this: All of the intelligence indicated that the Iranians were not being truthful when they said that their nuclear program was intended solely for civilian purposes. Rather, the intelligence indicated that the Iranians had built just enough centrifuges at Natanz and Qom to process enriched uranium for use in a nuclear weapon, but not anywhere near enough for a civilian nuclear power reactor.

In August 2010, the National Intelligence Council issued a draft National

Intelligence Estimate that essentially reversed most of the conclusions of the November 2007 estimate on the Iranian nuclear program. Based in part on information provided by Amiri, the 2010 intelligence estimate concluded that Iran was indeed developing nuclear weapons components and secretly enriching nuclear material that could be used in a nuclear weapon. But the estimate added that it was not known whether the Iranian government had made the decision to go one step further and actually build a nuclear weapon.

According to a 2011 interview with Michael Eisenstadt, the director of military and security studies at the Washington Institute for Near East Policy, the Iranians currently have enough enriched uranium for three to four nuclear weapons, but they would probably like to have a stockpile of uranium sufficient for about one hundred bombs, even if they do not actually move ahead and build the weapons themselves. Just having the raw materials on hand along with a viable bomb design would be as sufficient a deterrent as having the bombs themselves.

Deep differences remain within the U.S. intelligence community as to whether Iran has resumed work on building an atomic bomb. When asked in late 2010 for his opinion as to whether Iran was actively working on a nuclear weapon, one senior American intelligence official could only shrug his shoulders and say, "Your guess is as good as mine."

Arguably the toughest target that the U.S. intelligence community currently faces is the hypersecretive North Korean regime, which Joseph S. Bermudez Jr., one of the leading experts on the North Korean military outside of the U.S. government, has described as "the most closed and security-conscious society in the world."

The military threat posed by North Korea today is perhaps greater than at any time since the end of the Korean War in 1953. With an estimated 1.2 million men under arms, the North Korean military is a major threat not only to South Korea, where 28,000 U.S. combat troops are currently stationed, but also to Japan and other nearby Asian nations. The North Korean military has almost one thousand ballistic missiles in its inventory and is developing and building new missile systems at an alarming rate, including one missile, called the Taepodong-2, which can reach targets in the U.S.

But it is North Korea's nuclear weapons stockpile that gives American intelligence analysts the most cause for concern. North Korea tested its first nuclear weapon in October 2006. By 2009, U.S. intelligence officials believed that North Korea possessed somewhere between six and twelve low-yield nuclear weapons in its arsenal. Since then, the North Koreans have restarted plutonium production at their nuclear reactor complex at Yongbyon, which had been temporarily shut down in 2008. Pyongyang was believed at the time to be pursuing uranium nuclear weapons designs, but the intelligence community thought that North Korea was still years away from being able to produce the enriched uranium needed for these weapons.

However, the nature of the intelligence business is to be continually surprised by one's enemies. In November 2010, the North Koreans showed a delegation of foreign scientists led by a former head of the Los Alamos Nuclear Laboratory, Siegfried S. Hecker, a massive new underground uranium enrichment facility that they had just secretly constructed, forcing the U.S. intelligence community to scrap its previous estimates on the North Korean nuclear arsenal. Intelligence officials admit that they do not know how many uranium enrichment facilities the North Koreans have or how much material they are producing. But one thing is now clear to the analysts: Pyongyang might soon possess a much larger arsenal of nuclear weapons with significantly greater destructive power than previously believed.

Trying to gather intelligence about all of these subjects inside the paranoid and hypersecretive North Korean police state has always been an extremely difficult proposition. During the Korean War (1950–53), the CIA and the South Korean intelligence services failed miserably in their attempts to insert teams of agents into North Korea to collect intelligence. Former CIA official Samuel Halpern recalled that "it was tough because North Korea was a denied area, no one came from there, and no people traveled there. We were not successful in collecting [intelligence] about North Korea. Most people forget this."

Between 1954 and 1972, the South Korean intelligence services sent thousands of agents into North Korea. Few ever returned. In 1999, someone within the South Korean intelligence community leaked to a newspaper in Seoul that 7,726 South Korean agents had been killed or captured or had disappeared while conducting espionage missions in North Korea between 1950 and 1972.

Spying on North Korea has become even more difficult in recent years. Intelligence sources in the United States, Japan, and South Korea confirm that there is today a dearth of reliable intelligence information about what is going on inside North Korea. The U.S. intelligence community and its counterparts in South Korea have virtually no intelligence assets in North Korea. Recruiting North Korean diplomats outside the country is nigh on impossible because they always travel in twos, usually with a security officer in tow. There is the occasional refugee or low-level defector who manages to make it to Manchuria, and from there to South Korea, but the information obtained from these sources is at best anecdotal and not very reliable. Some of the CIA's foreign collaborators recruited aid workers who were allowed into North Korea to bring food and medicine to starving civilians in the 1990s, but most of what these sources reported was no better than what newspapers in the West were reporting.

As a matter of expediency, over the past decade the U.S. intelligence community has had to increasingly depend on Russia and China, North Korea's two remaining allies with any standing, for much of what it thinks it knows about what the Pyongyang regime is doing. But senior U.S. intelligence officials admit that although the Russians and Chinese have large embassies in Pyongyang, their level of access to the North Korean leadership is extremely limited, so the quality of their intelligence on what is going on in the country is dubious.

This means that the United States remains largely dependent on technical sources, such as spy satellites and signals intelligence, for what little intelligence we have about what is going on inside North Korea. These sources have obvious limitations. Spy satellites are the principal source of information available to the U.S. intelligence community about North Korea, with much of the focus being on North Korean nuclear weapons and ballistic missile production facilities and deployment sites. Almost every day one of the U.S. Air Force Global Hawk high-altitude reconnaissance drones based on the island of Guam can be found flying off the North Korean coastline taking pictures of targets deep inside the country that are more detailed than those coming from satellites. SIGINT remains an important source for information about North Korean military activities, but radio intercepts today are producing less intelligence because in the mid-1990s the North Korean government and military began shifting much of their internal communications to fiber-optic cables, which reduced significantly what NSA was able to discern about events taking place north of the Demilitarized Zone.

All this reduces the problem to a simple equation: How do the few American intelligence analysts who specialize in North Korea divine the intentions of the notoriously erratic regime with so little hard information to work with? For example, U.S. intelligence officials admit that the most detailed portrait of North Korea's reclusive and ailing leader, Kim Jong-il, who has ruled the country since 1994, was derived from the debriefing of the North Korean dictator's former Japanese sushi chef who goes by the pen name of Kenji Fujimoto, who returned to Japan in 2003 after having lived in North Korea since

1982, and Hwang Jang-yop, North Korea's former chief ideologue, who defected in Beijing in 1997 and spent his remaining days in South Korea until his death in October 2010 at the age of eighty-seven.

Taken together, these materials are slim indeed. Sometimes, a paucity of raw material spurs insightful work by intelligence analysts, who have to extract every ounce of usable data from what little they have to work with. The CIA psychological profilers used these materials to put together a series of detailed character and personality studies of Kim Jong-il that are considered to be some of the best analytic work produced by the agency since 9/11 and are required reading for analysts within the U.S. intelligence community.

According to a Japanese intelligence official, however, these materials are now badly out of date and do not cover what effect Kim Jong-il's August 2008 stroke had on his health. Also according to the official, virtually nothing is currently known about Kim's son and heir apparent Kim Jong-un, other than some vague impressions passed on by Chinese government officials based on their conversations in 2010 with his father.

The dearth of hard information explains why there are today significant differences of opinion within the U.S. intelligence community as to whether the horrific state of the North Korean economy has reduced the military threat posed by Pyongyang. According to some estimates, more than a million North Korean civilians died of starvation in the 1990s. Everyone agrees that famine remains widespread inside North Korea, and malnutrition is affecting the performance of not only the economy but also the North Korean military, leading some senior U.S. intelligence officials to believe that North Korea no longer poses much of a threat.

Other officials, principally low- and mid-level intelligence analysts who have followed North Korea for years, are not so sure. They believe that the massive 1.2-million-man North Korean military, the fourth largest in the world, is probably a bigger threat today than it was at the height of the Cold War, and they point to the November 2010 North Korean artillery attack on South Korea's Yeonpyeong Island as proof that the Pyongyang regime remains as dangerous as ever.

These analysts argue that despite the disastrous state of the North Korean economy, the Pyongyang regime has continued to direct whatever money it has to the military, even at the expense of feeding its own people. The North Koreans have not let up in their efforts to upgrade and modernize their armed forces. As far as the analysts at DNI headquarters at Liberty Crossing in Virginia can ascertain, the North Korean government's top spending priorities continue to be to build up the size of its small arsenal of nuclear weapons and increase the already considerable number of ballistic missiles in its inventory.

Regardless of which side of the debate people come down on, what worries everyone in the U.S. intelligence community is that the threat of war with North Korea is just as high today as it was at the height of the Cold War. Only this time, North Korea has nuclear weapons and the means to deliver them to targets throughout the Pacific.

Latin America, a backwater of American diplomacy for more than half a century, may currently pose the most complex set of problems for America's spies. The U.S. intelligence community continues to enjoy excellent relations with its counterparts in Brazil, Argentina, Peru, and Chile. The relationship between Washington and Bogotá remains close because of the U.S. intelligence community's continuing support of the Colombian government's efforts to subdue two Marxist guerrilla groups, the Fuerzas Armadas Revolucionarias de Colombia (FARC) and the Ejército Liberación Nacional (ELN), which have been trying to overthrow the Colombian government for more than forty years.

Despite long-standing efforts to crush them, the FARC and ELN insurgencies continue. The CIA station in Bogotá, the U.S. military intelligence services, and the DEA continue to provide substantial financial and technical support to the Colombian government's six military and civilian intelligence services. The U.S. Army is still secretly deploying small teams of SIGINT and HUMINT personnel to help the Colombian military destroy remaining elements of the FARC. Utilizing specialized airborne reconnaissance aircraft and Predator unmanned drones based at Apiay Air Base southeast of Bogotá, U.S. Army intelligence personnel provide realtime intelligence information to Colombian special forces in order to neutralize FARC insurgents and narcotics traffickers.

There are serious problems elsewhere in Latin America. The president of Ecuador, Rafael Correa, has been a thorn in the side of the U.S. government since he was elected in December 2006. Ecuador is suspected by the U.S. intelligence community of giving sanctuary to FARC guerrillas from neighboring Colombia. Ecuador severed diplomatic relations with Colombia in March 2008 after Colombian forces attacked a camp inside Ecuador, killing the leader of FARC, whose nom de guerre was Raul Reyes, and twenty-five other guerrillas. In February 2009, the Ecuadorian government expelled the CIA Quito station chief, Mark Sullivan, for what it termed "unacceptable meddling" in Ecuadorian internal affairs. Washington was hoping that Correa would keep the expulsion under wraps. Instead, he went on television and publicly announced, "Let's be clear, Sullivan was the director of the CIA in Ecuador."

President Evo Morales of Bolivia has also delighted in taunting the CIA, repeatedly accusing the agency of interfering in the internal affairs of his country. He has fired a number of Bolivian army and police officers who he alleged were on the CIA payroll, and in March 2009 he declared persona non grata the CIA station chief in La Paz, Francisco Martinez, for "activities not in consonance with his diplomatic functions."

But it is Venezuela and its mercurial president, Hugo Chávez, that most frustrate U.S. government officials. Elected in a landslide in 1998, Chávez was reviled by the Bush administration because he moved his country away from the United States toward countries generally deemed to be antagonistic to Washington, particularly Cuba, Russia, Belarus, China, Syria, Iran, and Vietnam. Diplomatic relations with Venezuela began deteriorating immediately after an abortive military coup d'état in April 2002, wherein the Bush administration recognized the short-lived government of the coup leader, Pedro Carmona. Once back in power, Chávez made it abundantly clear that he would never forgive Washington for what he deemed to be a naked attempt to unseat him from power. It has been all downhill ever since.

In August 2005, Venezuela accused the U.S. Drug Enforcement Administration of conducting espionage inside Venezuela and terminated all joint counternarcotics efforts. In November 2007, the Venezuelan security service leaked to the press the name of the CIA station chief in Caracas, as well as copies of what U.S. intelligence officials vehemently claim are forged documents about an alleged CIA plan called "Operation Pliers" to subvert the Venezuelan government. In September 2008, the U.S. Treasury Department froze the assets of the heads of Venezuela's two intelligence services, Hugo Carvajal Barrios and Henry de Jesus Rangel Silva, and former Venezuelan interior minister Ramón Rodriguez Chacin for "materially assisting the narcotics trafficking activities of the [Colombian terrorist group] FARC." In retaliation, on September 11, 2008, Chávez ordered the expulsion of the U.S. ambassador to Venezuela.

Despite the ups and mostly downs in U.S.-Venezuelan diplomatic relations, the U.S. intelligence community has never viewed Chávez or Venezuela as a very serious threat. Randall Fort, a former head of the State Department's intelligence staff, described Chávez in a leaked cable from October 2008 as "an annoyance with limited political influence within the region."

Still, Latin America watchers inside the U.S. intelligence community, and there are not many of them, counseled that whatever one's views of Chávez, he deserves careful scrutiny and even a certain degree of respect. A leaked 2007 State Department cable warned that "notwithstanding his tirades and antics, it would be a mistake to dismiss Hugo Chávez as just a clown or old school caudillo. He has a vision, however distorted, and he is taking calculated measures to advance it. To effectively counter the threat he represents, we need to know better his objectives and how he intends to pursue them. This requires better intelligence."

Since entering office in 2009, President Obama and Secretary of State Hillary Rodham Clinton have quietly tried to patch up the strained diplomatic relations with Venezuela, but progress has been slow because the Venezuelan economy has been in free fall since the global economic downturn of 2009. Today, Venezuela has the dubious distinction of being the only Latin American country whose economy is shrinking rather than growing.

Venezuela's expanding relations with Cuba remain a cause for concern in Washington, particularly the increasingly intimate relationship between the Cuban and Venezuelan intelligence services. According to a leaked 2006 State Department cable, "Sensitive reports indicate Cuban and Venezuelan intelligence ties are so advanced that the two countries' agencies appear to be competing with each other for the [Venezuelan government's] attention. Cuban intelligence officers have direct access to Chavez and frequently provide him with intelligence reporting unvetted by Venezuelan officers . . . Cuban intelligence officers train Venezuelans both in Cuba and in Venezuela, providing both political indoctrination and operational instruction."

Conclusion: The Past Is Prologue

The Lessons for U.S. Intelligence from Today's Battlefields

*Fools say that they learn by experience. I prefer
to profit by others' experience.*

—OTTO VON BISMARCK

So, is the U.S. intelligence community working the way it should ten years after
the tragedy of 9/11? The answer is: not yet. A number of important changes for
the better have taken place since 9/11, but it is abundantly clear that the intelligence community still has a very long way to go. As revealed in this book, not
only have many of the structural and procedural problems that afflicted the intelligence community prior to 9/11 not been fixed, but a host of new problems
have arisen that are challenging the ability of America's spies to perform their
mission. New high-tech intelligence collection systems, such as the much-
heralded unmanned drone, produce so much raw data that they are drowning
the intelligence analysts. Hundreds of new computer databases have been created to store the vast amount of data that the community's collection sensors
vacuum up every day, but analysts still cannot freely access much of this data
because many of these databases cannot communicate with one another.

As this book shows, strong leadership of the U.S. intelligence community
remains conspicuously lacking, which means that unity of command, cohe-
siveness, and a clear direction for the intelligence community still have not
been achieved a decade after 9/11. Attempts by DNI Admiral Dennis Blair
during the first sixteen months of the Obama administration to assert his
authority and make the CIA responsive to the DNI's commands were an un-
mitigated failure. Not only was Blair defeated at every turn by his opponents

within the Obama administration and the U.S. intelligence community, but he ultimately lost his job for his efforts. It remains to be seen if the new director of the CIA, General David Petraeus, will be more responsive than his predecessor, Leon Panetta.

Despite the passage of time, weak leadership at the top has meant that the intelligence community has not become any easier to govern. Although important changes for the better have taken place, all evidence indicates that the office of the DNI still has not been able to effectively integrate the vast number of appendages comprising the U.S. intelligence community into a cohesive organization that performs its mission in an efficient and efficacious manner. In fact, the intelligence empire has become so large and unwieldy, and the number of classified intelligence programs so numerous and opaque, that the intelligence community has become, in some important respects, more unmanageable than it was before 9/11.

America's spies have so much money that they are suffering from an embarrassment of riches. In May 2011, Congress passed a new intelligence spending bill that increased the amount of money for America's spies to over $85 billion, this coming at a time when politicians on Capitol Hill were talking about making deep cuts in Medicaid and Medicare spending for the elderly and infirm. More money has not necessarily made things better. The Tom Drake case described in chapter 2 shows that the intelligence community still has problems managing big-budget classified equipment procurement programs, in large part because the internal checks and balances that existed a decade ago to prevent fraud, waste, and abuse were swept away in the aftermath of the 9/11 terrorist attacks and have not been put back into place. Intensifying all of these problems is the fact that, in the opinion of many intelligence insiders, congressional oversight of the intelligence community has deteriorated over the past decade as partisan rancor and bickering have taken over what used to be a collegial and bipartisan endeavor.

Despite its outstanding performance in the events leading up to the killing of Osama bin Laden in May 2011, the intelligence community still has a long way to go before we can declare that all of the problems identified in the aftermath of 9/11 and the Iraqi WMD scandals have been fixed. Even with the change in administrations, the intelligence community is still experiencing problems getting its views heard, much less appreciated, in the upper reaches of the U.S. government, especially when the community's assessments differ from those of the White House and the Pentagon, as in the recent cases of

Afghanistan and Pakistan. As shown in chapter 7, in recent years the Obama White House has, like the Bush administration before it, been making public statements about the wars in Afghanistan and Pakistan that did not conform with what the intelligence community was reporting. Witness the example of the December 2010 NIEs on Afghanistan and Pakistan, and how they conflicted with President Obama's status report on these wars; later events were to prove that the intelligence community assessments were correct, and the statements originating from the White House exaggerated the successes being experienced in Afghanistan and Pakistan.

One of the biggest problems that the U.S. intelligence community still faces is the same conundrum it faced throughout the Cold War—it is collecting far more data than it can process, analyze, and report to its consumers. As Secretary of Defense Donald Rumsfeld put it in a declassified memo, the intelligence community produces "more data than we can translate into usable knowledge." Sources agree that less than 1 percent of the data collected every day gets reported to intelligence consumers in Washington and overseas, meaning that 99 percent of what gets collected ends up on the cutting room floor and is never used. And it has been suggested by intelligence insiders that rather than improving, the situation is getting worse because new high-tech collection sensors, such as the unmanned drones, produce so much raw video imagery and such vast amounts of signals intercepts that they literally are drowning the intelligence analysts in what is commonly referred to within the community as "data crush."

The quality of the analysis coming out of the intelligence community still leaves something to be desired. Despite the vast amount of raw data pouring into Washington every day from NSA's listening posts and the 170-plus CIA stations around the world, many senior U.S. intelligence officials worry that more than a decade after 9/11, we still don't know who our enemies are. Seven years ago, in December 2004, the commander of U.S. Central Command, General John Abizaid, wrote a classified memo to Secretary of Defense Rumsfeld arguing that "we remain largely ignorant of who fights us, why they fight and what their weaknesses are." The result is that we are still playing catch-up in our efforts to understand the enemies we face today.

For example, ten years after the U.S. invasion of Afghanistan in 2001, we still know far too little about the Taliban guerrillas that U.S. and NATO soldiers are up against. Despite outnumbering the Taliban by more than four to one, coalition forces are still unable to beat the ragtag Taliban guerrillas, in large part because of a poor intelligence appreciation of the fighting power and resiliency of the enemy we face. We do not even know much about the leaders of the Taliban insurgency. In 2010, an impostor was able to pretend for several weeks to be a high-level Taliban official sent to Kabul to negotiate a peace agreement with the Karzai government before being discovered. Beyond Afghanistan, we know very little about who actually rules Iran and whether they intend to build a nuclear weapon or not, and the dearth of knowledge about North Korea is so pronounced that much of what we know about the enigmatic leader of the country comes from his former sushi chef.

So what is the current state-of-play on the global intelligence battlefield? The challenges facing the intelligence community today are just as vast as they were in the days after 9/11. America's spies have achieved some commendable, albeit unheralded, successes in their efforts. Thanks to vast investments in new signals intelligence equipment and human intelligence resources, coverage of China has improved dramatically over the past decade, and there have been some unheralded operational successes in Russia and the former Soviet republics of Central Asia since 9/11. But high hurdles still remain.

In Afghanistan, the intelligence community has been playing catch-up since the Obama administration took office in 2009. There have been some improvements in our understanding of the Taliban's strategy and tactics, but our overall appreciation of the enemy we face is still nowhere near what it should be.

And there are signs that U.S. intelligence in Afghanistan has over the past year reverted to the bad habits that were the norm before Obama became president. Major General Mike Flynn, the director of intelligence in Afghanistan from June 2009 to 2010, returned to the United States and was replaced by Brigadier General Stephen G. Fogarty, who immediately reversed many of the changes made by his predecessor. For example, Fogarty ordered that the ISAF intelligence staff in Kabul reduce the amount of resources that General Flynn had dedicated to trying to understand the political, economic, and social dynamics of the Afghan battlefield, and instead return to the former emphasis on locating Taliban commanders so that they could be killed by commando raids by U.S. and NATO special forces.

According to senior U.S. and NATO intelligence officials, the reason for the dramatic shift in emphasis was that in the fall of 2010, senior Obama administration officials became convinced that the war in Afghanistan could not be won militarily, despite the fact that coalition forces had just made some noteworthy gains in the Taliban strongholds of Helmand and Kandahar provinces. These officials concluded that these gains were temporary at best, because the Obama administration was committed to begin withdrawing U.S. forces from Afghanistan in July 2011, and the weak and corrupt Afghan government forces had proven that they were incapable of holding the ground once the U.S. and NATO forces pulled out.

So in the fall of 2010, the emphasis secretly shifted to trying to negotiate a peaceful settlement of the Afghan conflict with the Taliban, while at the same time keeping up the military pressure on the Taliban through an intensified campaign of commando raids that targeted senior insurgent field commanders. The expectation was that these commando raids would induce the Taliban leadership in Pakistan to come to the negotiating table.

It remains to be seen if the Obama administration's new Afghan war strategy will ultimately succeed. But a number of intelligence officials in the United States and Europe point out that the fundamental problem with this risky strategy is that it has not worked in the past. They point to what happened in Vietnam between 1965 and 1968, when President Lyndon Johnson had hoped that massive B-52 air strikes on targets in North Vietnam would drive the Hanoi regime to the negotiating table. But CIA reporting revealed that the air strikes were causing little, if any, real damage to the North Vietnamese war effort, and had not altered in any meaningful way Hanoi's will to continue the war. The intelligence officials worry that the Obama administration may be making the same mistake that Johnson and his advisers made more than forty years ago.

The collapse of intelligence cooperation between the U.S. and Pakistan in early 2011 is a very serious development that has long-term implications for the U.S. intelligence community. American intelligence officials are now concerned that Pakistan will "unleash" its Afghan Taliban proxies, ramping up the tempo of fighting inside Afghanistan. The collapse of intelligence cooperation also bodes ill for the future of the intelligence community's campaign to destroy what is left of al Qaeda and the host of other terrorist groups that are still hiding in the northern part of the country. A number of joint intelligence collection and analysis projects have been terminated, and unmanned drone strike operations over northern Pakistan have been severely restricted since January 2011.

And just when officials in Washington and Islamabad thought that relations couldn't get any worse, they did. In June 2011, CIA officials alleged that someone in the Pakistani government or ISI had leaked to the Pakistani Taliban that the United States intended to launch drone strikes on one of the Taliban's two bomb factories in northern Pakistan. This led to yet another round of bitter recriminations between the U.S. and Pakistani governments and intelligence officials. Senior CIA officials in Washington told congressional officials that, in their opinion, Pakistan could no longer be trusted with any sensitive classified information.

Then there is the war on terror. Senior U.S. and European intelligence officials do not know if we are winning the war given the dramatic changes now taking place around the world. Even though Osama bin Laden is dead and al Qaeda in Pakistan has been whittled down to a small rump organization, new terrorist groups are taking shape around the world that are just as committed to killing Americans as bin Laden ever was. The intelligence community's decade-long counterterrorism operations against the al Qaeda affiliates in Yemen and Somalia are stalled, with no discernible progress to report in almost two years, and new al Qaeda–affiliated terrorist groups have sprung up in recent years across Africa. The U.S. government still cannot get the full cooperation of a number of its key Middle East allies, including Saudi Arabia, to cut off the flow of funds to the Taliban and other terrorist groups around the world. And the terrorist threat at home is rapidly evolving in new and potentially more lethal directions, to the point that U.S. intelligence officials are unsure who they should be looking for anymore.

Recent events in the Middle East and North Africa clearly show just how dangerous the world is, and how great the challenges facing the intelligence community are going to be in the future as threats to U.S. national security continuously evolve. The U.S. intelligence community did not foresee the sudden collapse of the pro-U.S. regimes in Egypt and Tunisia, the eruption of a civil war in Libya, and the escalating wave of street protests across the Middle East. Then again, no one else in the U.S. government or among our allies abroad did either.

If pundits in Washington are to believed, the next big threat to the security of the United States is something the experts call "cyber war," the new global battle being fought every minute of every day on the ethereal plane of the Internet. In its infancy during the 1980s and 1990s, cyber war was the exclusive domain of teenage hackers and cyber criminals, some of whom were backed by organized crime groups in Russia and elsewhere, who tried to steal passwords, bank account numbers, and other personal information so that they could loot bank accounts and cause other forms of criminal mischief.

As the antics of the hackers and cyber criminals began appearing with greater frequency in the press in the 1990s, the intelligence services of a number of countries decided that they needed their own corps of teenage hackers who could infiltrate foreign government communications networks and computer systems to gather secrets and, if necessary, attack and destroy these systems.

One of these was America's electronic eavesdropping Goliath, the National Security Agency, which has been secretly engaged in disrupting foreign computer systems and e-mail traffic for more than twenty years. Shortly after the end of the Cold War in the early 1990s, NSA set up a small unit called the Information Warfare Support Center to experiment with penetrating and disrupting foreign government communications systems and computer networks.

The concept was given a dry run during Operation Desert Storm in 1991, when NSA was able to electronically disrupt the French-made computers that controlled the Iraqi air defense system. But it was not until March 1999 that NSA first systematically applied its new cyber-attack capability when it electronically knocked down large parts of the communications and computers that supported the Yugoslav air defense system during the short war over the breakaway province of Kosovo.

In the run-up to the invasion of Afghanistan in October 2001, the United States tried to duplicate its success in Kosovo by using cyber attacks to degrade the Taliban air defense system, but the system was so antique and decrepit that it defied attack by electronic means.

The Pentagon took its first giant leap into the area of cyber war in January 2005 with the creation of a 125-person unit at NSA headquarters at Fort George G. Meade called the Joint Functional Component Command–Network Warfare, which was described at the time as the single largest conglomeration of computer hackers in the world.

As soon as the unit was created, teams of its personnel were secretly deployed to Iraq to begin mapping the communications networks of the Iraqi insurgents and al Qaeda foreign fighters opposing the U.S. military there. Over a period of almost two years, this small team of military computer surveillance specialists, called the Multi-National Force–Iraq Cyber Team, carefully watched the flow of e-mails and text messages inside Iraq. They managed to identify the electronic addresses of hundreds of computers and personal messaging systems that were then being used by the Iraqi insurgents.

As first reported by Shane Harris of the *National Journal*, several months before the beginning of General Petraeus's 2007 Baghdad surge offensive, the NSA was authorized by the White House to launch a cyber attack on all of the Iraqi insurgent e-mail and text messaging systems that the Cyber Team had located. According to intelligence officials, the cyber attack knocked off the air almost all of the communications of the Iraqi insurgents and al Qaeda in Iraq fighters around Baghdad for three days.

On April 27, 2007, while NSA was gearing up to launch its electronic offensive against Iraqi insurgents, right-wing Russian nationalists, enraged by the decision of the Estonian government to relocate a huge Stalin-era statue of a Soviet soldier in downtown Tallinn, the capital of Estonia, launched a concerted month-long cyber attack on virtually every Estonian computer server, router, Web site, and e-mail system that served the country's government ministries, banks, newspapers, and television and radio stations. According to a leaked State Department cable, "On April 28, less than 24 hours after the first cyber attacks, Russian-language internet forums . . . were exhorting people to attack specific GOE [government of Estonia] websites and offering links to software tools."

A year later, in August 2008, the Russian government itself launched a cyber attack on the communications and computer systems of the Georgian government and news media prior to the launch of a major military offensive to retake portions of the breakaway province of South Ossetia that had recently been captured by Georgian forces. A 2009 report by the NSA examining the cyber attack on Georgia found that the Russians managed to plant a Trojan Horse program into a number of Georgian government computer networks that allowed Moscow to launch continuous denial-of-service attacks on the host computers, temporarily knocking them out of commission. The Georgian government's computer experts were able to quickly put together an ad hoc communications system to replace the one being jammed by the Russians, but the incident highlighted the fact that cyber attacks, if done right, can be more effective than an artillery barrage or air strike in wreaking havoc on foreign computer and communications systems.

Leaked State Department documents reveal that the intelligence services of the People's Republic of China have become the world's foremost practitioners of cyber war. The scope of the Chinese cyber-war effort is massive. In March 2009, researchers in Canada and Great Britain discovered that someone in China was conducting a cyber-spying operation, which they named GhostNet, that involved inserting undetectable Trojan Horse viruses into computers around the world, including the personal computer of the Tibetan leader-in-exile, the Dalai Lama. Whoever was running the operation inside China was reading all of the e-mails sent to and from the targeted computers and monitoring which Web sites they visited, leading to the obvious conclusion that GhostNet was a Chinese government spying operation, though this remains to be proved.

The classified reporting of the U.S. intelligence community strongly suggests that GhostNet was but a small part of a much larger global cyber-spying operation by the Chinese government that has been going on for almost a decade. Leaked State Department documents show that since 2002, Chinese hackers have succeeded in penetrating a number of Canadian, French, and German government computer systems, some of them very high-level. For example, a secret 2008 report by the German equivalent of the FBI, the Federal Office for the Protection of the Constitution, reported that hundreds of Chinese cyber attacks had "targeted a wide variety of German organizations to include German military, economic, science and technology, commercial, diplomatic, research and development, as well as high-level government [computer] systems."

The main targets of the Chinese hackers have been the computer and communications systems of the U.S. government and military. According to a classified State Department report, "Since late 2002, USG [U.S. government] organizations have been targeted with social-engineering online attacks by [Chinese] actors." The Chinese have used the same techniques as mainstream computer hackers; the cable revealed that they had "relied on techniques including exploiting Windows system vulnerabilities and stealing login credentials to gain access to hundreds of USG and cleared defense contractor systems over the years." The cable confirmed that the cyber attacks have targeted virtually every department of the U.S. government involved in national security matters. According to the cable, "The majority of the systems [Chinese] actors have targeted belong to the U.S. Army, but targets also include other DoD [Department of Defense] services as well as DoS [Department of State], Department of Energy, additional USG entities, and commercial systems and networks."

In June 2009, Chinese hackers attempted to penetrate the computers of five State Department officials in the office of the special envoy for climate in Washington just as talks got under way in Beijing with the Chinese government over reducing greenhouse gas emissions. According to a leaked State Department cable, "The event appears to be a targeted spear-phishing attempt [attempting to acquire electronically sensitive personal or financial information, such as bank account passwords] and may be indicative of efforts [by the Chinese] to gather intelligence on the U.S.'s position on climate change issues."

Despite knowing about the Russian and Chinese cyber attacks on U.S. and allied computer systems, the U.S. government chose to do nothing about them, fearing that Russia and other foreign countries might use the attacks to force the enactment of binding international agreements that would restrict Washington's ability to conduct its own cyber attacks on targets deemed to be threats to U.S. national security. According to a leaked 2009 State Department cable, "U.S. policy remains that hackers and cyber criminals, not states, are the most urgent cyber threat. [U.S. delegation] should continue to oppose Russian arguments for arms-control-like constraints on information technology and offensive capabilities."

It was not until Chinese cyber attacks hit the giant American Internet service provider Google in January 2010 that the U.S. government finally was forced to take action. Although the U.S. intelligence community was certain that the attacks originated from inside China, no one knew exactly who launched them or why. According to a leaked State Department cable from the U.S. embassy in Beijing, "A well-placed contact claims that the Chinese government coordinated the recent intrusions of Google systems. According to our contact, the closely held operations were directed at the Politburo Standing Committee level." Another source, however, indicated that it was one of Google's Chinese competitors who launched the attack. When Google formally complained to the U.S. government about the attack, in an unprecedented move, America's eavesdropping giant, the National Security Agency, was ordered to help the Internet giant erect electronic defenses against further attacks.

The actual culprit was never identified, and probably never will be. But the revelations in the press had the salutary effect of spurring the U.S. intelligence community into action. According to senior U.S. intelligence officials, the Chinese attacks on Google resulted in cyber warfare being instantly elevated to the single most important priority item within the intelligence community. In testimony delivered before the Senate Select Committee on Intelligence in February 2010, DNI Denny Blair warned that "the recent intrusions reported by Google are a stark reminder of the importance of these cyber assets, and a wake-up call to those who have not taken this problem seriously."

On May 21, 2010, a new military organization called U.S. Cyber Command was created, which is responsible for directing all of America's offensive and defensive cyber-war activities, including conducting cyber attacks on foreign government computer systems if so ordered. Although nominally independent, U.S. Cyber Command is, in fact, an adjunct of the National Security

Agency. The director of the NSA, General Keith Alexander, is also the chief of the 1,100-person U.S. Cyber Command.

So what has Cyber Command been doing since becoming operational? No one knows for sure because of the secrecy surrounding its operations, but there are telltale signs that it is already active.

In July 2010, computer security experts discovered a new computer virus called Stuxnet, which the New York Times later described as "the most sophisticated cyberweapon ever deployed." We know nothing for certain about the origins of Stuxnet, or who wrote the program. The New York Times has opined that the virus was written jointly by U.S. and Israeli intelligence, but there is as yet no substantive evidence to support this allegation.

What we do know is that the person or persons who wrote the Stuxnet program designed the system for a very narrow and specific application, and with a very specific target in mind. Unlike previous computer viruses, Stuxnet did not target personal computers or the computer servers used by corporations or financial institutions. Instead, Stuxnet was designed to attack a specific piece of software made by the German high-tech giant Siemens AG. And we now know that Stuxnet's principal target was the computer system that regulated the operations of the nine thousand centrifuges at Iran's main uranium enrichment plant at Natanz in central Iran.

It also is clear that whoever designed Stuxnet was not a teenage hacker but rather one or more individuals working for a foreign intelligence agency who knew virtually everything about the Natanz plant. A detailed study of the virus shows that Stuxnet was designed based on a near-complete understanding of the computer system at Natanz, which could only have come from someone inside the plant providing the virus's designers with the schematics of the plant's computer hardware and software systems.

Moreover, Stuxnet was deliberately designed to attack computer systems that were not connected to the Internet for security reasons, as was the case at Natanz. In order to get around the firewall, the Stuxnet virus had to be loaded onto a CD or flash drive and then covertly downloaded into the computer system at Natanz. Once again, this could only be accomplished by an intelligence service with an agent at Natanz with access to the plant's computer systems. Once buried inside the targeted computer's software, analysis of the virus shows, Stuxnet was programmed to take control of the host computer system.

According to computer security experts, the Stuxnet virus was somehow covertly inserted into the computers at Natanz in mid-2009, knocking out of commission almost one thousand of the facility's nine thousand centrifuges in a single blow. But a recent report by the International Atomic Energy Agency indicates that the damage caused by Stuxnet was only temporary. Beginning in late 2009, IAEA video cameras at Natanz caught Iranian workers carting off the damaged centrifuges. Six months later, in early 2010, the cameras saw the same workers hauling in crates containing new centrifuges. U.S. intelligence experts now believe that the Natanz plant is back in full operation.

Even if the cyber attack on Natanz was only a temporary setback for the Iranian nuclear program, cyber-war proponents still believe that the weapon has utility in any future conflict. "Stuxnet may be the wave of the future," a former NSA official said in a recent interview. "Imagine a hundred Stuxnets, each aimed at the computer system of a specific foreign target, released simultaneously, and you have the potential for a cyber catastrophe—a perfect storm."

Acknowledgments

The author wishes to thank the dozens of government officials who assisted in the preparation of this book. Unfortunately, the vast majority of these individuals cannot be named here because the Obama administration, despite promising the American public a new era of transparency in government, has authorized the Justice Department to file criminal indictments against a number of current or former government officials alleged to have leaked classified information to the press. The administration also quietly fired a number of officials, some of them quite senior, who provided information to author Bob Woodward for his 2010 book *Obama's Wars*. In this oppressive atmosphere, it seems prudent not to identify the sources who provided information for this book, even if they were willing to have their names used.

Those individuals who can be thanked include Joseph S. Bermudez Jr., Dr. Michael Eisenstadt, Dr. Michael Elleman, Matthew Hoh, and the late Ambassador Richard Holbrooke. Three old friends, Dr. Richard J. Aldrich, Dr. Martin Rudner, and Dr. Cees Wiebes, directed me to a number of valuable declassified documents concerning the wars in Afghanistan and Pakistan.

First Lieutenant Ray "Radar" Geoffrey, USAF, Lieutenant Colonel Götz Haffke of the German Army, and Mr. Robert M. Hill of the ISAF Public Affairs Office in Kabul were very helpful in pointing me to declassified documents on a number of battles in Afghanistan. And Angela L. Moncur of the U.S. Army public affairs office at Fort Huachuca, Arizona, was a fount of knowledge about all things relating to U.S. Army intelligence.

I want to pay special tribute to Saleem Shahzad, one of the hardest working Pakistani journalists in Islamabad, who was of immeasurable help to me. His encyclopedic knowledge of the Pakistani intelligence service, the ISI, was unparalleled. On May 29, 2011, he disappeared from his home in Islamabad.

A few days later his body was found in an irrigation canal outside the Pakistani capital. He had been savagely beaten to death.

CIA officials in Washington are convinced that he was murdered on the orders of the director of the ISI because he had written a number of articles before his death alleging that the Pakistani Taliban had managed to infiltrate the Pakistani military and ISI. The Pakistani government has vehemently denied the charges, but friends in Islamabad report that the Pakistani police and security forces have done virtually nothing to find his murderers. His death says much about the tragic state of affairs in Pakistan today.

Special thanks go to Peter Ginna, my publisher at Bloomsbury Press, who suggested the subject of this book. Pete Beatty expertly edited the manuscript in record time, and Michael O'Connor put the manuscript in its final form. And, finally, my agent, Rick Broadhead, has my undying gratitude for fighting so hard on my behalf. Thank you.

Notes

GLOSSARY

AMEMBASSY = American Embassy
COMINT = Communications intelligence
DOD = Department of Defense
FOIA = Freedom of Information Act
FOUO = For Official Use Only
HCS = Human Intelligence Control System
NARA = National Archives and Records Administration
NOFORN = No Foreigners
SECSTATE = Secretary of State

INTRODUCTION

6   "In November 2009" Cable, Bogotá 003435, AMEMBASSY BOGOTA to SECSTATE WASH DC, "Scenesetter for Admiral Roughead's Dec 2–6 Visit to Colombia," November 24, 2009, WikiLeaks Cablegate Files. Secret/NOFORN.

6   "In December 2009" Cable, State 130330, SECSTATE WASH DC to AMEMBASSY SANAA, "USG Policy Toward Yemeni Arms Acquisitions," December 22, 2009, WikiLeaks Cablegate Files. Secret/NOFORN.

7   "In January 2010" Cable, State 002634, SECSTATE WASH DC to AMEMBASSY BEIJING, "Demarche Following China's January 2010 Intercept Flight-Test," January 12, 2010, WikiLeaks Cablegate Files. Secret/NOFORN.

7   "In February 2010" Cable, Riyadh 000182, AMEMBASSY RIYADH to SECSTATE WASH DC, "Scenesetter for Special Representative Ambassador Holbrooke's February 15–16 Visit to Riyadh," February 7, 2010, WikiLeaks Cablegate Files. Secret/NOFORN.

1: LIPSTICK ON A PIG

12   "June 2008 Pentagon report to Congress" U.S. Department of Defense, *Report on Progress Toward Security and Stability in Afghanistan*, June 2008, p. 5. Unclassified.

12 "Afghanistan is clearly on the road to recovery" General Dan McNeill, "Commander's Fore-word," *ISAF Mirror*, March 2007. Unclassified.

12 "McNeill caustically dismissed" John Ward Anderson, "Emboldened Taliban Reflected in More Attacks, Greater Reach," *Washington Post*, September 25, 2007, p. A11.

13 "According to an internal planning document" U.S. Embassy to Afghanistan and Head-quarters, U.S. Forces, Afghanistan, *United States Government Integrated Civilian-Military Campaign Plan for Support to Afghanistan*, August 10, 2009, p. 2. Unclassified/FOUO.

14 "By 2008, not only was corruption pervasive" Joint Chiefs of Staff, PowerPoint Presenta-tion, *Strategy for the Long War: 2006–2016*, various dates between September 27, 2006, and November 3, 2006, DOD FOIA. Secret.

14 "The venality of many of Karzai's closest advisers" Memorandum, McCaffrey to Meese, *After Action Report—General Barry R. McCaffrey USA (Ret): Visit to Kuwait and Afghani-stan—10–18 November 2009*, December 5, 2009. Unclassified.

14 "According to Dr. Thomas H. Johnson" Thomas H. Johnson and M. Chris Mason, "Refight-ing the Last War: Afghanistan and the Vietnam Template," *Military Review*, November–December 2009, p. 2.

15 "A classified 2009 State Department survey" Cable, Kabul 004182, AMEMBASSY KABUL to SECSTATE WASH DC, "Pervasive Corruption Undermining Ghazni Province's Public Administration," December 28, 2009, WikiLeaks Cablegate Files. Confidential.

15 "And the governor of neighboring Paktia" Cable, Kabul 004150, AMEMBASSY KABUL to SECSTATE WASH DC, "Above the Law: Corrupt Governor Thwarts Governance and Devel-opment in Paktya Province, Afghanistan," December 27, 2009, WikiLeaks Cablegate Files. Secret.

15 "Captain Carl Thompson" Report, Captain Carl Thompson, Maryland Army National Guard, *Winning in Afghanistan*, April 9, 2009. Unclassified.

15 "The situation was so apparent" Cable, USNATO 000453, "Allies Find Briefing on Afghan-istan NIE 'Gloomy,'" December 5, 2008, WikiLeaks Cablegate Files. Secret.

16 "A March 2010 report" ISAF, PowerPoint Presentation, *ISAF Joint Command Helping Af-ghans Succeed*, March 14, 2010. FOUO.

16 "Even the Pentagon's" U.S. Department of Defense, *Report on Progress Toward Security and Stability in Afghanistan*, June 2008, p. 6. Unclassified.

17 "A report prepared by" Elizabeth Lee Walker, ISAF Rule of Law adviser *Culturally-Attuned Government and Justice in Helmand Province, Afghanistan* (Washington, D.C.: International Media Ventures, April 2010), p. 5. FOUO.

18 "the CIA assessment overstates." Memorandum, Franks to Secretary of Defense, *Trends in Afghanistan*, October 1, 2002, DOD FOIA. Secret.

19 "As a declassified CIA history put it" Robert M. Hathaway and Russell Jack Smith, *Richard Helms as Director of Central Intelligence: 1966–1973* (Washington, D.C.: CIA History Staff, 1993), p. 2. Secret.

19 "According to Paul R. Pillar" Paul R. Pillar, "A Scapegoat Is Not a Solution," *New York Times*, June 4, 2004.

20 "August 2006, Defense Policy Board official" PowerPoint Presentation, Marin Strmecki, *Afghanistan at a Crossroads: Challenges, Opportunities, and a Way Ahead*, August 17, 2006, DOD FOIA. Secret/NOFORN.

20 "According to Neumann" Cable, Kabul 000746, AMEMBASSY KABUL to SECSTATE WASH DC, February 21, 2006, State Department FOIA. Secret.

21 "A secret NATO intelligence summary" Cable, USNATO 000115, USMISSION USNATO to SECSTATE WASH DC, "North Atlantic Council Readout—February 21, 2007," February 23, 2007, WikiLeaks Cablegate Files. Secret/NOFORN.

21 "Other classified reporting" Cable, Kabul 003719, AMEMBASSY KABUL to SECSTATE WASH DC, "PAG Makes First Recommendations to President Karzai," August 21, 2006, WikiLeaks Cablegate Files. Secret.

21 "These stark warning signs" Paul D. Miller, "Lessons for Intelligence Support to Policymaking During Crises," *Studies in Intelligence*, vol. 54, no. 2, June 2010. Unclassified.

22 "The intelligence community agreed" Seth G. Jones, *Counterinsurgency in Afghanistan* (Santa Monica, California: RAND Corporation, June 2008), p. 37. Unclassified.

22 "At the same time, the Pentagon was telling" See, for example, Lt. General Michael D. Maples, U.S. Army, Director, Defense Intelligence Agency, Statement for the Record Before the Committee on Armed Services, United States Senate, *Current and Projected National Security Threats to the United States*, February 27, 2008, p. 6. Unclassified.

22 "These divergent goals" Ismail Khan, "Omar Threatens to Intensify War: Talks with Karzai Govt Ruled Out," *Dawn (Pakistan)*, January 4, 2007.

23 "Mullah Sabir, a senior Taliban commander" Sami Yousafzai and Ron Moreau, "Taliban Two-Step: Can't Sit Down Yet," *Newsweek*, November 10, 2008.

23 "According to Major General Mike Flynn" Major General Michael T. Flynn, USA, Captain Matt Pottinger, USMC, and Paul D. Batchelor, DIA, *Fixing Intel: A Blueprint for Making Intelligence Relevant in Afghanistan* (Washington, D.C.: Center for a New American Security, January 2010), p. 9.

25 "The quality of the intelligence" Cable, Kabul 000165, AMEMBASSY KABUL to SECSTATE WASH DC, "CENTCOM Commander Petraeus Jan 20 Meeting with President Karzai," January 23, 2009, WikiLeaks Cablegate Files. Secret.

25 "When asked about this problem" Department of Defense, Office of the Assistant Secretary of Defense (Public Affairs), *Transcript of DoD News Briefing with Gen. McNeill from the Pentagon*, June 13, 2008. Unclassified.

25 "According to Captain Daniel Helmer" Captain Daniel Helmer, USA, "Twelve Urgent Steps for the Advisor Mission in Afghanistan," *Military Review*, July–August 2008, p. 76.

26 "According to Robert Baer" Robert Baer, "Taliban Imposter: The U.S. Doesn't Know Its Enemy," *Time*, November 28, 2010.

26 "The current chief of intelligence in Afghanistan" Major General Michael T. Flynn, USA, Captain Matt Pottinger, USMC, and Paul D. Batchelor, DIA, *Fixing Intel: A Blueprint for Making Intelligence Relevant in Afghanistan* (Washington, D.C.: Center for a New American Security, January 2010), p. 8.

26 "In November 2007" Senlis Afghanistan, *Stumbling into Chaos: Afghanistan on the Brink* (London: Senlis Council, November 2007).

27 "According to General McNeill's spokesman" "Taliban Control No More than Five Afghan Districts: NATO," *AFP*, December 3, 2007.

29 "Dr. Thomas Johnson" Thomas H. Johnson and M. Chris Mason, "Understanding the Taliban and Insurgency in Afghanistan," *Orbis*, vol. 51, no. 2, Winter 2007, pp. 82–83.

29 "Marine Corps Lt. Colonel Chris Nash" Lt. Colonel Chris Nash, USMC, PowerPoint Presentation, *Observations and Opinions IRT Operations in Afghanistan by a Former ETT OIC*, August 2008. FOUO.

29 "The parallels with the Soviet military's" U.S. Marine Corps, Battalion Landing Team 1/6,

24th Marine Expeditionary Unit, *After Action Review (AAR) and Lessons Learned from Operation Enduring Freedom Phase III*, September 25, 2008, pp. 23–24. Unclassified/FOUO.

29   "In Helmand Province" Cable, Kabul 000140, AMEMBASSY KABUL to SECSTATE WASH DC, "Vice President-Elect Biden and Senator Graham Discuss Security in Helmand," January 20, 2009, WikiLeaks Cablegate Files. Confidential.

29   "In the summer of 2008, the British Army garrison" Gerald Meyerle, *Encirclement of Patrol Base Armagh, Helmand Province, July–August 2008* (Arlington, VA: Center for Naval Analyses [CNA], November 14, 2008). FOUO.

30   "Clear . . . go back to FOB" Captain Jamison, USMC, Marine Corps Intelligence Activity Afghanistan Team, PowerPoint Presentation, *Afghanistan*, September 17, 2008. FOUO.

30   "Major Fred Tanner" Oral History, *Interview with Major Fred Tanner*, Combat Studies Institute, Fort Leavenworth, Kansas, March 4, 2010, p. 10. Unclassified.

30   "According to declassified data" Major General Paul Dettmer, USAF, Assistant DCS for ISR, PowerPoint Presentation, *Strategic Challenges of the 21st Century*, July 8, 2009. Unclassified.

31   "A restricted-access Marine Corps" Captain Jamison, USMC, Marine Corps Intelligence Activity Afghanistan Team, PowerPoint Presentation, *Afghanistan*, September 17, 2008. FOUO.

31   "On April 13, 2010" Colonel Joe Felter, PowerPoint Presentation, *COIN Advisory and Assistance Team & COIN in Afghanistan*, May 13, 2010. FOUO.

32   "According to a restricted-access" Captain Jamison, USMC, Marine Corps Intelligence Activity Afghanistan Team, PowerPoint Presentation, *Afghanistan*, September 17, 2008. FOUO.

32   "According to Major Jim Grant" Major Jim Grant, USA, "One Tribe at a Time: A Strategy for Success in Afghanistan," *Joint Center for Operational Analysis Journal*, vol. 11, no. 3, Fall 2009, p. 19.

32   "For instance, a 2009 study" Gerald Meyerle and Carter Malkasian, *Insurgent Tactics in Southern Afghanistan* (Arlington, Virginia: Center for Naval Analyses [CNA], June 2009). FOUO.

33   "according to a September 2008 Marine Corps report" U.S. Marine Corps, Battalion Landing Team 1/6, 24th Marine Expeditionary Unit, *After Action Review (AAR) and Lessons Learned from Operation Enduring Freedom Phase III*, September 25, 2008. FOUO.

33   "Even the lowliest Taliban fighters" Lt. Colonel Donald C. Bolduc, USA, *Bureaucracies at War: Organizing for Strategic Success in Afghanistan* (Carlisle Barracks, Pennsylvania: U.S. Army War College, November 13, 2008), p. 11.

34   "The Americans have the wristwatches" Thomas H. Johnson and M. Chris Mason, "Understanding the Taliban and Insurgency in Afghanistan," *Orbis*, vol. 51, no. 2, Winter 2007, p. 87.

34   Documentary sources for the Battle of Wanat are: Memorandum, TF Bayonet to Commander, Combined Joint Task Force 101, *AR 15-6 Investigation Findings and Recommendations— Vehicle Patrol Base (VPB) Wanat Complex Attack and Casualties, 13 July 2008*, August 13, 2008, Secret; U.S. Army, *Presentation of Collateral Investigation Results to the Family of 1LT Jonathan P. Brostrom*, October 23–24, 2008, For Official Use Only; U.S. Army, *Combined Responses from CJTF 101 and 173rd ABCT to Colonel David Brostrom*, October 23–24, 2008, Unclassified; Douglas R. Cubbison, *Battle of Wanat Historical Analysis* (Ft. Leavenworth, Kansas: U.S. Army Combat Studies Institute, June 25, 2009), For Official Use Only.

35   "Lieutenant Brostrom had no way of knowing it" Report, *14 JAN 2008 TF ROCK KLE (Waigul District Governor)*, January 14, 2008, WikiLeaks Kabul War Diary Files. Secret.

37   "According to a leaked State Department cable" Cable, USNATO 000453, "Allies Find Brief-
      ing on Afghanistan NIE 'Gloomy,'" December 5, 2008, WikiLeaks Cablegate Files. Secret.

38   "situation [in Afghanistan] has deteriorated" General David H. Petraeus, USA, PowerPoint
      Presentation to Center for a New American Security, *CENTCOM Update*, June 11, 2009.
      Unclassified.

2: LIBERTY CROSSING

41   "dismayed about the work of the intelligence committees" Memorandum for Record, *Meeting
      of Vice Chair Hamilton with SSCI Vice Chair Jay Rockefeller*, October 16, 2003, 9/11 Commis-
      sion Files, NARA, Washington, D.C. Unclassified.

42   "an almost unworkable bureaucracy." Memorandum for Record, *Interview of Carl Ford*, Oc-
      tober 22, 2003, 9/11 Commission Files, NARA, Washington, D.C. Secret.

42   "The intelligence community that Blair inherited" Confidential interviews. See also Office of
      the Director of National Intelligence, Conference Call with Dr. Ronald Sanders, Associate Di-
      rector of National Intelligence for Human Capital, *Results of the Fiscal Year 2007 U.S. Intelli-
      gence Community Inventory of Core Contractor Personnel*, August 27, 2008; Office of the Director
      of National Intelligence, Media Roundtable with Mr. Dennis C. Blair, Director of National In-
      telligence, ODNI Headquarters, McLean, Virginia, March 26, 2009; Office of the Director of
      National Intelligence, Media Conference Call with Director of National Intelligence Mr. Den-
      nis C. Blair, *2009 National Intelligence Strategy*, September 15, 2009, all Unclassified.

45   "The CIA's 5,000-person National Clandestine Service" The National Clandestine Service
      had been created in May 2006 by merging CIA's old Cold War clandestine organization, the
      Directorate of Operations, with the U.S. military's smaller clandestine organization, the
      Defense HUMINT Service.

45   "Pat Hanback, the CIA's former" Memorandum for Record, *Interview of Pat Hanback*, Septem-
      ber 12, 2003, 9/11 Commission Files, NARA, Washington, D.C. Top Secret/HCS/NOFORN.

45   "The Clandestine Service's performance prior to 9/11" Memorandum, Meigs to Secretary of
      Defense, *Answers to SecDef "23 Questions,"* July 28, 2001, DOD FOIA. Secret/Close Hold/
      NOFORN.

45   "diplomatic cover isn't going to get" Michael J. Sulick, *Human Intelligence*, March 22, 2007,
      p. 9, Seminar on Intelligence, Command and Control, Center for Information Policy Re-
      search, Harvard University, Cambridge, Massachusetts.

47   "There were also a couple of hundred FBI agents" For example, see Cable, Madrid 000154,
      AMEMBASSY MADRID to SECSTATE WASH DC, "Spain Details Its Strategy to Combat
      the Russian Mafia," February 8, 2010, WikiLeaks Cablegate Files. Secret/NOFORN.

47   "According to Federal Aviation Administration (FAA) records" The FBI aviation front com-
      panies are Northeast Aircraft Leasing Corp., Northwest Aircraft Leasing Corp., Southeast
      Aircraft Leasing Corp., Southwest Aircraft Leasing Corp., National Aircraft Leasing Corp.,
      and Worldwide Aircraft Leasing Corp.

48   "Unlike its larger cousins" National Reconnaissance Office, *Mission Ground Station Declassifi-
      cation Questions and Answers*, October 15, 2008, NRO FOIA via Dr. Jeffrey T. Richelson. Top
      Secret.

48   "As it was during the Cold War" Cable, Kyiv 001942, AMEMBASSY KYIV to SECSTATE
      WASH DC, "U.S.-Ukraine Nonproliferation Meetings September 23–24, 2009," December
      24, 2009, WikiLeaks Cablegate Files. Secret/NOFORN.

49 "NSA was a shambles" Memorandum, *The Threats and Opportunities: 9/11, al Qa'ida and Other 21st Century Challenges*, undated, p. 4, Records of the 9/11 Commission, NARA, Washington, D.C., Unclassified; Memorandum for the Record, *Interview with Rich Taylor, Former NSA Deputy Director for Operations, 1997–2001*, December 10, 2003, p. 6, Records of the 9/11 Commission, NARA, Washington, D.C. Top Secret COMINT.

49 "According to General Montgomery Meigs" Memorandum, Meigs to Secretary of Defense, *Answers to SecDef "23 Questions,"* July 28, 2001, DOD FOIA. Secret/Close Hold/NOFORN.

50 "In 2009, the president of Panama" Cable, Panama 000905, AMEMBASSY PANAMA to SECSTATE WASH DC, "Guidance Request: DEA Wiretap Program," December 24, 2009, WikiLeaks Cablegate Files. Secret/NOFORN.

51 "27 people, no capability—a total mess" Memorandum for Record, *Interview of Patrick M. Hughes, Assistant Secretary for Information Analysis, DHS*, April 4, 2004, 9/11 Commission Files, NARA, Washington, D.C. Unclassified.

51 "The U.S. State Department itself has become" Cable, State 080163, SECSTATE WASH DC to USMISSION UN ROME, "Reporting and Collection Needs: The United Nations," July 31, 2009, WikiLeaks Cablegate Files. Secret/NOFORN.

52 "As of 2009, the U.S. Army had a staggering 54,000 men and women" U.S. Army, Director of Military Intelligence, PowerPoint Presentation, *A Strategy to Rebalance the Army MI Force*, December 15, 2009, slide 7. Unclassified.

53 "But it was the unmanned reconnaissance drone" Unless otherwise noted, all data in this section were derived from Dr. Daniel L. Hauman, *U.S. Unmanned Aerial Vehicles in Combat, 1991–2003* (Bolling AFB: Air Force History Office, June 9, 2003), Unclassified; Headquarters U.S. Air Force, PowerPoint Presentation, *Air Force Unmanned Aerial System (UAS) Flight Plan 2009–2047*, July 23, 2009, Unclassified; U.S. Army UAS Center of Excellence, Fort Rucker, Alabama, *"Eyes of the Army": U.S. Army Roadmap for Unmanned Aircraft Systems: 2010–2036*, April 2010, Unclassified.

53 "The growth of the military's drone fleet" As of 9/11, the U.S. Army had only 54 Hunter and Shadow drones in its inventory. Today, the Army has 4,034 drones (42 medium-sized and 3,992 small drones) deployed in the United States and overseas. As of July 2009, the USAF had 158 drones in its inventory (118 Predator, 27 Reaper, and 13 Global Hawk).

59 "more data than we can translate into useable knowledge" Memorandum, "Visualizing the Intelligence System of 2025," attached to Memorandum, Rumsfeld to Cambone and Haver, *Intelligence System of 2025*, June 23, 2001, Rumsfeld.com. Unclassified.

59 "This is parochialism at its worst." Colonel Barry Harris, U.S. Army, *Intelligence Transition in the United States Army: Are We on the Right Path?* (Carlisle Barracks, Pennsylvania: U.S. Army War College, August 2009), p. 27. Unclassified.

59 "a hysterical group of Talmudic scholars" Department of State, Foreign Relations of the United States, 1969–1976, vol. 7, *Vietnam, July 1970–January 1972* (Washington, D.C.: Government Printing Office, 2010), p. 466.

60 "According to a restricted-access Pentagon briefing" Colonel Jack Jones, Military Assistant to the Deputy Under Secretary of Defense, PowerPoint Presentation, *ISR Trends & Challenges*, undated but circa 2010. FOUO.

60 "Information is like confetti" Brigadier General Michael Shields, Director, National Joint Operations and Intelligence Center (NJOIC), PowerPoint Presentation, *NJOIC Collaboration and Web 2.0*, April 22, 2010. Unclassified.

60 "fundamentally unreformed" Patrick C. Neary, "Intelligence Reform, 2001–2009: Requiescat in Pace?" *Studies in Intelligence*, vol. 54, no. 1, March 2010.

61   "be a train wreck" Memorandum, Rumsfeld to President, *Intelligence "Reform,"* September 11, 2004, Rumsfeld.com. Unclassified.

61   "looked at the reform brouhaha with detached bemusement" Patrick C. Neary, "Intelligence Reform, 2001–2009: Requiescat in Pace?" *Studies in Intelligence,* vol. 54, no. 1, March 2010.

62   "This reality was summarized succinctly" Draft Study, President's Foreign Intelligence Advisory Board, *Study of the Mission, Size, and Function of the Office of the Director of National Intelligence,* March 2010. Secret.

63   "undermining ODNI's credibility" Office of the Director of National Intelligence, Office of the Inspector General, *Critical Intelligence Community Management Challenges,* November 12, 2008. Unclassified.

63   "According to Patrick G. Eddington" Patrick G. Eddington, *Long Strange Journey: An Intelligence Memoir* (Shelbyville, Kentucky: Wasteland Press, 2011), p. 17.

63   "received a lot of resistance from [within] the FBI" Memorandum for Record, *Interview of Admiral David Jeremiah, USN (ret.),* October 22, 2003, 9/11 Commission Files, NARA, Washington, D.C. Top Secret Codeword.

63   "doubts whether the FBI can carry out reform" Memorandum for Record, *Meeting of Vice Chair Hamilton with SSCI Vice Chair Jay Rockefeller,* October 16, 2003, 9/11 Commission Files, NARA, Washington, D.C. Unclassified.

64   "Take the example of Thomas A. Drake" Indictment, *United States of America v. Thomas Andrews Drake,* April 14, 2010, U.S. District Court for the Northern District of Maryland. Unclassified.

64   "On June 9, 2011" DOD, Office of the Inspector General, *Requirements for the TRAILBLAZER and THINTHREAD Systems,* December 15, 2004, p. 27. Top Secret/COMINT.

65   "a culture that is emphatic about secrecy" Major General Michael T. Flynn, USA, Captain Matt Pottinger, USMC, and Paul D. Batchelor, DIA, *Fixing Intel: A Blueprint for Making Intelligence Relevant in Afghanistan* (Washington, D.C.: Center for a New American Security, January 2010), p. 9.

67   "For example, the U.S. Air Force had 34 Predator drones" Brigadier General Walt Davis, USA, Director of Army Aviation, PowerPoint Presentation, *Army Aviation,* January 13, 2009. FOUO.

67   "We also spent a lot of time, money, blood, and treasure" Russell W. Glenn and S. Jamie Gayton, *Intelligence Operations and Metrics in Iraq and Afghanistan* (Santa Monica, California: RAND Corporation, November 2008), p. 194. FOUO.

68   "the results of such missions were "lackluster" at best" Captain Kyle Greenberg, "Unmanned Aerial Systems: Quality as Well as Quantity," *Military Review,* July–August 2010, p. 53.

68   "a minimum of 72 hours" U.S. Army, *Operation Enduring Freedom: Combat Aviation Brigade in Afghanistan Initial Impressions Report,* November 2008. Unclassified/FOUO.

68   "Over 90% [of all detainees were] released due to insufficient evidence" U.S. Marine Corps, PowerPoint Presentation, *Military Police Support of the MAGTF: Case Study: 24th Marine Expeditionary Unit Operation Azada Wosa, Afghanistan 2008,* November 2008. FOUO.

69   All the information we need is available in ISAF." Brigadier General Michael Shields, Director, National Joint Operations and Intelligence Center (NJOIC), PowerPoint Presentation, *NJOIC Collaboration and Web 2.0,* April 22, 2010. Unclassified.

3: THE SWORD OF DAMOCLES

70 "He was referring to the Soviet military's disastrous" G. F. Krivosheev, *Grif sekretnosti snyat* [The Secret Seal Is Removed] (Moscow: Voyenizdat, 1993), pp. 401–5.

71 "The decision [to invade Afghanistan]" *CC CPSU Letter on Afghanistan*, May 10, 1988, in Svetlana Savranskaya, ed., *Afghanistan: Lessons from the Last War: The Soviet Experience in Afghanistan: Russian Documents and Memoirs*, October 9, 2001, National Security Archive Electronic Briefing Book 57, http://www.gwu.edu/~nsarchiv/NSAEBB/NSAEBB57/soviet.html

72 "In June 2006, the top Pentagon official" Memorandum, Vickers to President, *Transitioning to an Indirect Approach in Iraq*, June 12, 2006, Rumsfeld.com. Unclassified.

73 "many indicators suggest the overall situation" Memorandum, Headquarters, NATO International Security Assistance Force, Afghanistan (ISAF) to Secretary of Defense, *Commander's Initial Assessment*, August 30, 2009, p. 2-1. Confidential.

75 "I don't want to say we're clueless, but we are." Major General Michael T. Flynn, USA, Captain Matt Pottinger, USMC, and Paul D. Batchelor, DIA, *Fixing Intel: A Blueprint for Making Intelligence Relevant in Afghanistan* (Washington, D.C.: Center for a New American Security, January 2010), p. 9.

77 "The embassy of virtually every major foreign power in Kabul" ISAF CJ2, *Threat Report Other Rpt Kabul*, August 25, 2007, WikiLeaks Kabul War Diary Files. Secret.

78 "The CTPT teams, which are deployed at twenty-six firebases" The largest CTPT teams are based at Forward Operating Base (FOB) Asadabad in Kunar Province, Camp Dyer outside the city of Jalalabad in Nangarhar Province, FOB Salerno and FOB Chapman outside the city of Khost in Khost Province, FOB Lilley and FOB Orgun-e in Paktika Province, Spin Boldak in Kandahar Province, and FOB Geckho in central Helmand Province. There is also a CTPT Quick Reaction Force at Bagram Air Base that can be rapidly sent by helicopter anywhere in eastern Afghanistan at short notice.

79 "like the small agency-run listening post called Cardinal" Report, *231200Z TF Rock Conducts Boarder Flag Meeting IVO Ghaki Pass*, June 23, 2007, WikiLeaks Kabul War Diary Files. Secret.

86 "We now knew where all of the males in the village were" Personal Experiences Paper of Dwight C. Utley, SGM, *Operation ENDURING FREEDOM, Konar Valley, Afghanistan, May 15–December 1, 2004*, Combat Studies Institute, Ft. Leavenworth, Kansas, August 20, 2006, p. 10. Unclassified.

86 "The people here have an incestuous relationship with the Taliban" "Facilitating Development and Governance in Kunar Province," *Army*, May 2010, p. 66.

88 "On September 8, 2009, several hundred Taliban guerrillas" A sanitized version of the army's postmortem investigation into the attack on COP Keating can be found in HQ, Combined/Joint Task Force (CJTF)-82, Memorandum for Record, *AR 15-6 Report of Investigation into Operations in the Gangjal Valley, Konar Province, Afghanistan, 8 September 2009 (Executive Summary)*, November 25, 2009, ISAF FOIA. Secret.

88 "On October 24, 2009, the *Wall Street Journal* reported" Yochi J. Dreazen and Anand Gopal, "In One Province, Taliban Revive," *Wall Street Journal*, October 24, 2009.

89 "Since 2006, more Taliban attacks have occurred in Helmand" NATO, International Security Assistance Force, *Metrics Brief 2007–2008*, February 2009. FOUO.

90 "with a declassified Marine Corps report admitting" U.S. Marine Corps, PowerPoint Presentation, *2nd Battalion, 8th Marine Regiment OEF First 100 Days After Action Review*, November 2009. FOUO.

90 "complete lack of security in the provincial capital" Cable, Kabul 001677, AMEMBASSY KABUL to SECSTATE WASH DC, "Helmand Governor Mangal Upbeat, Hopeful in Meeting with Ambassador," June 27, 2009, WikiLeaks Cablegate Files. Confidential.

90 "almost all officials [in Helmand Province] are assessed to be in some way involved in" Elizabeth Lee Walker, ISAF Rule of Law adviser, *Culturally-Attuned Government and Justice in Helmand Province, Afghanistan* (Washington, D.C.: International Media Ventures, April 2010), p. 5. FOUO.

91 "When they got into the area that Daud controlled" Oral History, *Interview with Lt. Colonel Michael Slusher*, Combat Studies Institute, Ft. Leavenworth, Kansas, February 16, 2007, p. 15. Unclassified.

91 "It was hard to determine if folks were actually no-joke Taliban or just criminals" Oral History, *Interview with Major Stuart Farris*, Combat Studies Institute, Ft. Leavenworth, Kansas, December 6, 2007, p. 7. Unclassified.

94 "little was known by ISAF about the human terrain and insurgent dispositions in Marjah" Theo Farrell, Briefing Note, *Appraising Moshtarak: The Campaign in Nad-e-Ali District, Helmand* (London: Royal United Services Institute, June 23, 2010), p. 2. Unclassified.

95 "Karzai doesn't get it" Cable, Kabul 000693, AMEMBASSY KABUL to SECSTATE WASH DC, "Ahmed Wali Karzai: Seeking to Define Himself as U.S. Partner?" February 25, 2010, WikiLeaks Cablegate Files. Secret.

96 "demonstrates the fragility of European support for the NATO-led ISAF mission" CIA Red Cell, Special Memorandum, *Afghanistan: Sustaining West European Support for the NATO-led Mission—Why Counting on Apathy Might Not Be Enough*, March 11, 2010. Confidential/NOFORN.

96 "The situation on the ground was increasingly grim" International Security Assistance Force, Afghanistan (ISAF), PowerPoint Presentation, *ISAF Joint Command District Assessments*, April 8, 2010. NATO/ISAF Unclassified REL GIROA.

96 "there are growing fissures between [the Taliban] groups" Major General Bill Mayville, USA, "Ops Update: The State of the Insurgency," *The Afghan Hands Blog*, March 17, 2010, http://www.isaf.nato.int. Unclassified.

97 "Even the Pentagon's April 2010 assessment" Department of Defense, *Report on Progress Toward Security and Stability in Afghanistan and United States Plan for Sustaining the Afghanistan National Security Forces*, April 2010, p. 34. Unclassified.

4: THE ROOT OF ALL EVIL

100 "Pakistan's intermittent support to terrorist groups and militant organizations threatens to undermine" Cable, State 131801, SECSTATE WASH DC to AMEMBASSY ABU DHABI et al., "Terrorist Finance: Action Request for Senior Level Engagement on Terrorism Finance," December 30, 2009, WikiLeaks Cablegate Files. Secret/NOFORN.

102 "According to author Bob Woodward" Bob Woodward, *Obama's Wars* (New York: Simon & Schuster, 2010), p. 3.

102 "the lawless 10,000-square-mile area of northern Pakistan bordering Afghanistan called the Federally Administered Tribal Areas, or FATA" The FATA is an amalgamation of seven tribal agencies (Khyber, Kurram, Bajaur, Mohmand, Orakzai, North Waziristan and South Waziristan) and six frontier regions (Peshawar, Kohat, Tank, Banuu, Lakki, and Dera Ismail Khan). The FATA has a population of approximately 4 million people, almost all of whom are ethnic Pashtuns who make no secret of their sympathy for their Afghan Taliban brethren.

103 "I fear we are so mesmerized [by signals intelligence] that we find it impossible" Memorandum, Wolfowitz to Rumsfeld, *Al Qaeda Ops Sec.* July 19, 2002, DOD FOIA. Secret.

103 "looking for a silver needle in a stack of 6 million needles." Colonel Jasey Briley, U.S. Army Intelligence Center & Fort Huachuca, PowerPoint Presentation to the 2009 Fires Symposium, *Army Intelligence in an Age of Uncertainty*, March 18, 2009. Unclassified.

104 "some terrorist groups use family and communal relationships" Memorandum, "Visualizing the Intelligence System of 2025," attached to Memorandum, Rumsfeld to Cambone and Haver, *Intelligence System of 2025*, June 23, 2001, Rumsfeld.com. Unclassified.

104 "screen their recruits probably better than the U.S. government does" Michael J. Sulick, *Human Intelligence*, March 22, 2007, p. 8, Seminar on Intelligence, Command and Control, Center for Information Policy Research, Harvard University, Cambridge, Massachusetts.

105 "Over the next four years (2004–8), CIA Predator drones conducted 46 missile strikes" A breakdown of these CIA drone attacks is as follows: 2004: 1 strike; 2005: 1 strike; 2006: 3 strikes; 2007: 5 strikes; 2008: 36 strikes. Bill Roggio and Alexander Mayer, "Analysis: A Look at US Airstrikes in Pakistan Through September 2009," *The Long War Journal*, October 1, 2009.

106 "Senior Pakistani military officials asked for access" See, for example, Report, *260000Z CJTF82 CJ3 KLE PAK Military 11th Corps Cdr & 7th Div Cdr*, March 26, 2007, WikiLeaks Kabul War Diary Files. Secret.

107 "they are going to cooperate [with the CIA] to the least extent that they can get away with" Michael J. Sulick, *Human Intelligence*, March 22, 2007, p. 15, Seminar on Intelligence, Command and Control, Center for Information Policy Research, Harvard University, Cambridge, Massachusetts.

108 "al Qaeda had succeeded in regenerating itself in the sanctuaries afforded it in northern Pakistan" Director of National Intelligence, National Intelligence Council, National Intelligence Estimate, *The Terrorist Threat to the Homeland*, July 2007, Unclassified.

110 "by the time I left office (in January 2009), more than a dozen of those people [on the list] were dead" Mark Mansfield, "Reflections on Service: A Conversation with Former CIA Director Michael Hayden," *Studies in Intelligence*, vol. 54, no. 2, June 2010.

110 "shortly before dawn on the morning of September 3, 2008" This was the second known U.S. commando raid into Pakistan. Two years earlier, in March 2006, a forty-man U.S. special operation team was dropped inside Pakistan and attacked an al Qaeda camp near the town of Danda Saidgai in North Waziristan, killing Imam Asad, the Chechen commander of the Black Guard, the elite praetorian guard for Osama bin Laden and other senior al Qaeda leaders. A third cross-border commando raid by U.S. Navy SEALs in 2005, whose goal was to kill Osama bin Laden's deputy, Ayman al-Zawahiri, according to newspaper reports was called off at the last moment by the Pentagon.

111 "*may* still enjoy support from the lower echelons of the ISI." Department of State, Issue Paper for Vice President, *Counterterrorism Activities (Neo-Taliban)*, December 9, 2005, State Department FOIA. Secret. On file at the National Security Archive, Washington, D.C.

111 "Pakistani Intelligence Service (ISI) elements have an ongoing relationship with the Taliban." Joint Chiefs of Staff, PowerPoint Presentation, *Strategy for the Long War: 2006–2016*, various dates between September 27, 2006, and November 3, 2006, p. 25, DOD FOIA. Secret.

111 "The consensus opinion within the intelligence community at the time was" U.S. Army, TRADOC Intelligence Support Activity (TRISA), *HB 9 Paramilitary Terrorist Insurgent Groups: Afghanistan*, March 1, 2009. FOUO.

III   "But a restricted-access 2008 Marine Corps intelligence briefing concluded that Pakistani support" Captain Jamison, USMC, Marine Corps Intelligence Activity Afghanistan Team, PowerPoint Presentation, *Afghanistan*, September 17, 2008. FOUO.

II2   "Despite ten years of fierce denials" See, for example, Cable, Islamabad 001515, AMEMBASSY ISLAMABAD to SECSTATE WASH DC, "President Musharraf Meets with Codels Reyes and Tierney," April 6, 2007, WikiLeaks Cablegate Files. Secret/NOFORN.

II3   "Mullah Omar is under Pakistani protection" Cable, New Delhi 001051, AMEMBASSY NEW DELHI to SECSTATE WASH DC, "Indians Offer Bleak Assessment of Afghanistan and South Asian Region During CTJWG," March 2, 2007, WikiLeaks Cablegate Files. Secret.

II3   "The November 2008 National Intelligence Estimate on Afghanistan" Cable, USNATO 000453, "Allies Find Briefing on Afghanistan NIE 'Gloomy,'" December 5, 2008, WikiLeaks Cablegate Files. Secret.

II4   "The Pakistani military, the Directorate for Inter-Services Intelligence (ISI) in particular, sees the Taliban" Carter Malkasian and Gerald Meyerle, *How Is Afghanistan Different from Al Anbar?*, (Arlington, Virginia: Center for Naval Analyses [CNA], February 2009), p. 16. FOUO.

II4   "Pakistan believes the Taliban will prevail in the long term." Cable, USNATO 000453, "Allies Find Briefing on Afghanistan NIE 'Gloomy,'" December 5, 2008, WikiLeaks Cablegate Files. Secret.

II4   "Instead of standing and fighting, the Pakistani Army and police forces in the Swat Valley had abandoned their posts and fled" Cable, Islamabad 000236, AMEMBASSY ISLAMABAD to SECSTATE WASH DC, "Scenesetter for Special Envoy Holbrooke," February 4, 2009, WikiLeaks Cablegate Files, Secret; Cable, Islamabad 000270, AMEMBASSY ISLAMABAD to SECSTATE WASH DC, "CODEL Biden's Meeting With COAS Kayani and ISI Pasha," February 6, 2009, WikiLeaks Cablegate Files. Secret.

II5   "the decision to pull troops out of Swat was less about needed troops on the border with India" Cable, Peshawar 000002, AMCONSULATE PESHAWAR to SECSTATE WASH DC, January 3, 2009, WikiLeaks Cablegate Files. Secret.

II5   "The militant takeover of Swat in the Northwest Frontier Province (NWFP) is the most striking example" Cable, Islamabad 000385, AMEMBASSY ISLAMABAD to SECSTATE WASH DC, "Focusing the U.S.-Pakistan Strategic Dialogue," February 21, 2009, WikiLeaks Cablegate Files. Confidential.

II5   "The CIA station chief in Islamabad, John D. Bennett, whose cover position was counselor for regional affairs" Sixteen months later, on July 21, 2010, Bennett was called out of retirement and named the chief of the National Clandestine Service by CIA director Leon Panetta.

II6   "get control of the ISI." Cable, London 002651, AMEMBASSY LONDON to CDR USCENTCOM MACDILL AFB FL, "USDP Edelman's October 15 Meetings in London," October 21, 2008, WikiLeaks Cablegate Files. Secret/NOFORN.

II6   "the United States and Pakistan needed to have confidence in each other" Cable, Islamabad 000270, AMEMBASSY ISLAMABAD to SECSTATE WASH DC, "CODEL Biden's Meeting with COAS Kayani and ISI Pasha," February 6, 2009, WikiLeaks Cablegate Files. Secret.

II7   "The [Pakistani] government is losing more and more territory every day to foreign and domestic militant groups" Cable, Islamabad 000236, AMEMBASSY ISLAMABAD to SECSTATE WASH DC, "Scenesetter for Special Envoy Holbrooke," February 4, 2009, WikiLeaks Cablegate Files. Secret.

II7   "does not want a reckoning with the past" Cable, Islamabad 000365, AMEMBASSY

ISLAMABAD to SECSTATE WASH DC, "Scenesetter for General Kayani's Visit to Washington," February 19, 2009, WikiLeaks Cablegate Files. Secret.

118   "President Zardari and PM Gilani recognize Pakistan's greatest threat has shifted from India to militancy" Cable, Islamabad 000385, AMEMBASSY ISLAMABAD to SECSTATE WASH DC, "Focusing the U.S.-Pakistan Strategic Dialogue," February 21, 2009, WikiLeaks Cablegate Files. Confidential.

118   "divide and conquer strategy is not working." Cable, Islamabad 000478, AMEMBASSY ISLAMABAD to SECSTATE WASH DC, "New Waziristan Terrorist Alliance," March 4, 2009, WikiLeaks Cablegate Files. Secret/NOFORN.

119   "damaged, [but] not broken." Cable, USNATO 000453, "Allies Find Briefing on Afghanistan NIE 'Gloomy,'" December 5, 2008, WikiLeaks Cablegate Files. Secret.

119   "The U.S. has been remarkably successful in disrupting al-Qaida operations in Pakistan's tribal areas" Cable, Islamabad 000236, AMEMBASSY ISLAMABAD to SECSTATE WASH DC, "Scenesetter for Special Envoy Holbrooke," February 4, 2009, WikiLeaks Cablegate Files. Secret.

121   "Pakistan's arsenal of seventy to ninety nuclear weapons" Some analysts outside of government believe that the Pakistanis may have up to two hundred nuclear weapons in their arsenal. But several U.S. intelligence analysts interviewed for this book believe that this number is inflated.

123   "It appears that the drone attacks have increased [the] militants' motivation for terrorist activity." Master's Thesis, Irfan Ahmad, *Role of Airpower for Counterinsurgency in Afghanistan and FATA (Federally Administered Tribal Areas)* (Monterey, California: Naval Postgraduate School, June 2009), p. 76. Unclassified.

124   "Fear that the ISAF mission in Afghanistan will end without the establishment of a non-Taliban" Cable, Islamabad 002295, AMEMBASSY ISLAMABAD to SECSTATE WASH DC, "Reviewing Our Afghanistan-Pakistan Strategy," September 23, 2009, WikiLeaks Cablegate Files. Secret.

124   "Although Pakistani senior officials have publicly disavowed support for these [terrorist] groups" Cable, State 131801, SECSTATE WASH DC to AMEMBASSY ABU DHABI et al., "Terrorist Finance: Action Request for Senior Level Engagement on Terrorism Finance," December 30, 2009, WikiLeaks Cablegate Files. Secret/NOFORN.

124   "But what really angered American diplomats and intelligence officials was that the Pakistani Army had refused" Cable, Islamabad 002523, AMEMBASSY ISLAMABAD to SECSTATE WASH DC, "Terrorists Increase Activity in Advance of Waziristan Operation," October 16, 2009, WikiLeaks Cablegate Files. Secret.

5: WE HAVE TO KILL THEM ALL

126   "our way of life as a free and open society." Joint Chiefs of Staff, PowerPoint Presentation, *Strategy for the Long War: 2006–2016*, various dates between September 27, 2006, and November 3, 2006, DOD FOIA. Secret.

127   "The U.S. intelligence community's fight against al Qaeda and the hundreds of other foreign terrorist groups around the world is run from the National Counterterrorism Center" The following description of NCTC is derived from National Counterterrorism Center, PowerPoint Presentation, *National Counterterrorism Center*, March 2006, Unclassified; National Counterterrorism Center, *NCTC and Information Sharing: Five Years Since 9/11: A Progress Report*, September 2006, Unclassified; National Counterterrorism Center, PowerPoint

Presentation to 2008 USMC PS Division Security Conference, *National Counterterrorism Center (NCTC) Overview Briefing*, February 2008, Unclassified.

132 "According to the latest annual report from the National Counterterrorism Center" Director of National Intelligence, National Counterterrorism Center, *2009 Report on Terrorism* (Washington, D.C.: Government Printing Office, April 30, 2010), pp. 9–10. Unclassified.

133 "In Canada, over a dozen foreign terrorist groups" Cable, Ottawa 000154, AMEMBASSY OTTAWA to SECSTATE WASH DC, "Security Environment Profile Questionnaire—Spring 2009," February 27, 2009, WikiLeaks Cablegate Files. Secret/NOFORN.

133 "vigorously harassed" Cable, Ottawa 000918, AMEMBASSY OTTAWA to SECSTATE WASH DC, "Counselor, CSIS Director Discuss CT Threats, Pakistan, Afghanistan, Iran," July 9, 2008, WikiLeaks Cablegate Files. Secret/NOFORN.

133 "a stew of widespread criminality, drug trafficking, [and] corruption." Cable, Mexico 001487, AMEMBASSY MEXICO CITY to SECSTATE WASH DC, "Scene Setter for the Visit to Mexico of FBI Deputy Director John S. Pistole, May 21–23, 2008," May 16, 2008, WikiLeaks Cablegate Files. Secret.

133 "The cartels have assassinated government officials and policemen" Cable, Mexico 000027, AMEMBASSY MEXICO CITY to SECSTATE WASH DC, "Mexico—Country Terrorism Report for 2009," January 6, 2010, WikiLeaks Cablegate Files. Unclassified.

134 "Israel has evidence that foreign fighters" Cable, Tel Aviv 001580, AMEMBASSY TEL AVIV to SECSTATE WASH DC, "Mossad Chief to CODEL Corzine: Some Foreign Fighters Beginning to Leave Iraq," March 17, 2005, WikiLeaks Cablegate Files. Secret.

135 "For example, in the last three years a brand-new al Qaeda offshoot" Cable, Madrid 002023, AMEMBASSY MADRID to SECSTATE WASH DC, "Spain/CT: S/CT Coordinator Dailey Discusses Al-Qaida Threat and Encourages Further Bilateral Cooperation," October 24, 2007, WikiLeaks Cablegate Files. Secret/NOFORN.

135 "prickly, paranoid group." Cable, Algiers 000198, AMEMBASSY ALGIERS to SECSTATE WASH DC, "Scene Setter for A/S Welch Visit to Algeria," February 22, 2008, WikiLeaks Cablegate Files. Secret/NOFORN.

135 "Next door in Morocco" Cable, Rabat 001229, AMEMBASSY RABAT to SECSTATE WASH DC, "Gen. Ward Signs CISMOA; Discusses AQIM, ACSA, Guinea, Narcotics and Future Cooperation," January 4, 2010, WikiLeaks Cablegate Files. Secret.

136 "This has forced the U.S. intelligence community to expand its efforts to these countries." Cable, Rabat 00000005, AMEMBASSY RABAT to WHITE HOUSE WASH DC, "APHSCT Townsend's Visit to Morocco," July 31, 2007, WikiLeaks Cablegate Files. Secret/NOFORN.

136 "Another target is the notorious Lord's Resistance Army" Cable, Addis Ababa 000288, AMEMBASSY ADDIS ABABA to SECSTATE WASH DC, "AU Summit—A/S for African Affairs Carson Meets French Counterpart," February 11, 2010, WikiLeaks Cablegate Files. Secret.

139 "Many of the foreign fighters currently operating in Somalia" Cable, Nairobi 001801, AMEMBASSY NAIROBI to SECSTATE WASH DC, "Somalia—CODEL Marshall Scenesetter: How Iraq/Afghanistan Relate to Somalia," August 26, 2009, WikiLeaks Cablegate Files. Secret.

139 "The CIA and U.S. military tried to help the Somali government by secretly going after the leadership" Cable, Nairobi 001363, AMEMBASSY NAIROBI to SECSTATE WASH DC, "Somalia—Ayrow's Demise," June 3, 2008, WikiLeaks Cablegate Files. Secret/NOFORN.

140 "The area around Mogadishu was under relentless attack by al Shabaab militia forces" Cable, State 063860, SECSTATE WASH DC to Distribution List, "Diplomatic Security Daily," June 19, 2009, WikiLeaks Cablegate Files. Secret/NOFORN.

140 "Leaked State Department cables show that since 2006" Cable, Addis Ababa 001318, AMEMBASSY ADDIS ABABA to SECSTATE WASH DC, "Understanding the Ethiopian Hardliners," June 8, 2009, WikiLeaks Cablegate Files. Secret.

140 "hurt closer ties with the U.S." Cable, Asmara 000047, AMEMBASSY ASMARA to SEC-STATE WASH DC, "An Eritrean Overture to the United States," February 9, 2009, WikiLeaks Cablegate Files. Secret.

144 "the U.S. feared Yemen could become another Waziristan" Cable, Riyadh 000447, AMEM-BASSY RIYADH to SECSTATE WASH DC, "Counterterrorism Advisor Brennan's Meeting with Saudi King Abdullah," March 22, 2009, WikiLeaks Cablegate Files. Secret.

145 "Saleh's decision to reverse himself" Cable, Sanaa 001015, AMEMBASSY SANAA to SEC-STATE WASH DC, "Saleh Sees Foreign Hand Behind Yemen's Internal Woes," May 31, 2009, WikiLeaks Cablegate Files. Secret/NOFORN.

147 "The Houthis are your enemies too." Cable, Sanaa 001669, AMEMBASSY SANAA to SEC-STATE WASH DC, "Brennan-Saleh Meeting Sep 6, 2009," September 15, 2009, WikiLeaks Cablegate Files. Secret/NOFORN.

147 "the war against the Houthis is not a distraction from the CT fight." Cable, Sanaa 002230, AMEMBASSY SANAA to SECSTATE WASH DC, "Yemen's Counter Terrorism Unit Stretched Thin by War Against Houthis," December 17, 2009, WikiLeaks Cablegate Files. Secret/NOFORN.

148 "Over and over again since 9/11, the Political Security Bureau has withheld information from the CIA" Cable, Sanaa 001989, AMEMBASSY SANAA to SECSTATE WASH DC, "Townsend-Saleh Meeting Provides Opening for Additional CT Cooperation," October 30, 2007, WikiLeaks Cablegate Files. Secret/NOFORN.

148 "there continue to be frequent and troubling lapses in the [Yemeni government's counter-terrorism] performance" Cable, Sanaa 001790, AMEMBASSY SANAA to SECSTATE WASH DC, "Priorities for Washington Visit: Saleh Needs to Be Part of the Solution," June 28, 2005, WikiLeaks Cablegate Files. Secret.

149 "The Saudi Arabian foreign intelligence service, the General Intelligence Directorate" Ca-ble, Riyadh 00090, AMEMBASSY RIYADH to SECSTATE WASH DC, "Saudi Arabia: General Jones' January 12, 2010 Meeting with Prince Mohammed Bin Naif, Assistant Min-ister of Interior," January 19, 2010, WikiLeaks Cablegate Files. Secret/NOFORN.

149 "President Saleh will not allow any CIA or U.S. military intelligence personnel to work out-side the city limits" Cable, Sanaa 000271, AMEMBASSY SANAA to SECSTATE WASH DC, "ROYG Unveils Intel-Sharing Center to Better Coordinate CT Operations," February 10, 2010, WikiLeaks Cablegate Files. Secret/NOFORN.

150 "We'll continue saying the bombs are ours, not yours." Cable, Sanaa 1430, AMEMBASSY SANAA to SECSTATE WASH DC, "General Petraeus' Meeting with Saleh on Security As-sistance, AQAP Strikes," January 4, 2010, WikiLeaks Cablegate Files. Secret/NOFORN.

150 "countering financial support for al-Qa'ida" Cable, State 131801, SECSTATE WASH DC to AMEMBASSY ABU DHABI et al., "Terrorist Finance: Action Request for Senior Level En-gagement on Terrorism Finance," December 30, 2009, WikiLeaks Cablegate Files. Secret/NOFORN.

150 "disrupt any Taliban-related financial activity that can be identified in the UAE." Cable, Abu Dhabi 000009, AMEMBASSY ABU DHABI to SECSTATE WASH DC, January 7, 2010, WikiLeaks Cablegate Files. Secret/NOFORN.

151 "Qatar's overall level of CT cooperation with the U.S. is considered the worst in the region." Cable, State 131801, SECSTATE WASH DC to AMEMBASSY ABU DHABI et al., "Terrorist

Finance: Action Request for Senior Level Engagement on Terrorism Finance," December 30, 2009, WikiLeaks Cablegate Files. Secret/NOFORN.

151 "it has been an ongoing challenge to persuade Saudi officials" Cable, State 131801, SEC-STATE WASH DC to AMEMBASSY ABU DHABI et al., "Terrorist Finance: Action Request for Senior Level Engagement on Terrorism Finance," December 30, 2009, WikiLeaks Cablegate Files. Secret/NOFORN.

154 "In the fall of 2006, a team of U.S. government officials and consultants" Joint Chiefs of Staff, PowerPoint Presentation, *Strategy for the Long War: 2006–2016*, various dates between September 27, 2006, and November 3, 2006, DOD FOIA. Secret.

6: MEN OF ZEAL

155 "tiny, uncomfortable, low-ceilinged, windowless room." Henry Kissinger, *White House Years* (Boston: Little, Brown, 1979), p. 315.

157 "During the first ten months of 2009" Los Angeles Joint Regional Intelligence Center/LA-RTTAC, *Synopsis of Recent Terrorist Arrests*, October 26, 2009, Unclassified; City of Phoenix, Homeland Defense Bureau, TLO Intelligence Brief, *2009 Year in Review: Homegrown Terrorist Plots on the Rise in 2009*, 2010, Controlled Unclassified Information/FOUO.

157 "The second, David C. Headley, was arrested in Chicago" Joint FBI-DHS Bulletin, Intelligence Bulletin no. 331, *Two Arrested for Conspiring to Commit Terrorist Act Overseas*, October 27, 2009, Unclassified/FOUO; Cable, New Delhi 000367, AMEMBASSY NEW DELHI to SECSTATE WASH DC, "FBI Director Mueller Discusses Headley Case with Indian Home Minister," February 26, 2010, WikiLeaks Cablegate Files, Secret.

157 "Two months later, on Christmas Day 2009, a twenty-three-year-old Nigerian national" Federal Bureau of Investigation, Terrorist Explosive Device Analytical Center, *Preliminary Analysis of the Device Used in the Attempted Bombing of NWA Flight 253*, December 26, 2009. Unclassified/FOUO.

158 "to inform Hasan's military chain of command and Army security officials" U.S. Senate, Committee on Homeland Security and Governmental Affairs, *A Ticking Time Bomb: Counterterrorism Lessons from the U.S. Government's Failure to Prevent the Fort Hood Attack*, February 3, 2011, p. 8. Unclassified.

158 "Insofar as Umar Farouk Abdulmutallab was concerned, three separate internal reviews of the incident" White House, Report, *Summary of the White House Review of the December 25, 2009 Attempted Terrorist Attack*, January 7, 2010, Unclassified; U.S. Senate, Senate Select Committee on Intelligence, *Unclassified Executive Summary of the Committee Report on the Attempted Terrorist Attack on Northwest Airlines Flight 253*, May 18, 2010, Unclassified.

160 "Full intelligence-sharing relations were restored with New Zealand in August 2009" Cable, AMEMBASSY WELLINGTON to SECSTATE WASH DC, "Scenesetter for Visit of US Secretary of State Hillary Clinton to New Zealand," January 6, 2010, WikiLeaks Cablegate Files. Secret/NOFORN.

160 "The only problem area was the U.S. intelligence community's relationship with the Mossad" For an example of continuing disagreements with the Israeli intelligence services about whether Iran intends to build a nuclear weapon, see Cable, Tel Aviv 003586, AMEMBASSY TEL AVIV to SECSTATE WASH DC, "General James L. Jones' First Meetings in Israel," December 20, 2007, WikiLeaks Cablegate Files, Secret; Cable, Tel Aviv 2502, AMEMBASSY TEL AVIV to SECSTATE WASH DC, "40TH JPMG: NEA Regional Discussion (Part 3 of 4)," November 18, 2009, WikiLeaks Cablegate Files. Secret.

160 "and responded quickly to the growing narco-violence in Mexico" Cable, Mexico 003061, AMEMBASSY MEXICO CITY to SECSTATE WASH DC, "Director of National Intelligence Dennis Blair's Meeting with President Calderon, October 19," October 23, 2009, WikiLeaks Cablegate Files, Secret/NOFORN; Cable, Mexico 003077, AMEMBASSY MEXICO CITY to SECSTATE WASH DC, "Director of National Intelligence Dennis Blair's Meeting with General Galvan Galvan, October 19," October 26, 2009, WikiLeaks Cablegate Files, Secret/NOFORN.

160 "On Saturday, May 1, 2010 at 9:30 P.M." Joint FBI-DHS Intelligence Bulletin, *Destructive Device Found in Parked Vehicle at Times Square, New York City*, May 2, 2010, Unclassified/FOUO; U.S. Department of Homeland Security, Office of Intelligence and Analysis, *01 May 2010: Attempted Bombing in New York City*, May 2, 2010, Unclassified/FOUO.

161 "The Sit Room senior watch officer immediately called John Brennan" White House Times Square Bombing Incident Timeline, released to author by White House on May 4, 2010. Unclassified.

165 "an American Muslim population that remains hostile to jihadist ideology" Brian Michael Jenkins, *Would-Be Warriors: Incidents of Jihadist Terrorist Radicalization in the United States Since September 11, 2001* (Santa Monica, California: RAND Corporation, 2010), p. vii.

174 "You get a clear sense of the conundrum facing the FBI and U.S. law enforcement" Department of Homeland Security, Federal Bureau of Investigation, and National Counterterrorism Center, *Identifying Homegrown Violent Extremists Before They Strike: An Information Needs Review*, 2010. Unclassified/FOUO.

176 "The British government, for example, is spending" See, for example, Cable, London 001933, AMEMBASSY LONDON to SECSTATE WASH DC, "UK Government Seeks Deeper Counter-Radicalization Coordination," August 21, 2009, WikiLeaks Cablegate Files, Confidential; Cable, London 002005, AMEMBASSY LONDON to SECSTATE WASH DC, "UK's Assistance Strategy," August 28, 2009, WikiLeaks Cablegate Files, Confidential.

177 "risks reinforcing the idea that the United States is somehow at war with Islam itself." Remarks by John O. Brennan, Assistant to the President for Homeland Security and Counterterrorism, "A New Approach to Safeguarding Americans," Center for Strategic and International Studies, James S. Brady Press Briefing Room, Washington, D.C., August 6, 2009.

177 "fundamentally troubling . . . that there remains no federal government agency" Peter Bergen and Bruce Hoffman, *Assessing the Terrorist Threat: A Report of the Bipartisan Center's National Security Preparedness Group* (Washington, D.C.: Bipartisan Policy Center, September 20, 2010), p. 29.

178 "The Internet has expanded as a platform for spreading extremist propaganda" Robert S. Mueller III, Director, Federal Bureau of Investigation, Statement Before the Senate Committee on Homeland Security and Governmental Affairs, Washington, D.C., September 22, 2010.

178 "According to a May 2008 secret assessment by the British foreign intelligence service, MI6" Cable, London 1224, AMEMBASSY LONDON to SECSTATE WASH DC, "CODEL Smith Discussed Iraq and Counterterrorism Issues with MOD, MI-6, and DFID Officials," May 1, 2008, WikiLeaks Cablegate Files, Secret/NOFORN.

184 "Dondi, an Asian elephant, had died suddenly at the Southwick Zoo" Central Florida Intelligence Exchange (CFIX), *Domestic Security Intelligence Report*. August 6, 2010, Sensitive But Unclassified.

7: Distant Battlefields

194 "Particularly important was the CIA's intimate relationship with the Egyptian General Intelligence" Cable, Cairo 002543, AMEMBASSY CAIRO to SECSTATE WASH DC, "Scenesetter for General Petraeus' Visit to Egypt," December 21, 2008, WikiLeaks Cablegate Files. Secret/NOFORN.

194 "The FBI worked closely with the Egyptian State Security Service" Cable, Cairo 003348, AMEMBASSY CAIRO to SECSTATE WASH DC, "FBI Deputy Director Meets with Head of State Security," November 28, 2007, WikiLeaks Cablegate Files. Secret.

196 "Assad has continued to thumb his nose at the United States since Obama became president in 2009." Cable, Damascus 000390, AMEMBASSEY DAMASCUS to SECSTATE WASH DC, "Scenesetter for Visit of Special Envoy Mitchell to Damascus," June 4, 2009, WikiLeaks Cablegate Files. Secret.

196 "According to U.S. intelligence officials, Syria remains one of the top state sponsors of terrorism in the world." See, for example, Cable, Damascus 000146, AMEMBASSEY DAMASCUS to SECSTATE WASH DC, "Reactions to Makhluf Designation," February 28, 2008, WikiLeaks Cablegate Files. Secret.

196 "Classified intelligence reports reviewed by the author reveal that" See also Cable, Damascus 000389, AMEMBASSY DAMASCUS to SECSTATE WASH DC, "CODEL Pelosi Meets Syria's President Asad," April 25, 2007, WikiLeaks Cablegate Files, Confidential; Cable, Damascus 000252, AMEMBASSY DAMASCUS to SECSTATE WASH DC, "CODEL Lynch Meets Asad, Muallim," April 6, 2009, WikiLeaks Cablegate Files, Confidential.

196 "Inside Syria, [Iraqi] insurgent leaders could take refuge" Carter Malkasian and Gerald Meyerle, *How Is Afghanistan Different from Al Anbar?* (Arlington, Virginia: Center for Naval Analyses [CNA], February 2009). FOUO.

197 "telling a group of analysts in Washington in June 2009" General David H. Petraeus, USA, PowerPoint Presentation to Center for a New American Security, *CENTCOM Update*, June 11, 2009. Unclassified.

197 "In another ominous portent of things yet to come, the U.S. government's relations" Cable, Baghdad 000011, AMEMBASSY BAGHDAD to SECSTATE WASH DC, "Najaf Clerical Leaders Fear Iranian Ideological Dominance," January 5, 2009, WikiLeaks Cablegate Files, Secret; Cable, Baghdad 000197, AMEMBASSY BAGHDAD to SECSTATE WASH DC, "Rubaie Claims He Carried Message of Confident Iraq in Visit to Iran," January 26, 2009, WikiLeaks Cablegate Files. Secret/NOFORN.

197 "Since at least 2003, Brigadier General Qasem Soleimani" Cable, Baghdad 002992, AMEMBASSY BAGHDAD to SECSTATE WASH DC, "Iran's Efforts in Iraqi Electoral Politics," November 13, 2009, WikiLeaks Cablegate Files. Secret.

198 "Over the past decade, Dubai and the other principalities" Cable, Abu Dhabi 000877, AMEMBASSY ABU DHABI to SECSTATE WASH DC, September 3, 2009, WikiLeaks Cablegate Files. Secret/NOFORN.

199 "according to a leaked State Department cable, banks in Dubai currently hold about $12 billion" Cable, Riyadh 009095, AMEMBASSY RIYADH to SECSTATE WASH DC, "xxxxxxxxxxx on Iranian Threats," December 16, 2006, WikiLeaks Cablegate Files. Secret/NOFORN.

202 "According to Lt. General Ronald L. Burgess Jr., the director of the Defense Intelligence Agency" Lt. General Ronald L. Burgess, USA, Director, Defense Intelligence Agency, Statement Before

the Committee on Armed Services, United States Senate, *Iran's Military Power*, April 14, 2010. Unclassified.

202 "Iran is also continuing to provide clandestine support to a number of extremist Shiite groups in Iraq." Cable, Baghdad 000011, AMEMBASSY BAGHDAD to SECSTATE WASH DC, "Najaf Clerical Leaders Fear Iranian Ideological Dominance," January 5, 2009, WikiLeaks Cablegate Files, Secret; Cable, Baghdad 000197, AMEMBASSY BAGHDAD to SECSTATE WASH DC, "Rubaie Claims He Carried Message of Confident Iraq in Visit to Iran," January 26, 2009, WikiLeaks Cablegate Files, Secret/NOFORN; Cable, Baghdad 001103, AMEMBASSY BAGHDAD to SECSTATE WASH DC, "Iran in Iraq: Strategy for Pressuring IRGC-QF," April 24, 2009, WikiLeaks Cablegate Files, Secret/NOFORN; Cable, Baghdad 002992, AMEMBASSY BAGHDAD to SECSTATE WASH DC, "Iran's Efforts in Iraqi Electoral Politics," November 13, 2009, WikiLeaks Cablegate Files, Secret.

203 "may have attempted to conceal its activities from other branches of the Iranian government." Cable, USNATO 000520, USMISSION NATO to SECSTATE WASH DC, "North Atlantic Council Readout—September 19, 2007," September 20, 2007, WikiLeaks Cablegate Files. Secret/NOFORN.

203 "enemy of my enemy" Joint Chiefs of Staff, PowerPoint Presentation, *Strategy for the Long War: 2006–2016*, various dates between September 27, 2006, and November 3, 2006. Secret.

203 "Iran has opposed Afghan reconciliation talks with the Taliban" Director of National Intelligence, *Annual Threat Assessment of the Intelligence Community for the Senate Select Committee on Intelligence*, February 12, 2009, p. 11. Unclassified.

204 "According to a leaked State Department cable, these three men" Cable, Kabul 000467, AMEMBASSY KABUL to SECSTATE WASH DC, "Negative Influence of Certain Karzai Advisors," March 2, 2009, WikiLeaks Cablegate Files. Confidential.

204 "This new information formed the basis for a controversial November 2007 National Intelligence Estimate" Cable, Berlin 002157, AMEMBASSY BERLIN to SECSTATE WASH DC, "German Response to U.S. National Intelligence Estimate on Iran's Nuclear Program," December 3, 2007, WikiLeaks Cablegate Files. Secret/NOFORN.

207 "it was tough because North Korea was a denied area" Ralph E. Weber, ed., *Spymasters* (Wilmington, Delaware: Scholarly Resources Books, 1999), p. 115.

207 "In 1999, someone within the South Korean intelligence community leaked" "ROK Spies Who Died After Infiltrating NK Number 7,726," *Korea Times*, July 27, 1999.

210 "The CIA station in Bogotá, the U.S. military intelligence services, and the DEA continue to provide" Cable, Bogotá 004983, AMEMBASSY BOGOTA to SECSTATE WASH DC, "FARC/ELN: Terrorist Takesdowns Reflect USG-GOC Intel Cooperation," June 5, 2006, WikiLeaks Cablegate Files, Secret; Cable, Bogotá 011380, AMEMBASSY BOGOTA to SECSTATE WASH DC, "UAVS—'Eyes in the Sky' for COLMIL Operations," December 20, 2006, WikiLeaks Cablegate Files, Secret.

210 "Ecuador is suspected by the U.S. intelligence community" Cable, Quito 000015, AMEMBASSY QUITO to SECSTATE WASH DC, "Whither Correa: A Shift Further Left," January 14, 2009, WikiLeaks Cablegate Files. Secret/NOFORN.

211 "In September 2008, the U.S. Treasury Department froze the assets" Cable, State 014070, SECSTATE WASH DC to Distribution List, "Russia's Anticipated Transfer of IGLA-S (SA-24) MANPADS to Venezuela," February 14, 2009, WikiLeaks Cablegate Files. Secret/NOFORN.

211 "Randall Fort, a former head of the State Department's intelligence staff" Cable, Wellington 000356, AMEMBASSY WELLINGTON to SECSTATE WASH DC, "A/S Fort's October 9-10 Visit to New Zealand," October 24, 2008, WikiLeaks Cablegate Files. Secret/NOFORN.

212 "notwithstanding his tirades and antics" Cable, Santiago 000983, AMEMBASSY SANTI-AGO to SECSTATE WASH DC, "A Southern Cone Perspective on Countering Chavez and Reasserting U.S. Leadership," June 18, 2007, WikiLeaks Cablegate Files. Secret.

212 "Sensitive reports indicate Cuban and Venezuelan intelligence ties" Cable, Caracas 000219, AMEMBASSY CARACAS to SECSTATE WASH DC, "Cuba/Venezuela Axis of Mischief: The View from Caracas," January 30, 2006, WikiLeaks Cablegate Files. Secret/NOFORN.

CONCLUSION: THE PAST IS PROLOGUE

214 "It remains to be seen" Harold P. Ford, "Why CIA Analysts Were So Doubtful About Vietnam," *Studies in Intelligence*, Semiannual Unclassified Edition no. 1, 1997, p. 88; Bruce Palmer Jr. "US Intelligence and Vietnam," *Studies in Intelligence*, Special Edition vol. 28, no. 5, 1984, pp. 42–44, CIA Electronic FOIA Reading Room, document no. 0001433692, http://www.foia.cia.gov.

219 "As first reported by Shane Harris of the *National Journal*" Shane Harris, "The Cyberwar Plan," *National Journal*, November 14, 2009.

220 "On April 28, less than 24 hours after the first cyber attacks" Cable, Tallinn 000375, AMEMBASSY TALLINN to SECSTATE WASH DC, "Estonia's Cyber Attacks: Lessons Learned," June 6, 2007, WikiLeaks Cablegate Files. Secret.

221 "For example, a secret 2008 report by the German equivalent of the FBI" Cable, State 116943, SECSTATE WASH DC to Distribution List, "Diplomatic Security Daily," November 3, 2008, WikiLeaks Cablegate Files. Secret/NOFORN.

221 "Since late 2002, USG [U.S. government] organizations have been targeted" Cable, State 116943, SECSTATE WASH DC to Distribution List, "Diplomatic Security Daily," November 3, 2008, WikiLeaks Cablegate Files. Secret/NOFORN.

221 "The event appears to be a targeted spear-phishing attempt" Cable, State 063860, SECSTATE WASH DC to Distribution List, "Diplomatic Security Daily," June 19, 2009, WikiLeaks Cablegate Files. Secret/NOFORN.

222 "U.S. policy remains that hackers and cyber criminals" Cable, State 093327, SECSTATE WASH DC to Unknown, "FSC Fall 2009 Opening Round Guidance," September 8, 2009, WikiLeaks Cablegate Files. Secret/Sensitive.

222 "A well-placed contact claims that the Chinese government" Cable, Beijing 207, AMEMBASSY BEIJING to SECSTATE WASH DC, "PRC Role in Attacks and Responsive Strategy," January 26, 2010, WikiLeaks Cablegate Files. Secret.

222 "In testimony delivered before the Senate Select Committee on Intelligence in February 2010" Dennis C. Blair, Director of National Intelligence, *Annual Threat Assessment of the Intelligence Community for the Senate Select Committee on Intelligence*, February 2, 2010, p. 2. Unclassified.

222 The following section on Stuxnet is based largely on interviews conducted over the past two years with a number of U.S. government cyber-security experts, as well as two intelligence analysts who specialize in cyber-warfare issues.

223 "the most sophisticated cyberweapon ever deployed." William J. Broad, John Markoff, and David E. Sanger, "Israeli Test on Worm Called Crucial in Iran Nuclear Delay," *New York Times*, January 15, 2011.

Index

A Note on the Author

Matthew M. Aid is a leading intelligence historian and visiting fellow at the National Security Archive in Washington, D.C. His *The Secret Sentry* has been hailed as the definitive history of the National Security Agency. He is a regular commentator on intelligence matters for the *New York Times*, the *Financial Times*, the Associated Press, CBS News, NPR, and many other media outlets. He lives in Washington, D.C.